GLOBAL DOMESTIC WORKERS

Intersectional Inequalities and Struggles for Rights

Sabrina Marchetti, Daniela Cherubini and
Giulia Garofalo Geymonat

BRISTOL
UNIVERSITY
PRESS

First published in Great Britain in 2021 by

Bristol University Press
University of Bristol
1–9 Old Park Hill
Bristol
BS2 8BB
UK
t: +44 (0)117 954 5940
e: bup-info@bristol.ac.uk

Details of international sales and distribution partners are available at bristoluniversitypress.co.uk

British Library Cataloguing in Publication Data
A catalogue record for this book is available from the British Library

ISBN 978-1-5292-0788-0 paperback
ISBN 978-1-5292-0791-0 OA ePub
ISBN 978-1-5292-0790-3 OA PDF

Cover design by blu inc.
Front cover image: Domestic workers' sit-in 'Give Visibility to the Invisible' on Jantar Mantar Road, New Delhi, 7 January 2014. Photo by Sabrina Marchetti. Bristol University Press uses environmentally responsible print partners. Printed and bound in Great Britain by CMP, Poole.

This publication has received funding from
the European Research Council under the
European Union's Horizon 2020 Research
and Innovation programme
(GA n.678783 DomEQUAL).

Università
Ca'Foscari
Venezia

European Research Council
Established by the European Commission

Contents

List of Abbreviations

The following acronyms and abbreviations are those most frequently used throughout the book, in the original language; the translations are our own, and where applicable we indicate the relevant country.

ACLI-COLF   Associazioni Cristiane Lavoratori Italiani – Collaboratrici Familiari (Christian Associations of Italian Workers – Domestic workers, Italy)

ALLWIES   Alliance of Workers in the Informal Economy/Sector (Philippines)

ATH-ELE   Asociación de Trabajadoras de Hogar/Etxeko Langileak Elkartea (Association of Domestic Workers, Spain)

ATRH   Asociación de Trabajadoras Remuneradas de Hogar (Association of Paid Domestic Workers, Ecuador)

C189   Convention No. 189 concerning Decent Work for Domestic Workers of the International Labour Organization

DGB   Deutscher Gewerkschaftsbund (Trade Union Confederation, Germany)

EFFE   European Federation for Family Employment and Home Care

ENS   Escuela Nacional Sindical (National Trade Union School, Colombia)

EU   European Union

FENATRAD   Federação Nacional das Trabalhadoras Domésticas (National Federation of Domestic Workers; Brazil)

Filcams-CGIL   Federazione Italiana dei Lavoratori del Commercio, Alberghi, Mense e Servizi – Confederazione Generale Italiana del Lavoro (Italian Federation of Workers in Trade, Hotels, Canteens and Services – Italian General Confederation for Labour, Italy)

GDP   Gross domestic product

IDWF	International Domestic Workers Federation
IDWN	International Domestic Workers Network
ILO	International Labour Organization
ITUC	International Trade Union Confederation
LEARN	Labour Education and Research Network (Philippines)
NDWM	National Domestic Workers' Movement (India)
NGO	Non-governmental organization
NPDW	National Platform for Domestic Workers (India)
PDWR	Platform for Domestic Workers' Rights (India)
SEDOAC	Servicio Doméstico Activo (Active Domestic Work, Spain)
SEWA	Self Employed Women's Association (India)
SINDIHOGAR/ SINDILLAR	Sindicato Autónomo de Trabajadoras de Hogar y del Cuidado/Sindicat Independent de Dones Treballadors de la Llar i les Cures (Independent Trade Union of Domestic Workers and Caregivers, Spain)
SINTRAIMAGRA	Sindicato Nacional de Trabajadores de la Industria de Alimentos (National Union of Food Workers, Colombia)
SINUTRHE	Sindicato Unitario de Trabajadoras Remuneradas del Hogar de Ecuador (Unified Trade Union of Domestic Workers of Ecuador)
SUMAPI	Samahan at Ugnayan ng mga Manggagawang Pantahanan sa Pilipinas (Home Workers' Association and Linkage in the Philippines)
TIWA	Taiwan International Workers' Association (Taiwan)
TWG	Domestic Work Technical Working Group (Philippines)
UN	United Nations
UNITED	United Domestic Workers of the Philippines
UNTHYA	Unión Nacional de Trabajadoras del Hogar y Afines (National Union of Domestic Workers and Allies, Ecuador)
US	United States
UTRASD	Unión de Trabajadoras Afrocolombianas del Servicio Doméstico (Afro-Colombian Domestic Workers' Trade Union, Colombia)
WIEGO	Women in Informal Employment: Globalizing and Organizing

About the Authors

Sabrina Marchetti is Associate Professor in Sociology at Ca' Foscari University of Venice, and Principal Investigator in the project DomEQUAL since 2016. She specializes primarily in issues of gender, racism, labour and migration, with a specific focus on the question of migrant domestic work. She has also done extensive work as research consultant for non-governmental organizations, institutions and other research centres. Finally, she is an active member of several research networks active at a European level, among them, the Research Network for Domestic Workers' Rights.

Daniela Cherubini is Assistant Professor of Sociology of Culture at the University of Milano-Bicocca, Italy. She was Assistant Professor at Ca' Foscari University of Venice and researcher for 'DomEQUAL. A global approach to paid domestic work and global inequalities', from 2017 to early 2020. She is also part of the research group 'OTRAS. Feminist perspectives in social research' at the University of Granada, Spain. Her research focuses on gender, migration and citizenship, care and domestic work, gender-based violence and intersectionality, mainly from a qualitative and mixed-method perspective.

Giulia Garofalo Geymonat is Senior Research Fellow at Ca' Foscari University of Venice. A sociologist in the fields of gender, sexuality, labour and disability, she joined Ca' Foscari University of Venice and the DomEQUAL project in 2017 after working at Lund University as a Marie-Curie Intra-European Fellowship Post-Doctoral fellow. Her research focuses on intimate labour and social movements, especially with regard to issues of sex work, domestic work, migration and trafficking and disabilities. She has expertise in researching grassroots collective organizing in relation to sensitive and stigmatized topics and identities.

Acknowledgements

The idea for this book probably began on the day the picture on the cover was taken, during the protest of Indian domestic workers demanding the ratification of C189 (Convention No. 189 concerning Decent Work for Domestic Workers). Sabrina's participation on that day inspired us to attempt to connect that protest to similar situations we had witnessed in other parts of the world: what was different and what was similar in the experiences of these domestic workers demanding apparently the same thing, but in different contexts? The first thank you thus goes to our friend and colleague Sonal Sharma, who accompanied Sabrina to that demonstration on the Jantar Mantar Road in New Delhi on 7 January 2014.

Another big thank you goes to Anna Triandafyllidou, and to all other colleagues at the Robert Schuman Centre of the European University Institute in Florence who encouraged Sabrina to dare to submit an application for such an ambitious project. Their comments and support have been amazing, from the design of the project to its very first steps. Thanks also to the coordinators of the Research Network for Domestic Workers' Rights, with whom Sabrina shared her initial ideas. We all thank the Administrative Staff and the Faculty of Department of Philosophy and Cultural Heritage of Ca' Foscari University of Venice for their inestimable support on our work for this project, in all phases of the research.

A very big thank you also to a long list of all the other people who read the project proposal and to those who commented on the first draft of the book manuscript (and sometimes both!): Margarita Barañano Cid, Laura Bartolini, Margot Béal, Barbara G. Bello, Eileen Boris, Davide Calenda, Rosie Cox, Kostantinos Eleftheriadis, Silvia Federici, Ruby Gropas, Caterina Francesca Guidi, Eléonore Lépinard, Ingo Linsenmann, Helma Lutz, Luca Nutarelli, Timea Pal, Karin Pape, Flavia Piperno, Valeria Ribeiro Corossacz, Alexandra Ricard-Guay, Anna Rosinska, Raffaella Sarti, Helen Schwenken, Cristina Vega Solís and Francesca A. Vianello. Their suggestions have been very precious to us.

We also want to thank all the other scholars who served on our advisory board: Luz Gabriela Arango Gaviria, Jurema Brites, Aurora De Dios,

Donatella Della Porta, Dirk Hoerder, Eleonore Kofman, Pei-Chia Lan, Daria Mendola, Rachel Parreñas, Neetha Pillai, Maria Grazia Porcedda, Ruth Rubio Marín and Ilse Van Liempt. They supported the project and offered their advice at various stages of its development. Special thanks to Gloria Wekker for the inspiration.

Above all, writing this book would not have been possible without the collaboration of Anna Di Bartolomeo, Beatrice Gusmano and Vincenza Perilli as members of the DomEQUAL research group in Venice. They have been exceptional teammates on the road to realizing this goal. Thanks. We also want to mention Myrssini Antoniou, Sophie Roumat, Caterina Sartori, Heleen Schroeder and Paul Sheppard, who have collaborated with the copy-editing, video production and web design. A special thank you also to Neil Howard, Penelope Kyritsis, Katharina Lenner and Cameron Thibos, and to Open Democracy/Beyond Trafficking and Slavery, with whom we joined forces to produce the documentary film and book *Domestic Workers Speak*.

At the same time, we would not have had anything to write about if it weren't for the work done by Thays Almeida Monticeli, María Gabriela Alvarado Pérez, Beatrice Busi, María Fernanda Cepeda Anaya, Madhurima Das, Pei Chieh Hsu, Silvina Monteros Obelar, Marlene Seiffarth and Verna Dinah Q. Viajar. They did a great job in collecting the interviews and giving us every possible opportunity to gain further insights into their national contexts. In this respect we also want to thank Teresita Borgonos, Mylene Hega and Mina Tenorio in the Philippines. In Italy, Charito Basa and Raffaella Maioni offered us an amazing source of local knowledge and insight. Thanks also to Lokesh, Divya Jain and Juan Sebastian Yanez Paz, Sabrina's research assistants during preliminary fieldwork periods in India and Ecuador. We also want to thank the International Labour Organization officers Gianni Rosas, Claire Hobden and Maria Gallotti and the workers' representatives who welcomed and supported Daniela at the International Labour Conferences in Geneva in 2018 and 2019.

It is also important to us to express our gratitude for the participation of all the academics, experts and workers who joined the workshops organized by our country experts in Rio de Janeiro and Quito (September 2017), Bogotá and Hamburg (October 2017), Rome and Madrid (December 2017) and Taipei and Quezon City (January 2018). Likewise, we want to thank scholars and activists who joined the symposiums we organized in Venice: 'Global Views on Paid Domestic Work' (March 2017), 'The Global Struggle for Domestic Workers' Rights' (June 2017) and 'The Challenges of Intersectionality' (March 2018). Furthermore, we have received precious inputs from the activists who joined our stakeholders' workshop in Venice (June 2017): Marcelina Bautista Bautista, Marissa Begonia, Zita Cabais, Ip

Fish, Luciana Mastrocola, Ai-Jen Poo, Elizabeth Tang, Nerisa F. Valerio and Myrtle Witbooi. All these opportunities for feedback and discussion were fundamental to enabling us to elaborate on the theory and methodology behind this book.

Equally important to the writing of this manuscript was the feedback we got on early drafts of various parts of this book that we presented as papers in the following conferences: the ATGENDER (European Association for Gender Research, Education and Documentation) Spring Conference in Vilnius and the IV Congreso latinoamericano y caribeño de ciencias sociales in Salamanca in 2017; the ECPR (European Consortium for Political Research) Joint Sessions' workshop in Nicosia, the International Sociological Association's conference in Toronto, the 10th European Feminist research conference in Göttingen, and the IV Congress of AIBR (Network of Iberoamerican Anthropologists) in Granada in 2018; the 'International Intersectionality Conference' in Los Angeles, the 'Feminist Alliances: The Discourses, Practices and Politics of Solidarity among Inequalities Conference' in Florence, the 'Global Carework Summit' in Lowell and the 'Global Labor Migration' conference in Amsterdam in 2019; and finally, the 'Genere e r-esistenze in movimento' conference in Trento in 2020. Thanks to the chairs and discussants in our sessions. We also want to thank the editors and the anonymous peer-reviewers with whom we discussed earlier elaborations of our thoughts: Rossella Ciccia, Elisabeth Evans, Rossella Ghigi, Eléonore Lépinard, Alice Mattoni, Elena Pavan and Catherine Rottenberg.

Last but not least, our warmest thanks go to the community of domestic workers' rights activists who, since the very beginning, have given all possible means of support to our project. Thus our thanks goes to Elizabeth Tang and Myrtle Witbooi as representatives of the International Domestic Workers Federation. Thanks also to all the leaders and activists who have been interviewed by the country experts and whose names are listed in the Appendix to this book. Thanks to all these women, for their energy, knowledge and political vision, which have been the main source of inspiration for us in writing the pages which follow.

1

Introduction

Domestic workers tend to universally epitomize the figure of the low-skilled, low-valued, precarious, hidden and unorganized labourer. Overwhelmingly women, migrant and working class, they are also commonly low-caste, Black and indigenous. Belonging to society's most marginalized groups, they are largely excluded from labour protection laws and are significantly impacted by the social shifts brought about by globalization. The growth in urbanization and migration; the reconfiguration of class structures, gender norms, life-styles and families; and the structural adjustment in the Global South, coupled with the crisis of welfare and care provision in the Global North, have all shaped the sector in different and at times complex ways.

Concomitantly, since the beginning of the 21st century the situation facing paid domestic workers has increasingly garnered attention and action has been taken to improve the rights of those working in the sector. Among those making this change happen are international organizations such as the International Labour Organization (ILO) and the Commission on the Status of Women, as well as non-governmental organizations (NGOs), trade unions and grassroots domestic workers' organizations active at national, regional and transnational levels.

As the workers themselves progressively mobilize and become more visible, paid domestic work grows in prominence as an issue of global governance, and this has led to an accompanying improvement in labour laws and policies affecting the sector. These increasingly visible mobilizations appear to challenge the boundaries between labour movements, feminist struggles and so-called identity-based activism. They may offer a space of convergence between several issues of social justice that have traditionally been seen as distinct, such as struggles for the rights of workers, women, carers, racialized minorities and migrants.

These new developments have been especially true for the years under analysis in this book, the decade 2008–18. This notable period corresponds to what we call the 'C189 process', triggered by the ILO decision to put domestic work on the agenda. This process produced the first international convention regulating the sector, namely Convention No. 189 concerning Decent Work for Domestic Workers (C189), and the related Recommendation 201, adopted at the end of the International Labour Conference in June 2011 in Geneva. The convention set international labour standards for paid care and domestic work, equating the labour rights of these workers to those of other workers in ratifying countries. This crucial event at the transnational level has filtered down to the local context through myriad paths, with international standards and global campaigns on the issue being received, appropriated or resisted in different ways by institutional and non-institutional actors, including domestic workers' organizations.

Feminist scholarship since the 1960s has used many different terms to refer to the labour that is performed in the household – connecting it to its larger function of 'reproduction' or to its dimension of 'care'. While we engage with these concepts throughout the book, our research takes as its objects of analysis paid 'domestic work' and remunerated 'domestic workers' – also increasingly called 'household workers'. Broadly speaking, domestic workers provide personal and household care in the frame of a formal or informal employment relationship, which means that they work for one or more households for a wage or for other forms of remuneration. Occupations and tasks which domestic work is considered to encompass vary across countries: workers may cook, clean, do the laundry and ironing, take care of children, the elderly and the disabled, tend to the garden or pets, or drive the family car. They may work part time, full time or on an hourly basis, and may or may not live in the home of their employer. However, domestic work is defined according to the workplace, which is the household. The familial rather than business-like character of the employers and the apparently 'private' nature of the home are given as justification for the discrimination that affects these jobs. This is compounded by the difficulty in defining some of the tasks involved, in measuring their productivity and by cultural assumptions around women's and other subaltern groups' natural disposition to care and service, upon which these tasks are based.

Such usage of the term 'domestic work' is consistent with the definition adopted by the ILO and, in particular, C189, which refers to domestic work as 'work performed *in* and *for* the household'. It is also consistent with the language deployed by the global domestic workers' movement, which provides a common English translation for several local terms used in the different national contexts (see, among others, ILO, 2013: 7). The ILO definition is an attempt to cover the broad range of domestic work that exists around the world. However, the definition has been contested by some domestic workers' organizations. For instance, in the Indian context many domestic workers' organizations would prefer to narrow the definition to that of work performed *in* the household rather than *for* the household, since the conditions of the largely female workforce in the home, who, for instance, engage in cooking and cleaning, are very different to those of the predominantly male gardeners or drivers, and in practice the two groups organize separately (Agarwala and Saha, 2018).

With these elements in mind, we went on to develop the research project which led to this book. 'DomEQUAL: A Global Approach to Paid Domestic Work and Global Inequalities' (2016–21), is a project funded by a Starting Grant of the European Research Council, and which analysed domestic workers' conditions and struggles across nine countries and three continents. In Asia, it covered India, the Philippines and Taiwan; in South America, Colombia, Ecuador and Brazil; and in Europe, Spain, Italy and Germany. Our goal within DomEQUAL has been to contribute to the understanding of the multi-layered transformation that has seen domestic work become an object of governance, conflict and negotiation, entailing processes of political subjectification and collective organizing on the part of a category of workers conventionally regarded as 'unorganizable'. In our approach, the struggles for domestic workers' rights present a useful case for exploring the question of how transformations of intersectional inequalities take place in a global context. Some of the themes that emerge may therefore contribute to a better understanding of the organized struggles not only of domestic workers but also of other multiply marginalized groups globally.

In the remainder of this chapter we will introduce the analytical directions which have guided our research project by setting out the conceptual tools and the scholarly debates we have drawn on. In the first section we argue that domestic workers' struggles, especially in relation to the 'C189 process', represent a good case to explore how what come to be identified as 'global rights', in this case the rights of domestic workers, are imported to the level of local struggles. In the second section we argue that domestic workers' struggles are useful in examining how intersectional politics may actually be practised on the ground. In the third section we argue that domestic workers' struggles can be used to interrogate the role that feminist and women's rights activists play in the fight for the rights of multiply marginalized women. In the fourth and final section we introduce our multi-layered approach to analysing the transformations in domestic workers' rights, an approach which looks at the sector itself, at domestic workers' rights organizations, at the 'field of action' mobilizing for domestic workers' rights and at the 'interpretative frames' used by the actors in this field. The chapter ends by providing details about our methodology and summarizing the contents of the book.

Domestic workers' rights go global

In 2017, DomEQUAL organized two meetings at Ca' Foscari University of Venice, bringing together leaders of the global domestic workers' rights movement, including representatives of the International Domestic Workers Federation (IDWF). They were joined by academics from the Research Network for Domestic Workers' Rights.[1] Following the meetings, we became aware of the urgency of finding ways to compare contexts that were profoundly different, yet which were all, in their own ways, engaged in processes of change towards similar end goals. In other words, examining how a global right can be realized at the local level.

This change began with what we have called the 'C189 process' and the promulgation of ILO C189 in 2011. The Convention, counting 31 ratifications as of January 2021,[2] has continued to represent a motor for change globally in the years since its enactment. It is important to note that the ILO process itself only came about as a result of the activism of domestic workers and their allies. Indeed, in some contexts, organizing for domestic workers' rights preceded the Convention and was not the result of initiatives of the ILO or other international actors based in or associated with the Global North, including European Union (EU) institutions (such as the one financing our project). Clearly, a number of domestic workers' movements that emerged in the Global South had a lot to teach organizations based in other parts of the world in terms of organizing, alliance making, radical critiques of reproduction, inequalities and the care crisis, among other things. The networks promoting domestic workers' rights were particularly active in Asia and Latin America, and less so in Europe, while the Convention itself had been ratified in many countries of the Global South, where it has become an important tool for activists demanding greater rights. However, it has been received and used in diverse ways, which require some elaboration.

In 2008, the ILO decided to put what later became C189 on the agenda of their next assemblies, immediately prefiguring the possibility of a revolutionary shift. For many, it was incredible to think of a convention for a sector which traditionally suffered from an immense lack of rights, and for a form of work which in most countries was not even recognized as such. Where it was recognized, it was given second-class status for not being considered 'real work'. Given this scenario, having gathered the opinions of experts and activists, the ILO suggested that domestic workers should be treated as other workers in their respective countries. Equality was conceived in terms of salary, but also in terms of protection in the workplace. The ILO also demanded that the expansion of labour rights had to be accompanied by the creation of new forms of association and, where possible, trade unions formed by domestic workers themselves. Finally, these legal and socio-political transformations could not happen without a cultural change at the level of the social representation of these workers, with a view to countering the stigma attached to them. In so doing, the Convention combined the fight for the specific cause of domestic workers' labour rights with a wider struggle for the human rights of particularly vulnerable subjects, from undocumented migrants to low-caste and racialized women. C189 incorporates an intersectional approach, appealing simultaneously to issues of gender, race, ethnicity, religious and class-based discrimination at work, and advocating for the protection of the most vulnerable categories of domestic workers, with special reference to migrant workers (Schwenken, 2013; Fish, 2017). It is indeed this capacity of C189 to include previously invisible subjects which epitomizes what Clifford Bob (2011) refers to as a 'new right', meaning 'new' international human rights ascribed to groups traditionally neglected by society, as in the case of disabled people internationally or Dalit people in India.

Correspondingly, in the years 2008–18, the case of paid domestic workers gradually emerged as a matter of political debate involving a growing number of international actors, attracted by the emergence of domestic workers' rights as an increasingly pressing policy issue at the global level. Actors who had already been involved found new legitimation. As a result, we see a large range of actors in the field, from political parties, trade unions and grassroots workers' groups to humanitarian NGOs, religious organizations and international organizations for workers' rights, such as the International Trade Union Confederation (ITUC) and the global network Women in Informal Employment: Globalizing and Organizing (WIEGO). International bodies such as the ILO, UN-Women, the Commission on the Status of Women, and the European Parliament have also taken a stand (Fish, 2017). Finally, the founding of the IDWF in Montevideo in 2013 (previously the International Domestic Workers Network, IDWN) is evidence of the global expansion of the movement.

Against this backdrop, we set out to explore the impact of C189 as an instrument for the governance of global rights in a back-and-forth relationship between the national and transnational level. An expanding literature on the Convention has begun to address this issue in recent times. Indeed, scholars have seen the mobilization around C189 as a pivotal moment in the scaling-up of local and national movements and the formation of the IDWF as transnational collective actor. For instance, they have described the key role played by the IDWN and by some regional and national organizations in the drafting of the Convention in Geneva in 2011 (Schwenken, 2016; Fish, 2017; Acciari, 2019). Louisa Acciari (2019) suggests that this process constitutes a paradigmatic example of the ability of 'subaltern groups' from the Global South to generalize their demands and produce new rights. Other scholars have focused on the legal advancements brought about by signing the Convention into national law (Albin and Mantouvalou, 2012), while others still have looked at the impact of C189 on national or regional social movements and on the political processes related to the campaigns for its ratification and consequent implementation (Schwenken, 2013; Blofield and Jokela, 2018).

A comparative study of the transformations in the working conditions of domestic labourers in the nine countries which are the object of this research constitutes a strong vantage point from which to observe the different dynamics engendered by the C189 process. Each represents distinct positioning within the process of globalization, with differing socio-cultural contexts, mobilizations for domestic workers' rights and levels of involvement in the C189 process. All the countries we selected for the present study have been impacted by processes of change in the field of domestic work in the last decade, and in all of them activists and lawmakers have proposed bills to better the conditions of domestic workers, albeit with different outcomes. We included countries that have been involved in the C189 process, and countries where this process was marginal or even absent. Indeed, in the context of Europe, we included two countries which have ratified C189 – Italy and Germany – and Spain, which has not. In Latin America, we included two countries which have ratified it and Brazil, which hadn't at the time of our investigation.[3] As for Asia, we included the Philippines, the only country in Asia which has ratified C189, India, which has not, and Taiwan, which is exceptional in that it cannot ratify C189, since it is not a member of the United Nations (UN).

These countries also represent a combination of areas differently positioned in the processes of globalization across the Global North–South divide, and where various social inequalities are played out in the domestic work sector. Crucially, the nine countries are clustered in three geographical areas – Latin America, Asia and Europe – rather than from more dispersed locations, so as to allow not only global, but also intra-regional comparisons. For instance, international migration and segmentation by national origin strongly marks the sector in the three European countries, as well as Taiwan. Internal migration from rural and impoverished areas to major cities shapes domestic work in many of the countries of the Global South included in the study, such as India, Brazil and Colombia, while the combination of internal mobility and emigration of workers characterizes Ecuador and the Philippines.

Intersectionality in action

Self-organized groups of domestic workers, that is, trade unions, associations and networks composed of and led by women employed in the sector, have emerged as prominent in the politicization of domestic workers and in the struggle for their rights across all the countries studied. Interestingly, domestic workers' organizing represents a form of collective action developed by workers who, being subjected to both economic and symbolic exclusion, fight simultaneously for labour rights, human dignity and social recognition. Domestic workers are typically multiply marginalized – be that on the basis of gender, class, caste, nationality, race, ethnicity or rural background. As a result, the organizations involve and seek to represent these social groups, in addition to domestic workers per se. For all of these reasons, as we have said, domestic workers' mobilizations challenge the boundaries between labour movements, feminist struggles and what is sometimes referred to as identity-based activism (Fish, 2017). Namely, they may provide opportunities for encounter and convergence between struggles for labour rights and class equity, women's rights and gender equality, the right to care for dependent and disabled people, cultural recognition for ethnic and racialized minorities, and anti-racism and migrants' rights.

This coming together may make room for solidarity, coalitions and alliances across different social movements and political projects. At the same time, the regulation of domestic work is a contentious issue, revealing conflicting interests and power asymmetries among and within social movements that can affect the relationship between domestic workers' rights groups and other actors in the field. For all these reasons, we believe that domestic workers' movements put 'intersectionality in action' and may be fruitfully analysed through an intersectional approach.

Originating in Black, postcolonial, lesbian feminisms and critical race theory, intersectional analyses reveal the interplay of several axes of social division (such as race, gender, class, age, sexuality, ability, religion, origin, nationality and so on) in shaping people's lives and identities, social inequalities and the organization of power in society (Marchetti, 2013; Hancock, 2016; Romero, 2017; Collins and Bilge, 2020). As such, since the second half of the 1990s the idea of intersectionality has been taken up as a critical tool to explore a vast array of political projects and social movements (Cho et al, 2013: 800–4).

In our view, the ways in which authors in this expanding field of study have addressed these questions may be divided into two categories. A first research direction focuses on the difficulties that many social movements and organizations face when dealing with complex inequalities, trying to address issues such as multiple marginalization and power imbalances among their members. Studies cast light on the disempowering and exclusionary outcomes of movements that seek equality along a single dimension (for example, only gender, or only class, or only ethnicity) and fail to tackle the intersection between specific categories of identity and related forms of oppression (Crenshaw, 1991; Ferree and Roth, 1998; Strolovitch, 2007). A second set of studies focuses on the uses of intersectionality as 'a social movement strategy' (Chun et al, 2013; Evans, 2016). These studies concentrate on cases in which an intersectional approach to complex inequalities is involved in processes of empowerment and organizing from the margins, leading to the formation of new political subjectivities, groups or coalitions through which multiply marginalized subjects can make their voices heard. Taken together, these two streams suggest that intersectionality is increasingly seen as an inspiring idea and political praxis for social struggles beyond feminist and anti-racist movements.

Some authors suggest that the mapping of the various uses, forms of resistance and outcomes of intersectionality on the ground is a useful task that deserves further analysis (Bassel and Lépinard, 2014; Woehrle, 2014; Irvine et al, 2019; Evans and Lépinard, 2020a). Different proposals have been advanced for how this could be done. In-depth studies on women's and other social movements have investigated the use of an intersectional framework in relation to different aspects of a social movement, such as the construction of collective identity (Roth, 2004; Carastathis, 2013; Cherubini, 2018), the framing processes and cultural repertoires that a movement adopts (Cruells López and Ruiz Garcia, 2014; Lépinard, 2014; Okechukwu, 2014) and, finally, the conflicts, coalitions and alliances it may spark (Cole, 2008; Townsend-Bell, 2011; Predelli et al, 2012; Verloo, 2013). More broadly, Patricia Hill Collins and Sirma Bilge (2020) conceive of intersectionality as a critical praxis reflected in a vast array of social justice movements, guiding activists and practitioners in dealing with social problems that come with complex social inequalities. Ange-Marie Hancock (2011) identifies intersectionality as a justice-oriented framework for exercising solidarity and building political coalitions across differences, which may be embraced by collective actors in order to overcome what she calls the 'Oppression Olympics', that is, a detrimental competition among oppressed groups. Lastly, Elizabeth Evans and Éléonore Lépinard (2020b) argue that intersectionality can be practised in feminist and queer movements as a collective identity involved in the construction of multiple-axis organizations, as a strategy to build coalitions across differences and movements or, finally, as a repertoire for ensuring the inclusion of women and subjects from minority groups into existing organizations.

Drawing on these contributions, in this book we wish to embrace the question of how social movements make intersectionality on the ground, by applying it to the case of domestic workers' movements. Our analysis focuses on settings and types of movements that have rarely been researched in the literature on intersectionality discussed earlier. Indeed, when we look at the empirical cases investigated in this literature we can see that – with a few exceptions (such as Coll, 2010; Alberti et al, 2013; Bernardino-Costa, 2014; Cherubini and Tudela-Vázquez, 2016; Agarwala and Chun, 2019a; Tilly et al, 2019) – the studies largely concentrate on feminist movements, while very little attention is given to movements that may not define themselves as feminist (Molyneux, 2001). Such movements include women workers' movements (Cobble, 2005) and, in particular, movements for an informal, precarious and mostly female workforce, such as domestic workers. Further, we have also observed that most studies have taken place in contexts of the Global North and have been focused at the national level, although the recent expansion of the field is rapidly changing this picture. In contrast, in this book we focus on the women's labour movement, and we use a large-scale comparative analysis which includes both Global Northern and Southern contexts.

Some relevant methodological issues arise when engaging with the narratives of these movements in a comparative way. Firstly, we draw on notions of the 'translocality' and 'transtemporality' of social divisions, as developed by Nira Yuval-Davis (2015) and Floya Anthias (2012), to look at the way social categories can have different meanings and imply different power relations in different national contexts and historical periods. Secondly, we pay attention to issues of language. As scholars and activists we – the authors – contribute to academic and political spaces in which 'intersectionality' is a widespread and highly debated word. However, many of the groups we met through the project, including domestic worker activists, tend to use different language and do not always use the terms 'intersectionality' and 'intersectional' to refer to the phenomenon of overlapping experiences of gender, class, race, migration and so on that they personally live through. We may say that they use intersectionality as a 'form of critical praxis' without necessarily using the term (Collins, 2015), and that they develop an 'intersectional consciousness' and 'intersectional-like thinking' (Hancock, 2016). In short, according to our interpretation, these workers 'make intersectionality', although often under other names, as the analysis throughout the book will show.

Feminism and domestic workers' struggles

Feminist perspectives have greatly contributed both to our activism as feminists growing up in Italy and to our academic training in the social sciences in different western European countries in the 2000s. Building on this knowledge and experience, we have made sense of domestic workers' demands for equal rights as aligned with feminist claims for the general improvement of women's conditions around the world and as a paradigmatic case for the valorization of reproductive labour, which has been advocated in feminist debates (Federici, 1975; Picchio, 1992; Folbre, 2001). The same approach to domestic work as 'a feminist issue' was shared by many of the feminist scholars, policy makers and activists whom we encountered during the research, including interviewees for the project fieldwork (see section on 'Methodology').

However, when domestic work becomes a paid activity, troubles arise within feminist debates and this touches on power differentials and hierarchies existing between women. We also noticed that feminist organizations only rarely engaged directly in struggles for domestic workers' rights, and the conceptual linkages that we see do not automatically correspond to the formation of alliances between the two movements. Moreover, domestic workers' groups are often reluctant to define themselves as feminist, in a similar vein to other women activists who mobilize in support of workers' rights or against social marginalization. In fact, the perception of being at a distance from the feminist movement is a recurrent topic in the accounts of domestic workers' activists across different national contexts and time periods. This is at least partly connected to the fact that in a number of contexts feminists delegate care and domestic tasks, and they therefore become employers of domestic workers. This is especially true in contexts in which there is little public provision of care and these tasks remain mainly women's responsibility. This scenario is likely to give rise to a conflict of interests, and even to affect political interventions by feminists in the field of domestic workers' rights (Tronto, 2002; Pitch, 2004; May, 2011).

The complicated relationship between domestic workers' rights activism and feminist movements merited further study. We began by examining the conditions that made it possible to have feminist organizations allied with struggles for domestic workers' rights in certain countries and not in others. As will become apparent, to understand this diversity one must take into account the different feminist traditions, the other actors involved in domestic workers' rights and also, importantly, the interpretative frames that have been mobilized in each context to promote them, which will be discussed in the following chapters.

In this book we argue that despite the fact that in many contexts there has been a disconnection between the two movements at the practical level, they nevertheless share a great deal in their common critique of contemporary capitalist societies and the exploitation of women, migrants and domestic workers within them. Domestic workers' rights activists often seem to build their arguments on the same anti-capitalist interpretative frames used by feminist groups, yet they expand them through an intersectional analysis so as to include racialized, lower-class, migrant and other minority groups in ways which few feminist movements have accomplished. This capacity to rework existing frameworks becomes a creative force at the level of discourse, where different alliances may take place, and indeed it has been argued that it can contribute to the revitalization of contemporary feminisms (Federici, 2016). In order to understand our argument about this discursive convergence and creativity, it important that we begin by highlighting the main elements of those feminist approaches which provide an interpretation of domestic workers' labour conditions and social positioning.

Reproductive labour

The first feminist debate that is relevant to domestic workers' rights is the one on reproductive labour. This debate goes back to the 1960s, when feminist scholars in numerous countries concentrated their attention on what they called reproductive labour, with the aim of shedding light on the specificity of women's oppression within the political economy of capitalist societies. The notion of reproductive labour refers to the material and relational work necessary for the creation and recreation of the workforce through time. Such work includes all activities aimed at the well-being and survival of societies and, in particular, tasks relating to nurturing, tending to and assisting children and the sick, as well as to carrying out chores such as cleaning, cooking and washing, which benefit all members of the household. This reproductive labour has historically been a normative obligation for women, as opposed to the assignment of productive labour to men, that is, work for the production of material goods. This dichotomy has been reinforced by moral, religious and pseudo-scientific views that emphasize women's ostensibly natural aptitudes and skills in this realm, considered inferior to men's sphere of activity. Challenging these assumptions, feminists have long argued for the valorization of reproductive labour within capitalist economies in the same manner as productive work (Larguía and Dumoulin, 1976; Pateman, 1988; Picchio, 1992). Many women around the world have launched campaigns emphasizing the need to recognize the value of these activities, not only in terms of their social value but in terms of the economic contribution that they bring to society (Sarti et al, 2018). This has led, for instance, to the International Wages for Housework Campaign. The campaign is inspired by, among others, Silvia Federici, Mariarosa Dalla Costa and Selma James and has influenced dozens of groups of women in Italy and the United States (US) (Dalla Costa and James, 1975; Federici, 1975; Dalla Costa, 2008, Toupin, 2014; Gissi, 2018b).

Care economy and migration

Over the years, a strand of the feminist movement has preferred to use the term 'care' rather than 'reproductive labour'. In fact, the notion of care draws more links between labour done inside and outside the home, and more attention to the aspects of the work which are perceived to be 'emotional' (Palmer, 1989; Roberts, 1997; Zelizer, 2009), as well as to the needs of children, the ageing and the ill (Mahon and Robinson, 2011; Williams, 2011).

The questions of 'care' have been made particularly relevant by the crisis of welfare states and the intensification of different forms of commodification of reproductive labour, which became visible in most industrialized countries at the beginning of the 1990s. During this time, with the beginning of a crisis in state welfare systems, the refamiliarization of care provision, which was previously taken up by the state, provoked the expansion of a market of home-based care work. This has fostered the spread of a conception of care as a commodity and has made feminist economists speak of a 'care economy': a specific form of economy which differs substantially from others, given the intimate and personalized character of the service provided (Folbre, 2001; Zelizer, 2009).

Although the states that had previously engaged in direct care provision have mostly withdrawn from it, they maintain other functions which greatly influence the sector. Firstly, states have an important regulatory function over these markets, since they provide the normative framework and the regulations that allow private companies or individuals to offer their services inside households (Boris and Klein, 2012). Secondly, states play a key role in dictating the rules and conditions regarding the recruitment of migrant workers, which is of paramount importance today, given the high percentage of international migrants employed in all forms of care provision in many parts of the world. The composition of each labour force has a different character, depending on existing bilateral agreements with workers' countries of origin, including pre-departure training programmes and quota-based policies (Kofman and Raghuram, 2015).

This brings us to the social stratification between workers in the sector, which establishes hierarchies between migrants along nationality, class and gender lines, contributing to their differential inclusion in the labour market. Migrant women are disadvantaged by policies privileging skilled migration as well as by legislation denying work permits to those who have migrated to reunite with their families. The ways in which these racialized and gendered representations inform the organization of domestic and care labour have attracted the scholarly attention of those investigating the idea of a 'cultural' predisposition for caring among women (and men) of certain nationalities (Lan, 2006; Marchetti, 2014; Gallo and Scrinzi, 2016). This stratification perpetuates the devaluation of these jobs, as far as these are considered 'naturally' assigned to the most vulnerable and stigmatized subjects in each context (Gutiérrez-Rodríguez, 2010).

Challenging sisterhood

Finally, feminist scholars have also discussed the unequal distribution of reproductive labour *between* women, since this is often delegated by middle-class, racially privileged women to those from working-class and racialized groups (Nakano Glenn, 1992). It is particularly important to consider these differences when domestic workers are migrants in industrialized countries. Rhacel Parreñas (2001) introduced the concept of the 'international division of reproductive labour' to expand the view from a 'racial' division (Nakano Glenn, 1992) to the global level. On this view, globalization is the scenario within which reproductive work is divided and passed on, from one woman to another – less-privileged – woman. Building on this, Arlie Russell Hochschild (2002) later developed the notion of 'global care chains' to draw attention to the 'care drain' from the Global South to the Global North, with the improved family life of employers occurring at the price of workers' own family lives (Yeates, 2004; Pratt, 2012).

In some countries, the differences between women as employers and employees are strongly inflected by the legacies of slavery and of colonial domination (Marchetti, 2014; Ribeiro Corossacz, 2018; Masi de Casanova, 2019). In parts of the Global South, such legacies have remained alive even after independence and the end of slavery, with the continued existence of indentured labour and servitude. The corresponding racialization of social differences is still evident in contemporary societies, for example in the disparity between different areas of the country and in social stratifications in urban settings. Such differences are of the utmost importance in the relationship between employer and employee, for example when the former belongs to the racially privileged urban middle class and the latter is a racialized woman from a rural background living on the outskirts of a major city, or when women of indigenous heritage work for households belonging to the racially privileged group. Colonial legacies likewise play a major, albeit different, role in the relationship between migrant domestic workers and their employers in the Global North. Here the process of racialization and stereotyping of employees by their employers is rooted in a cultural imagery deriving from the colonial past, and often from the colonial history's erasure from collective memory. This tends to be reinforced by differences in immigration and citizenship status between the employers and the employees, related to the restrictive migration policies present in the Global North.

The inequality affecting the employer–employee dyad therefore challenges notions of 'sisterhood' between women. Assumptions about a mutual understanding based on 'common' gender roles are counterbalanced by class-based hierarchies that simultaneously intertwine with differences based on age, religion, race or ethnicity (Momsen, 1999; Yeoh and Huang, 1999; Haskins, 2001). Women in this dyad have very different social positions and this asymmetry leads to a wide spectrum of phenomena, from abuse, to benevolent, maternalistic support. Through the latter, employers unwittingly exercise their power over subjects who are dependent on them for their legal status and for making a living (Marchetti, 2016a; Barua et al, 2017).

A multi-layered approach to domestic workers' rights

Throughout the DomEQUAL project and the writing of this book, our main research question has been to understand how advancement is made, or not made, in the field of domestic workers' rights. Drawing upon the tools and contributions of social movement, intersectional and feminist scholarship as discussed earlier, we came to study these changes through a multi-layered approach which focuses on the various objects and levels of analysis where change may take place. In choosing this approach we were inspired by the input of activists who, in their narratives, intertwine definitions about domestic workers' identities and considerations about the policing of the sector, as well as discussions on how to organize for the advancement of domestic workers' rights. Yet they often also stress the importance of the relationships between domestic workers' rights organizations and other organizations, institutions and movements. Further, activists also concern themselves with questions regarding the representation of domestic workers in the public sphere and how their organizations can shape this for the better. Therefore, we selected four objects and levels of analysis, which are not to be taken as exhaustive, or as representing a hierarchical or nesting relationship (Walby, 2007). They are the following:

1. The labour sector: we investigate the main features of the domestic work sector, the legal provisions regulating workers' rights and the labour conditions of domestic workers.
2. Domestic workers' rights organizations: we focus on the collective organizing of domestic workers as a social movement. We look at how the collective identity of 'domestic worker' is created through the organizing process, how it acquires political relevance in the eyes of the workers and how it is reflected in the claims, goals and activities of the domestic workers' organizations active in the field.
3. The domestic workers' rights field of action: we come to see domestic workers' groups as embedded within a larger field of action, and we analyse the whole field, made up of actors that variously engage with

the struggle as supporters but also as opponents. This is due partly to the nature of the struggles for domestic workers' rights, which tend to go beyond the bounds of traditional forms of organizing. In so doing, we make use of strategic action field theory, developed by Neil Fligstein and Doug McAdam (Fligstein, 2008; Fligstein and McAdam, 2012) to describe a meso-level dimension in which individual and collective actors interact with each other through a shared purpose. The authors make use of Bourdieu's idea of social fields to provide a means of interpreting the behaviour of collective actors, their reciprocal moves, how they frame their actions, goals and results and how actors 'strategically' (although not always consciously) decide to engage in a specific field in order to achieve certain results.

4. The frames used in the field: we explore the discursive frames that these actors mobilize in this process. Interpretative frames (Benford and Snow, 2000; Johnston and Noakes, 2005) prove to be decisive in shaping these concerns and the corresponding strategic field of action. Specific frames provide actors with tools to understand their problems and identify possible solutions, build consensus and take action. Different formulations of such narratives or emphasis on certain topics to create a shared political agenda may (or may not) pave the way to alliances between groups.

Methodology

In order to address the four levels of analysis illustrated earlier, we developed a quali-quanti methodology, combining, for each country, in-depth interviews with key informants, policy documents, materials written by domestic workers' organizations and other relevant actors, short periods of participant observation, as well as relevant statistical data.

The multi-local fieldwork and the simultaneous collection of data in the nine countries were possible thanks to the work of the country experts, that is, local researchers with previous expertise in the field, coordinated by the Principal Investigator, Sabrina Marchetti, and the senior researchers in Venice. For Latin America, the country experts were Thays Almeida Monticelli in Brazil, María Gabriela Alvarado Pérez in Ecuador and María Fernanda Cepeda Anaya in Colombia (coordinated by Daniela Cherubini); for Europe they were Beatrice Busi in Italy, Silvina Monteros Obelar in Spain and Marlene Seiffarth in Germany (coordinated by Anna Di Bartolomeo); and for Asia they were Madhurima Das in India, Verna Dinah Q. Viajar in the Philippines and Pei-Chieh Hsu in Taiwan (coordinated by Giulia Garofalo Geymonat).

The qualitative in-depth interviews were conducted with key informants, such as activists, organizers, policy makers, legal professionals and experts, between April 2017 and March 2018 by the nine country experts. There were 195 in total (with 200 key informants), of whom 24 were in Brazil, 24 in Colombia, 22 in Ecuador, 22 in Spain, 21 in Germany, 20 in Italy, 19 in the Philippines, 20 in India and 23 in Taiwan. The interviewees were selected after mapping the relevant actors in the field, in collaboration with the country experts – and through a continuous back-and-forth between us and them. Most of the informants were protagonists and/or specialists in the field of care and domestic work, but we also included actors from other fields which, depending on the country, were relevant to the struggle for domestic workers' rights, such as activists for labour, feminist, anti-racist, ethnic minority and disability rights, sex workers' rights, and media practitioners. A minority of the interviewees (22 activists and domestic workers' leaders and one politician) also had former or present experience of working as a domestic worker.

The interview strategy was developed through a pilot of 27 interviews, which allowed us to cluster our participants into three types of key informants, namely (i) academics, (ii) activists and policy makers and (iii) legal experts – even though we were aware that these categories overlap to some extent. Out of the 200 interviewees (of whom 163 identified as women and 37 as men), 70 were academic experts (of whom 61 identified as women and 9 as men), 97 were activists and policy makers (of whom 78 identified as women and 19 as men) and 33 were legal experts (of whom 24 identified as women and 9 as men). Each of these three groups was approached with a different interview guideline to explore their views regarding the condition of domestic workers in their country, and their own involvement in the strategic field of action and knowledge production in respect of domestic workers' rights. We also formulated, in collaboration with country experts, ad hoc questions for activists working in the fields of women's rights, migrants' rights and the media.

The analysis of the interview material was supported by the appraisal of policy documents, texts produced by paid domestic workers' organizations and other relevant actors, and by ongoing dialogue with the country expert for the duration of the project. Further, our interpretation of each country case was supported by the participant observation that we carried out and the conversations that we had with interviewees during our visits to each country, as well as by the information gathered through the workshops with local actors, which we held from late 2017 to early 2018.[4] The project also collected statistical data describing the main demographic trends of each country, including international migration flows. It looked at the main features of the domestic work sector in terms of the size and composition of the workforce and the make-up of the employers, as well as in terms of the country's working conditions and levels of formalization. Here the work of Anna Di Bartolomeo, who worked as senior researcher during the first two years of the project, was pivotal.

The participants had the opportunity to choose various levels of anonymity, and a small minority preferred to have their name (and/or the name of their organization) protected, while the great majority chose to make them public. The interviews were conducted in many languages: Italian, English, Spanish and Portuguese, which we were able to read in the original, but also German, Mandarin, Tagalog and Hindi, which the country experts translated into English. For the analysis of such a large body of text, we used MAXQDA, creating a system of 135 codes divided into 11 clusters, which supported our analysis, in terms both of content and of discourse concerning labour issues, laws and social policies, collective actions, the relationship between actors and so on. The organization and coding of this empirical material was carried out with the contribution of two research assistants based in Venice, Vincenza Perilli and Beatrice Gusmano.

It is worth pointing out that the analysis of the interviews that we provide in this book should be taken as our interpretation of the interviewees' reflexive accounts on collective activities, identity making and processes of social and legal change that they have, to varying degrees, participated in. These subjective accounts were produced by activists and organizations under different circumstances and through different interactions (such as interviews, DomEQUAL workshops, public events and documents). In the case of individual activists, they do not fully represent or capture the entire orientation and action of their groups. The picture we can present as researchers working with interpretations of interpretations (Geertz, 1973), within a qualitative approach, is always partial and situated. Moreover, in our case, the interviews were conducted by country experts, who also informed the interview material with insider knowledge, at least partly following their own activist and research agendas.

We selected the country experts independently, rather than in partnership with an academic or other institution. At the time, they were independent researchers or postgraduate students, and many of them were involved in activism in the field of women's or migrants' rights, trade unionism and human rights more generally. Some of the country experts have already produced their own publications based on their fieldwork with DomEQUAL (see Monticelli and Seiffarth, 2017; Monteros Obelar, 2019; Busi, 2020).

The country experts not only conducted the fieldwork to gather in-depth interviews, but also facilitated our general understanding of the legal, economic and socio-political background of each case. In particular, they were asked to prepare material concerning the general socio-economic and political profile of the country, with a specific focus on the domestic work

17

sector and other relevant fields (for example, migrants' and women's rights); a timeline of the major events that influenced the domestic work sector; and, finally, (at the end of the fieldwork) a self-reflective interview retrospectively commenting on their research experience and on the DomEQUAL research design and approach.

Lastly, the role of country experts was particularly visible during our visits to their countries, during which they provided us with the opportunity to see some of the places where domestic workers gather, to meet a number of the organizations and interviewees and to join them in public events such as demonstrations, parliamentary hearings and public assemblies. In the case of the Philippines, our travel was facilitated by the presence of Charito Basa, a Filipina migrant activist and community researcher based in Italy. Furthermore, the country experts co-organized the local workshops which brought together many of the interviewees.

The trips were unique moments of insight for the authors travelling from Italy. Firstly, we were better able to understand the ways in which the debate on domestic work is constructed differently in each national context. Secondly, we were able to gain a greater understanding of the relationships existing between the actors involved in the research and the country experts working for DomEQUAL. Finally, and this was crucial, the visits helped us to better see the position we occupied as researchers.

Indeed, positionality has emerged as an important issue throughout the research process, with respect to a complex web of negotiations and power-loaded relationships. Certainly, the entire research process has been deeply influenced by our position as White women academics from a university located in southern Europe, working in a well-funded EU research project. Furthermore, the position that the country experts themselves occupied vis-à-vis the participants and the domestic workers' movements has been very important. Writing this book has been nourished by the recognition of the pitfalls and potentialities of our specific (personal and research) standpoints. Indeed, becoming aware of these positionings and of the power relationships they imply is a fundamental yet inevitably ongoing process in feminist research (Haraway, 1988; Alcoff, 1991; Naples, 2003). In the following, we share some of our reflections and strategies regarding these matters.

Each of the country experts brought to the research their own background, resources and strategies to simultaneously negotiate their collaboration with us, as their research supervisors based in Italy, and their relationships with participants. The latter had to include not only grassroots activists, but also policy makers and experts. The country experts shared some characteristics as women, as junior academics and, in most cases, as nationals of the countries they studied. Yet, they had different positionings in relation to other important aspects, including those concerning class, sexuality, ethnicity and level of personal engagement in social movements. Each of the nine country experts worked for the project in a relationship of constant communication and supervision with us, while simultaneously, at least partly, following their own research and activist research agendas. Some of them started to volunteer for domestic workers' organizations, others activated their networks in labour or feminist movements or made beneficial use of their previous work experience at a variety of institutions, including universities and the ILO. This has in turn influenced both the relationship with us and the production of different qualitative materials, with some being more activist oriented, others more focused on policy reforms, some more intimate, others more formal and so on. These differences were also apparent in the self-reflective document that they submitted at the end of their collaboration.

The position of the three of us as authors and coordinators of this research certainly needs to be read as one of privilege vis-à-vis the country experts, the research participants and, crucially, domestic workers' movements (Federici, 2009; Chesters, 2012; Lasalle, 2020). Outside Europe in particular, we experienced reciprocal expectations and stereotypes, accompanied by the risks of knowledge exploitation from our side in relation to the country experts, the local scholars and the activists. We have tried to respond to this complex situation in a variety of ways. This includes eliciting the country experts' and our own reflections, during supervisions, informal conversations and in the self-reflective document mentioned earlier. Furthermore, we sought to address the issue through the inclusion of local academics in the advisory board of the project and the mobilization of the Research Network for Domestic Workers' Rights, of which Sabrina has long been a part. As for the relationship with activists, this was particularly important in the early and later phases of the project. In 2017 we were able to invite a group of leaders of the domestic workers' rights movement from various countries to Venice, as explained at the beginning of this chapter. Together with Beyond Trafficking and Slavery–Open Democracy, we developed the documentary film entitled *Domestic Workers Speak*[5] and published the open access volume *Domestic Workers Speak: A Global Fight for Rights and Recognition* (Garofalo Geymonat et al, 2017), both collecting the voices of the domestic workers' organizers around the world. In autumn 2021 we launched the web documentary series called *Domestic Workers' Rights: Intersectionality in Action*. The development of these projects of knowledge dissemination has been essential to the research process as a whole, not least because it helped us partially to redefine our relationship with some of the activists and participants in a more collaborative way.

Structure of the book

Following this introduction, our book is divided into four chapters, each of them reflecting our attention to the different levels of analysis presented earlier. These are: the main features of the domestic work sector, its legal provisions and workers' rights (Chapter 2), transformations in the strategic field of action of domestic workers' rights (Chapter 3), the collective identity and activities of domestic workers' organizations (Chapter 4) and the frames used to promote domestic workers' rights, with special attention to feminist approaches to reproductive labour and the commodification of care (Chapter 5).

Chapter 2 in particular aims to give a background to the different pathways through which domestic workers' rights emerged as a political terrain in the nine national contexts, over a period of time that precedes and includes the decade 2008–18. For each country, we focus on the changes and turning points that this sector has gone through in recent decades. We look at the size of the sector, its relevance and composition and the profiles and conditions of workers and (where possible) employers. Importantly, we connect such transformations to the demographic, socioeconomic, cultural and political changes that mark each country. In each case, we also trace the (albeit partial) history of domestic workers' rights, focusing on both the regulation of rights through legal reforms and policy interventions and the struggle for rights through collective organizing and mobilization in the field.

Building on this background, Chapter 3 discusses the role of C189 and, in particular, the ways that C189 as a tool of global governance of domestic workers' rights was incorporated, promoted or resisted in each country. We interrogate the ways in which what we identify as a global right can be applied to the level of local struggles. In particular, we offer an analysis of the dynamics created by the C189 process in each of the nine countries under study, by using a strategic action field perspective. We describe how, in each country, the main elements characterizing the strategic field of action – namely the actors, their goals and their relationships – have evolved over the period 2008–18. We also introduce the interpretative frames that have animated the field in giving meaning to the issue of domestic workers' rights in each country. In this analysis, we suggest that the C189 process was what Fligstein and McAdam (2012) call an 'external shock' which affected each country, yet prompted different dynamics depending on contextual factors. Building on this discussion, we elaborate a comparative assessment of what has happened in the nine countries in relation to the C189 process. We describe how it has been incorporated, challenged, modified or even opposed, depending on comparable local factors that relate to the socioeconomic, cultural and political context in which the C189 process took place at the national level.

Chapter 4 switches the focus of analysis by looking at domestic workers' groups, associations and trade unions. Among those we encountered in our fieldwork, we focus on organizations that were particularly active in the years 2008–18. We engage with the question of the 'making of intersectionality' on the ground, exploring the possible use of intersectionality as a social movement strategy. Keeping this question at the centre of our inquiry, we look at the way domestic workers make sense of their specific experience of marginalization and, on that basis, how they build a collective identity as organized workers and how they develop their actions and articulate their political demands.

The question of intersectionality returns in Chapter 5, which addresses the complicated relationship between the domestic workers' and the feminist and women's rights movements. In Chapter 5 we try to make sense of the different positions that the latter groups took in the strategic field of action of domestic workers' rights across our nine countries in the years 2008–18. In our view, it is important to take into consideration the possible connection that may exist at the discursive level between these movements. Indeed, our interview material indicates that, in several instances, actors in the field of domestic workers' rights draw upon prominent feminist discourses in framing their struggles for domestic workers. Notable among these are those related to reproductive labour and the commodification of care. Yet, when doing so, these actors crucially negotiate and elaborate on such feminist discourses, typically complicating the exclusively gender-based analysis that some feminist tendencies promote.

2

Scenarios of Domestic Workers' Rights

Paid domestic workers are estimated to make up a population of at least 67 million across the world, the majority of whom (80 per cent) are women (ILO, 2013),[1] while around 11.2 million are international migrants (ILO, 2015).[2] ILO global estimates indicate that at least 11.5 million children below the legal age of employment were involved in paid domestic work in 2012 (ILO, 2017b). This labour sector is particularly important in the Global South, where it mainly provides jobs for low-status, racialized, indigenous, rural girls and women and (in the case of India) the low-caste population. From a quantitative point of view, for instance, the sector employs one in four female workers in Latin America and the Caribbean and almost one in three in the Middle East (ILO, 2013). Moreover, many countries in the Global South and in the periphery of the West are impacted by the phenomenon, as a portion of their (mostly female) population consistently leave to take up care and domestic work abroad. This is especially the case in Asia-Pacific countries, South America and Eastern Europe, which feed South-to-North, South-to-South, but also North-to-North global migration flows. At the same time, in many Global Northern countries, remunerated domestic work has always been a significant sector for the employment of female workers. In the past, this was particularly the case for internal and intraregional rural-to-urban migrants, while in the last few decades (with different timing, depending on the context) the role has been increasingly filled by international migrants responding to the welfare crisis and the care needs of affluent and ageing societies. Some of the dynamics sketched out so far often coexist, as some countries may be both senders and receivers of migrant domestic workers, as in the case of those countries that have both a large overseas and internal domestic workforce. In other words, domestic work has a global nature, yet it has different characteristics in each national and regional context, and across time.

Within this scenario, what does domestic work look like in the nine countries and the different regions of the world involved in the DomEQUAL study? What common elements and connections link together such diverse contexts, and what local specificities did we observe? Importantly, what rights have domestic workers already achieved, and what rights are they still struggling for?

In this chapter we try to answer these questions by presenting an overview of the main trends characterizing paid domestic work in each of the nine countries, and focusing on domestic workers' exclusion from and entitlement to rights. We see this chapter as a global journey whereby we explore the various pathways through which domestic workers' rights emerged as a political terrain, in the different national contexts taken into account in the study. This means that we look at how domestic work became an object of governance, conflict and negotiation involving several actors, and how it came to entail processes of political subjectification and collective organizing by part of a socially and politically marginalized sector of society, a category of workers conventionally regarded as 'unorganizable'.

Such analysis will provide the context for the cases we discuss in the rest of the book, insofar as it reconstructs the background against which the issue of workers' rights has developed in the nine countries, up until the period we focus on. For this reason, the time frame of the present chapter is broader and not limited to the late 2000s and the 2010s. It is also flexible, on the basis of local specificities and temporalities in relation to the dynamics of the domestic workers' movement and the history of inclusion and exclusion from rights in each national context.

What we propose here as a presentation of each case is based on three kinds of sources. First, our reading of the existing literature on the matter, including academic research, and reports compiled by international and national bodies, NGOs, trade unions and experts. Second, the secondary analysis of the available statistical data collected by the country experts and supervised by demographer Anna Di Bartolomeo (see Chapter 1). Third, the qualitative data, including the accounts and interpretations shared by the interviewees during interviews and in the local workshops, as well as our own observations and those that the country experts shared with us during the fieldwork.

Philippines

With domestic work being the first occupation among the 2.4 million Filipinos working abroad (source: Survey on Overseas Filipinos, Philippine Statistics Authority-PSA, year 2015), the Philippines occupies a unique role in the global care chain. Since the 1990s the Philippines has progressively become one of the leading countries in the promotion of migrant domestic workers' rights (Chavez and Piper, 2015). It is perhaps less known that there is also a large domestic workforce in the Philippines, and that the country has a long tradition of domestic work undertaken by women and girls for their extended families or communities. In 2017, the official estimate of domestic workers in the Philippines was 1.85 million (source: Filipino Labour Force Survey, Philippine Statistics Authority-PSA, year 2017). This number is considered an underestimate for several reasons. First, it excludes important parts of the workforce, such as those under the age of 15 (who are not officially allowed to work in the country), those providing domestic work as a secondary occupation and those working in the homes of wealthier relatives without pay, in exchange for shelter, education or daily subsistence for themselves or their children (ILO, 2011; Daway, 2014). More generally, a large portion of domestic work is known to belong to the informal economy, which in the Philippines was estimated in 2008 to occupy 15.6 million workers, which is 38 per cent of the total working population (source: Informal Sector Survey, year 2008).[3]

The distribution of paid domestic work reflects the significant socioeconomic inequalities in the country, especially along lines of class, rural/urban residency and region of origin; the Gini Index was 44.4 in 2015, the Multidimensional Poverty Index 0.024, or 7.3 per cent of the population vulnerable to multidimensional poverty in 2019. Domestic work is mostly provided by women (84 per cent, versus 38 per cent of all workers) and young people (34 per cent of women domestic workers and 29 per cent of men domestic workers are 15–24 years old, versus 19 per cent of all workers) (ILO, 2011) migrating to metropolitan areas from rural areas. Live-in arrangements are still common, but have been in decline, falling from about 30 per cent in 2010 to about 20 per cent in 2016 (King-Dejardin, 2018). Most domestic workers come from the Visayas and Mindanao provinces, both characterized by poverty and environmental problems, and parts of which have been involved in armed conflicts since the end of the 1960s. Recruitment of domestic workers is mostly through friends and relatives, although agencies may also be involved. Households that employ domestic workers are concentrated in the Metro Manila Region and the surrounding provinces of Cavite, Laguna, Batangas, Rizal and Quezon (known collectively as Calabarzon). A typical middle-class household employs one or two live-in domestic workers, but lower middle-class families also often have some form of domestic help, in a context where almost no public support for childcare and care for the elderly is available (ILO, 2011).

The Philippines has a national law regulating domestic work, called the Kasambahay Law (2011), which provides, among other things, for minimum wage rates (for full-time workers) that may be increased periodically, as well as mandatory social protection coverage, weekly days off and written contracts of employment.[4] However, the law has some significant limitations, especially in its implementation, and regarding part-time workers. While the law provides that domestic workers can join labour organizations of their choosing and create their own trade unions, issues of mediation, grievance handling and collective bargaining remain weak. The law requires employers to register domestic workers for the social security system, health insurance (Philhealth) and housing benefits (Pag-Ibig) schemes. Yet the number of employers who do so is very limited – although slowly increasing for full-time, live-in workers – with the percentage of live-in domestic workers contributing to social security increasing from 3.4 per cent to 6 per cent and 13 per cent in 2005, 2010 and 2015, respectively (ILO, 2017a). The minimum wage was officially raised in 2018, and for Metro Manila it has gone up from P2,500 (in 2013) to P3,000 (equivalent to approximately USD56) per month for full-time workers – to which food and accommodation is added for live-in workers. However, this salary is still notably lower than for other workers – for instance, the minimum wage in Metro Manila's manufacturing sector in 2018 was set at a *daily* figure of P475.

The condition of domestic workers started to become an issue of public concern in the Philippines in the 1990s, in connection with legal cases against Filipino domestic workers accused of murder in Singapore (Flor Contemplacion, executed in 1995) and in the United Arab Emirates (Sarah Balabagan, repatriated in 1996). The cases were broadly publicized in the Philippines and mobilized public opinion, overseas workers, NGOs, religious groups and embassies. During those years, the Filipino government introduced measures to promote the welfare of Filipinos working abroad, in particular the Migrant Workers and Overseas Filipinos Act of 1995. In 1994 it launched the Technical Education and Skills Development Authority, a system of skill certification for overseas Filipino workers that includes domestic workers. Civil society was fast developing in the new democracy, with women's initiatives and non-traditional political parties representing marginalized groups, such as the Akbayan Citizens' Action Party, which has been supporting domestic workers' struggles. Following these mobilizations, the Anti-Violence against Women and Their Children Act was passed in 2004, and the Reproductive Health Law in 2012.

During the 2000s, the Philippines became a key player in the international debate on domestic work, and in the C189 process in Geneva. Ratification of C189 was signed by President B. Aquino III in 2012, following a fast and low-profile lobbying strategy, and the Kasambahay Law was quickly passed by Parliament in 2013, whereas previous Bills on domestic workers had been proposed since the 1980s without any follow-up. This phase of rapid policy change, which continued until President Duterte came to power in 2016, was notably led by the Domestic Work Technical Working Group (TWG), a primarily ad hoc tripartite institution created in 2009, which was very active up until 2016. The TWG, initially invited by the ILO Regional Office, includes state representatives (in particular what is now called the Bureau of Workers with Special Concerns at the Department of Labour and Employment, and the Philippine Commission on Women), employers' organizations (the industry-based Employers' Confederation of the Philippines) and workers' organizations (ILO, 2009; King-Dejardin, 2018). As regards workers' organizations, key actors that became involved in the field around the C189 process were the trade unions Federation of Free Workers, Sentro, the Trade Union Congress of the Philippines and the Alliance of Workers in the Informal Economy/Sector (ALLWIES) (Ogaya, 2020). Some NGOs that had previously done most of the work on domestic workers' rights also became part of the TWG. These were NGOs against trafficking and child labour (in particular, Visayan Forum), for migrant rights (such as Migrant Forum in Asia and the Centre for Migrant Advocacy) and religious organizations, in particular, the Catholic Bishops' Conference of the Philippines. Visayan Forum was also pivotal in promoting Home Workers' Association and Linkage in the Philippines (SUMAPI),[5] the first domestic workers' group in the country, created in 1995 and active until 2012, when Visayan Forum was involved in a famous corruption scandal with its main funder, US Agency for International Development (Fontana, 2020).

Generally speaking, domestic workers have started to organize collectively only recently. In 2012, the domestic workers' organization UNITED was created, with the support of labour organizations Sentro (formerly Alliance of Progressive Labour) and the Labour Education and Research Network (LEARN). United was registered as a workers' organization at the Labour Department in 2016 and has been part of the TWG, but has been struggling to gain recognition as a proper trade union. Other organizations were created in 2015, such as the ALLWIES-Kasambahay chapter and the Federation of Free Workers Taumbahay-FFW (*taumbahay* means 'person who stays at home'). In this process, central roles were played by the ILO (D'Souza, 2010), by the IDWF and by international cooperation organizations, among others, the Swedish International Development Cooperation Agency, and the Germany-based Friedrich Ebert Foundation.

Feminist organizations were not particularly active during these years of change, but some individual women's rights activists were pivotal, acting alone or as part of organizations supporting domestic workers' rights. These include labour organizations, as well as the workers in the Informal Sector Council of the Anti-Poverty Commission, some of whom are part of the global network WIEGO.

Taiwan

Taiwan represents a special case in our research. Since the country is not a member of the UN, intergovernmental organizations, and in particular the ILO, are absent there. The country cannot formally ratify international conventions, including C189, even though activists do at times refer to it in their campaigns. However, Taiwan has the possibility to commit to international conventions in an autonomous way, through introducing national laws, and indeed the government did so in 2009 with the UN International Covenant on Political and Civil Rights and the International Covenant on Economic, Social and Cultural Rights, and in 2011 with the Convention on the Elimination of all Forms of Discrimination against Women (Chen, 2019).

Until the 1980s, domestic and care work in Taiwan had been almost completely performed without payment by female family members. However, from the beginning of the 1990s the rapid economic growth and the progressive entry of Taiwanese women into the labour market caused an increased demand for paid domestic and care services in private households (Michel and Peng, 2012). This is connected to the rapidly ageing population – with people aged 65+ representing 14 per cent of the total population in 2018 (source: Statistical Bureau Taiwan, year 2018) – in addition to a family-based welfare model and to the lack of publicly funded care services. In 2017, migrant workers represented the majority of workers in the sector, with a total number of migrant caregivers and domestic workers in private households reaching about 247,000, of which 99 per cent were women, originating from the Philippines, Indonesia, Thailand and Vietnam (source: Ministry of Labour, year 2017). A limited number of Taiwanese caregivers and domestic workers are still engaged in live-out, part-time housekeeping and childcare – jobs from which migrant workers are de facto excluded – while migrants are mostly live-in, work full time and provide care to elderly and disabled people.

Taiwan is generally characterized by low inequality (the Gini Index was 33.8 in 2018) and by a high level of public support for social equity and redistribution (Peng and Wong, 2010), yet the field of care and domestic work represents an exception. Even though the official position of the country's governments in the decade under analysis has been to keep supporting women's entrance into the labour market, and to decrease reliance on the migrant workforce in this sector, in reality these promises have not been fulfilled. Indeed, the reforms proposed – in particular the Long-term Care Services Act, first developed in 2010 and introducing the certification of nursing aides (8,368 in 2015, 92 per cent women) – cover only a limited extent of the care needs of disabled and elderly people in the community, and have been severely criticized for, among other things, excluding foreign workers. Among the 760,000 long-term care recipients, only 12 per cent are supported by the government's long-term community care services, while family members account for 59 per cent and migrant caregivers provide for 30 per cent (Chen, 2016). In reality, the recruitment of migrant women is the main public response to care needs, a practice that has been steadily expanding since it started in 1992 under the newly established democratic regime.[6] At the same time, the migration system has been run since then as a temporary guest programme, strongly criticized for failing to provide good-quality care or to prevent the mistreatment of migrants. Migrant workers are allowed to stay for only limited periods of time and are unable to settle, nor are they allowed to have their own families or children with them. Indeed, until 2002, women were subjected to a compulsory pregnancy test and repatriated if found to be pregnant. While the Taiwanese state exerts strict control over who is allowed to apply for a migrant caregiver, it delegates migrants' recruitment and placement to certified private placement agencies, which take periodic fees from the workers and have a vested interest in maintaining this temporary migration system. Under this system, changing employers remains very difficult for migrant workers, and they are prohibited from forming their own unions.

While these conditions are shared by all migrant workers, such as those in manufacturing and construction, it is only caregivers and domestic workers working in private households who have been excluded from the protection of the labour code (Labour Standard Act),[7] and are not therefore entitled to the minimum wage, regulated work hours, weekly days off and health insurance. According to the Ministry of Labour, in 2015 the monthly wage for migrant care workers was equivalent to USD642 (NT19,643), which was below the national minimum wage (USD734, NT22,000), while it was also remarkably lower than the salary earned by Taiwanese certified nursing aides (USD984, NT30,106). The same data revealed that migrant caregivers work an average of 13 hours a day, and up to 34.5 percent don't have any days off all year. These conditions often lead to cases of physical and mental illness and abuse. This explains the phenomenon of so-called 'run-away workers': migrant workers who leave their legal employment and prefer to become illegal and work irregularly.

Some improvements in the conditions of migrant workers have been introduced by the government since the early 2000s. The government of the progressive DPP party, in power for the first time in 2000, was committed to making Taiwan a country based on human rights, and keen on protecting its international image (Cheng and Momesso, 2017). This image was particularly damaged in the 2000s by the poor reviews Taiwan received in the US-based Trafficking in Persons (TIP) Report and

Country Report on Human Rights Practices. Both explicitly criticized Taiwan for the situation of female migrants, including migrant domestic and care workers, and the TIP Report classified Taiwan as Tier 2 in the years 2005–9 (and Tier 2 Watchlist in 2006).[8] In 2002 the government eliminated the compulsory pregnancy test that had previously been imposed on migrant women, and included migrants in the Act of Gender Equality in Employment (2002), which in principle gives them rights regarding pregnancy, maternity leave and protection from sexual harassment. In 2005 it introduced the possibility of changing employers, if only for exceptional reasons such as the death of the care receiver or serious abuse. Finally, in 2009 the Human Trafficking Prevention and Control Act was introduced. However, the changes introduced have failed to confront the system of agencies that produces the conditions of exploitation and abuse of migrants. In practice, the anti-trafficking system is the framework that supports migrants in the country, in particular through a government-run hotline and government-funded shelters for migrants with grievances. In fact, some of the shelters are managed by migrants' rights' organizations, such as the Serve the People Association. The latter also supports the first organization of migrant domestic workers in Taiwan, the Domestic Caretakers' Union, established in 2016 in Taoyuan; and the Taiwan International Workers' Association (TIWA), which works closely with migrants' organizations, such as the Filipino KaSaPi[9] and the Indonesian IPIT.[10]

The violation of migrant workers' rights in private households has been denounced by both national and international organizations. This criticism has grown louder since the 2000s, when the first progressive government since the end of the dictatorship came to power. The international organizations Asia Pacific Mission for Migrants, Migrante International–Taiwan Chapter, the Action Network for Marriage Migrants' Rights and Empowerment and the Migrant Forum in Asia have all been vocal in this denunciation. At the national level, while large unions in the country have done little for migrants' rights, one organization of migrants' workers rights, TIWA, has been particularly active. Created in 1999, since 2003 it has organized biannual rallies for migrants' rights with migrants themselves.[11] In 2003, TIWA also launched the Promoting Alliance for the Household Services Act (renamed the Migrants Empowerment Network in Taiwan, in 2007), at least partly in reaction to the death that year of famous writer and ex-policy adviser Liu Shia at the hands of her migrant caregiver, an event that brought the dangers connected to the dire working conditions of migrant caregivers to the fore. The alliance was joined by religious and human rights organizations and supported by a number of care receivers' organizations as well as by the prominent feminist organization, the Awakening Foundation. This coalition drafted the Household Services Act, proposed in 2004, calling for laws to provide protection for caregivers and domestic workers' rights, both Taiwanese and migrant, and a transition towards a public care system. This proposal has not been taken up by the government, and has been met with opposition, predictably, from agencies well connected to the political class, but also from a coalition of care receivers. Indeed, a number of disabled and elderly people's groups have defended the existing system, at least partly out of fear that if migrants were granted greater labour rights, disabled and elderly people would no longer be able to afford care services (Chien, 2018).

India

India is said to be the second-largest employer of domestic workers in the world, following Brazil (ILO, 2011). Many Indian households hire either men or women, and sometimes children (an illegal practice), for everyday domestic and care work, often paying them in kind. The distribution of paid domestic work reflects the country's strong socioeconomic inequalities (Gini Index 35.7 in 2011, Multidimensional Poverty Index 0.123 in 2019, or 19.3 per cent of the population vulnerable to multidimensional poverty, according to the United Nations Development Programme). This is particularly the case along intersecting lines of gender, caste, tribe and internal migration.[12] However, the situation has changed markedly in the decade under study, due on the one hand to the increased industrialization and urbanization of the country, and on the other to the high degree of mobilization for the rights of domestic and informal workers.

In 2011, the National Sample Survey found that there were 2.5 million domestic workers in India (source: Employment and Unemployment, National Service Scheme, year 2011–12). Estimates of the numbers of domestic workers are particularly difficult to produce in the Indian context, given the considerable size of the informal economy, to which domestic workers largely belong. This sector (called the 'unorganised sector') employs 93 per cent of the total workforce and contributes around 60 per cent of the gross domestic product (GDP); within it, 54 per cent of female workers are estimated to work in private households, largely in domestic work (National Commission for Enterprises in the Unorganized Sector, 2007; Sharma and Kunduri, 2015).

In terms of gender, domestic work has undergone a remarkable transformation: while historically, men also used to be employed as domestic workers, today the sector is highly feminized, with women representing 85.8 per cent of domestic workers in 2011 (source: National Sample Survey, year 2011–12). Studies indicate that the majority of domestic workers are illiterate, first-generation rural migrants (Mehrotra, 2010; Palriwala and Neetha, 2010; Rao, 2011). In the Delhi area, for instance, these internal migrants are usually from neighbouring regions like Punjab, Bihar, Uttar Pradesh, Rajasthan, Haryana, Orissa or Andhra Pradesh. According to Mehrotra (2010), 86 per cent of female domestic workers in Delhi are migrants, while only 14 per cent were born in Delhi. Many of these migrants come from tribal areas, and indeed 'scheduled tribes'[13] account for 4.5 per cent of domestic workers in the country (source: National Sample Survey, year 2011–12).

In its intersections with gender, age and migration from rural areas, caste brings particular notions of shame and stigma which are still largely attached to those who perform domestic work in India (Sharma and Kunduri, 2015). Indeed, within the traditional vision of social hierarchy based on the caste system, religious codes concerning domestic tasks play a fundamental role, so that each task (like sweeping the floor, cleaning the toilet, doing the laundry, cooking and washing dishes, or collecting household waste) is expected to be performed by a different person, depending on their caste position. People from low castes also have internal hierarchies and refuse to perform tasks which they consider too impure for themselves (Ray and Qayum, 2009; Sharma, 2014). Data confirm the significant over-representation of low-caste people among domestic workers, with scheduled caste workers representing 29.7 per cent of all domestic workers, despite making up only 16.6 per cent of the total population living in the country in 2011 (source: National Sample Survey, year 2011–12). In the year 2011–12, more than one out of every three domestic workers (34.2 per cent) belonged to a scheduled tribe or a scheduled caste (source: National Sample Survey, year 2011–12). Similarly, even though domestic workers have traditionally been Hindu, Christian and Muslim women have also recently entered the sector.

The employment conditions of domestic workers constitute another remarkable change that took place in the period under study (Agarwala and Saha, 2018). Until the 1990s, most domestic workers lived in and worked full time, with domestic workers and their families being passed on from generation to generation in the employer's household. This provided not only food and shelter, but also social protection. Since the 1990s, however, increased industrialization and migration have contributed to modifying families' home-making patterns. In this new context, the profile of live-in workers has changed, and an increasing number of workers are live-out. Remaining live-in workers are often young unmarried women, who migrate alone, send remittances to their villages and experience their migration as temporary. They find work through recruitment and placement agents, who have an interest in regularly changing their employers and add an extra layer of exploitation to their vulnerability to abuse, including, at times, trafficking. Live-out domestic workers, by contrast, tend to be married, middle-aged women who migrate with their families. Live-out workers usually find their way to the city through kinship networks, rent a home in informal settlements on the outskirts, and spend hours commuting to work each day (Agarwala and Saha, 2018).

The debate about domestic work as a labour issue is a not recent one in India, with many Bills introduced by Parliament after the first in 1959. Yet remarkable 'governmental resistance' (Palriwala and Neetha, 2010) meant that no change was possible up until the 2000s. Domestic workers' rights have emerged in their contemporary form as part of the work conducted in the country by NGOs providing support for people living in poverty and fighting child labour and trafficking. While some of these NGOs emerged from religious traditions, such as the National Domestic Workers' Movement (NDWM), others emerged from feminist approaches, such as Stree Jagriti Samiti in Bangalore or Jagori in Delhi, and the Self Employed Women's Association (SEWA). A large movement for the rights of domestic workers then started to become visible and national, especially through a very large national coalition, called the National Platform for Domestic Workers (NPDW), created in 2012 to demand comprehensive legislation for domestic workers (SEWA, 2014). Among the components of the NPDW are important domestic workers' organizations such as the NDWM, mentioned earlier, an NGO originally linked to the Catholic Bishops' conference of India. Founded in 1985 in Maharashtra, it has become India's largest domestic workers' organization across 23 states. It promoted the creation of the National Domestic Workers Union, chapters of which have emerged in various states since 2010, has been present in 15 states since 2017 and has been united under the National Domestic Workers' Federation since 2014 (NDWTU, 2015). The National Platform includes all of the previously mentioned organizations, as well as labour unions of the informal economy, groups fighting for the rights of minority groups (low-caste and untouchable) and religious groups such as the Jesuit organization Adivasi Jeevan Vikas Samatha. Feminist standpoints are well represented, in particular by organizations such as SEWA, the trade union for women workers in the informal sector, and the NGOs Jagori and Women's Voice. Also important in the field are organizations fighting against trafficking, such as Shakti Vahini in New Delhi. While traditional trade unions have excluded women workers – with some exceptions, such as Pune Shehar Molkarin Sangathan, the Communist Party in Maharashtra – they started to become more involved with domestic workers in relation to the C189 process. The IDWF and ILO have played important roles in this process by facilitating the coordination of meetings and rallies.

These organizations have obtained some important rights, though most of these rights do not have national application and are valid in only some states. By 2017, more than half of India's states had included domestic work in their minimum wage provisions, and since 2012 domestic workers have been included in a health insurance scheme for those below the poverty line (known as the Rashtriya Swasthya Bima Yojana), while a few states have passed Bills to regulate and register placement agencies. At the national level, while these rights still do not apply, domestic workers are now covered by the Child Labour Act (2006) and were able to be included in the Unorganised Workers' Social Security Act (2008) and in the Sexual Harassment of Women at Workplace (Prevention, Prohibition and Redressal) Act (2013) – from both of which they had initially been excluded. Moreover, in Geneva in 2011 this movement successfully lobbied India to change its vote from being against C189 to being in favour. However, India is still far from ratifying C189, nor has it accepted the proposal for a national law on domestic work that the NPDW has demanded and that would recognize domestic work as work.

Brazil

Brazil has the largest domestic worker sector in the world, with more than ten million household employers, and roughly six million workers. This represents 6 per cent of the total employed population and 16.9 per cent of employed women (source: National Household Sample Survey, Brazilian Institute of Geography and Statistics,[14] year 2015). Despite the sector's size, domestic workers are nevertheless among the most vulnerable workers in a country, which has the highest indicators of inequality in the world (for example the Gini Index was equal to 53.5 in 2017, World Bank).

These inequalities persist despite the country witnessing an improvement in labour opportunities, minimum wage and labour market participation since the late 2000s (Paes de Barros et al, 2006; IPEA, 2013). In particular, inequality in labour income and work opportunities remains significantly affected by race (Soares Leivas and Moreira Aristides dos Santos, 2018) and gender (Costa et al, 2016). This is important, since domestic work in Brazil is largely an occupation performed by Afro-descendant women; in 2010, over 56 per cent of domestic workers self-identified as such (44.3 per cent self-identified as 'brown', 12.2 per cent as 'black'), followed by 35.5 per cent identifying as 'white'[15] (source: National Household Sample Survey, year 2010). On the employers' side, the 2009 Family Budget Survey (POF)[16] showed that 85.7 per cent of families employing a domestic worker belonged to the richest sectors of society, with 72.2 per cent of the women employers declaring themselves to be White. There is consensus among scholars and activists that this racialized and gendered configuration of domestic work is rooted in Brazil's history of colonialism and slavery (Bernardino-Costa, 2007; Pinho and Silva, 2010; Acciari, 2019). Moreover, a significant portion of domestic workers have migrated within Brazil, especially from rural to urban areas. For instance, the percentage of (first-generation) internal migrants working in the domestic sector is 93.6 in São Paulo (mostly originating in the north-east, 52.7 per cent, and north, 44.1 per cent). The figure is 87.6 per cent in Brasília, while it is only 17.4 per cent in Rio de Janeiro (source: National Household Sample Survey, year 2015). Domestic work is significantly more feminized than other sectors (93 per cent of workers are women in this sector, while women make up 42.6 per cent of the total employed population) and workers have lower levels of education (6.3 years of schooling on average versus 8.9 years for the total employed population).

In terms of labour conditions, there is a sizeable wage gap between domestic workers and other workers, with the former earning 60 per cent less than the average earned by other workers (DIEESE, 2013). Compliance with minimum wage regulations is significantly lower than in other sectors: for instance, in 2009, 40.9 per cent of domestic workers had wages equal to or above the minimum wage, compared to 79.8 per cent of other workers (Oelz and Rani, 2015: 18). In addition, domestic work is characterized by a high degree of informality: more than two-thirds of domestic workers do not have a formal labour contract, while less than a third lack a contract among the general working population (source: National Household Sample Survey, year 2015).

In Brazil, domestic workers' labour rights were recognized as equal to those of other workers in 2013 under the constitutional reform known as PEC das Domésticas[17] and the subsequent law passed in 2015.[18] Before these reforms, the first law regulating the sector was introduced during the military dictatorship of Emílio Médici in 1972.[19] The new democratic constitution promulgated in 1988 significantly expanded the labour rights granted to domestic workers, but did not fully equate them to those of other workers. The legislation in force since 2015 gives domestic workers the same entitlements and provisions as the country's other workers, including minimum wage, the right to collective agreement, full access to social security and family benefits, health protection, a 13th-month payment, extra pay for night work and for working overtime, rest time, holidays, sick leave and parental leave. In this context, the ratification of C189 at the beginning of 2018 (just as our fieldwork came to an end) happened in a top-down manner under Michel Temer's neoliberal government, without any involvement of domestic workers' trade unions. In fact, according to our interviewees, after debating the opportunity to do so, the movement decided against campaigning for its ratification. A significant part of the movement considered the legislation in force since 2015 as actually providing more than that which would be afforded by C189. Thus, ratifying C189 was not considered a priority, despite the fact that Brazilian domestic workers' trade unions played a key role in the C189 process (Fish, 2017; Acciari, 2019).

Brazil has a strong and well-structured trade union movement for paid domestic workers, highly articulated at the local, national and international levels. It comprises the National Federation of Domestic Workers (FENATRAD),[20] which is made up of 27 organizations distributed across 15 Brazilian states, and is part of the National Trade Union Centre.[21] The movement was born in the 1930s[22] with the creation of the first domestic workers' association[23] in Santos (São Paulo state) by Laudelina de Campo Melo, an Afro-Brazilian domestic worker and organizer coming from the Black movement and the Communist Party. These political forces, together with the Catholic Workers Youth,[24] supported the expansion of the movement with the creation of more domestic workers' trade unions around the country in the following decades. Eleven national congresses of domestic workers have been held between the end of the 1960s and the present day. The movement has historically been connected to workers', feminist and Black activism (Oliveira, 2008; Bernardino-Costa, 2014; Fraga, 2016; Monticelli, 2017).

Following the military dictatorship (1969–82), organized domestic workers took part in the struggle for the democratization of the country and were directly involved in the constitution-writing process. Yet, the final draft of the constitution was a great disappointment, since it continued to define domestic workers as a subordinate class with fewer rights than other workers. Since the late 2000s, domestic workers have campaigned for the aforementioned PEC das Domésticas, the constitutional reform that was largely supported by feminist and Black feminist movements, national trade unions, academia, institutional representatives and public figures. Among the latter two was the rapporteur of the reform, Senator Benedita da Silva, a prominent Afro-Brazilian feminist organizer, politician and former domestic worker. Notable among the feminist and women's rights organizations supporting the domestic workers' campaign were Themis,[25] SOS Corpo[26] and Criola.[27]

The reforms achieved in the mid-2010s were facilitated in part by the governments led by Luiz Inácio Lula da Silva (2003–11) and Dilma Rousseff (2011–16) of the Workers' Party.[28] The radical change in the political context in the second half of the 2010s, with President Rousseff's impeachment process and the government of Michel Temer (2016–18), fractured this supportive relationship and triggered a period of confrontation in which domestic workers' demands were sidelined by state actors. Since 2018, the situation for domestic workers and all social justice movements in the country has deteriorated under Jair Bolsonaro's rule, which began after we had completed our fieldwork.

Colombia

When our fieldwork began in 2017, the Colombian domestic work sector employed around 681,000 people, that is, 3 per cent of all workers and

6.3 per cent of working women (source: Household Survey, National Institute of Statistics,[29] year 2017). Workers' conditions in the sector are shaped by two main factors: firstly, the territorial, socioeconomic and racial inequalities rooted in colonial legacies, and secondly, the impact of the internal armed conflict that has taken place since 1964 between the government, paramilitary groups and political groups (such as the Revolutionary Armed Forces of Colombia, People's Army (FARC-EP) and the National Liberation Army (ELN)).

According to the Gini Index (49.7 in 2017, World Bank) Colombia is the fourth-most unequal country in the world, after Brazil, Honduras and Panama. In rural contexts, 49.8 per cent of men and 48.3 per cent of women are living below the poverty line (source: Multidimensional Poverty Index, United Nations Development Program, year 2011). These inequalities intersect with the situation of racialized ethnic groups belonging to the Afro-Colombian minority or to indigenous communities[30] (Wade, 1993; Barbary and Urrea Giraldo, 2004; Pardo et al, 2004; Meertens et al, 2008; Posso, 2008; Urrea Giraldo et al., 2015). The armed conflict has produced 6.7 million internally displaced people. Among the civilian population, rural, indigenous and Afro-Colombian people – women in particular – have been most affected by the conflict. Fifteen per cent of Afro-Colombians and 10 per cent of indigenous people have been forcibly displaced, while 87 per cent of the displaced population are from rural backgrounds (source: United Nations High Commissioner for Refugees). This forced migration of millions of racialized and rural women greatly influenced the supply of paid domestic work in Colombian cities. They settled in the poorest urban areas of major Colombian cities, such as Bogotá, Medellín or Cali, and have tended to occupy positions with the most substandard working conditions. In fact, 41 per cent of domestic workers are internal migrants and/or refugees (source: Census, National Institute of Statistics, year 2005). In the regions of Bogotá, Valle del Cauca and Antioquia – where four out of ten of the country's domestic workers are employed, most of them in the departments' capital cities – these ratios stand at 87 per cent, 57 per cent and 23 per cent, respectively. Another transformation in recent decades concerns live-in work, formerly the most common arrangement in the sector (Castro, 1993; Huyette, 1994; Alzate Arias, 2005), which, according to the experts we interviewed, is being progressively replaced by live-out and per-day employment, especially in the urban centres. Domestic workers are more likely to be women (91 per cent versus 51 per cent of the total working population), aged over 30 and lower educated (only 19 per cent have post-secondary school level education versus 26 per cent of the total workforce).

An ILO report on national data shows that in 2011 the share of domestic workers subscribed to social security was 9.5 per cent, significantly lower than the country's total female workforce (26.5 per cent), and the average wage was around 64 per cent of the wage of other working women (Valenzuela and Sjoberg, 2012: 64–5). According to a 2013 report on domestic work in the cities of Bogotá, Bucaramanga and Cartagena, between 87 per cent and 75 per cent of workers did not receive social security or healthcare coverage; 98 per cent of surveyed workers did not have contracts and only 19 per cent of them earned equal to or above the minimum wage (Fundación José Antonio Galán, 2013). Another study carried out with Afro-Colombian domestic workers in Medellín in 2012 shows that most of the women surveyed, 85.7 per cent, did not make the statutory minimum wage and belonged to the lowest socioeconomic strata, classified according to the Colombian system as 1 (47.6 per cent of the women surveyed) and 2 (40.5 per cent of the women surveyed).[31] Finally, most of those surveyed reported that they worked more than the legal working day; 91 per cent of live-in workers said that they worked 10–18 hours a day, while 31 per cent of live-out workers worked between 11 and 14 hours a day (Morales Mosquera and Muñoz Cañas, 2013).

Colombia has a long history of mobilizations for domestic workers' rights. From the late 1930s until the early 1960s, the Catholic union Acción Católica assisted in the creation and development of the first organizations in support of domestic workers[32] (Plata Quezada, 2013). The first secular organizations were founded in the late 1970s and 1980s; among them, the Domestic Workers' Trade Unions SINTRASEDOM[33] and UTRAHOGAR[34] are still active today (Donaldson, 1992). In the 1980s, major mobilizations took place in this field, such as national demonstrations on a significant scale demanding social security rights in 1985 and 1987, and the First National Domestic Workers' Colloquium in 1987 (Donaldson, 1992; León, 2013). Further, a ten-year action research and awareness-raising project on the conditions of domestic workers was carried out in several provinces, gaining unprecedented attention from the media and public opinion (León, 2013). This period of mobilization led to new legislation facilitating access to social security, pensions and healthcare.[35] In the 1990s and 2000s, these mobilizations progressively weakened, but the 2010s was once more a period of visibility for domestic workers, including at a national level.

According to our analysis, diverse factors contributed to this upsurge in activity. Firstly, in the context of the peace process that had been developing over the previous decade,[36] the Colombian state promoted restorative policies towards the affected population. For instance, the Victims' Law in 2011[37] provided assistance, attention and reparation to the victims of armed conflict, as well as land restitution (Rettberg, 2015a). Secondly, the 'victims' started to emerge as new political subjects, both by responding to these institutional interventions and through collective organizing from below (Mosquera, 2015;

Rettberg, 2015b). In this same framework, grassroots women's movements fostered awareness of the gendered impact of the armed conflict and of the specific needs of racialized women therein (Paarlberg-Kvam, 2019). These interventions helped to raise the profile of Black women among displaced people, internal migrants and refugees; that is, the same social groups that are largely employed in the country's domestic work sector. Further, during the years of the C189 process, the topic of domestic work drew the attention of Colombian trade unions (above all, the Colombian Workers' Central Trade Union)[38] and of the Ministry of Labour, which, together with other civil society actors, were involved in the preparation process. This also attracted non-profit organizations such as the Colombian National Trade Union School (ENS)[39] and Bien Humano Foundation,[40] the US-based Care International and the German Friedrich Ebert Foundation,[41] all of which began providing technical and financial support to domestic workers' organizing. As a result, the 2010s were marked by the creation of new organizations, such as the Afro-Colombian Domestic Workers' Trade Union (UTRASD)[42] in 2013 in Medellín, and the domestic workers' chapter of the National Union of Food Workers (SINTRAIMAGRA)[43] in Bucaramanga in 2012. At the time of our fieldwork (2017–18), these organizations were joining efforts in the construction of a common trade union platform called Intersindical, aimed at scaling up the movement to the national level.

On the institutional side, C189 was ratified in 2012[44] and thereafter a number of legislative measures that included this category of workers within the general social security system were adopted.[45] In 2016 the right to a 13th-month payment was extended to domestic workers, thanks to the so-called Ley de Prima.[46] Such achievements came after a three-year campaign promoted by a coalition comprised of UTRASD, ENS and the Bien Humano Foundation, and with the support of two feminist congresswomen of the Green Party, Ángela María Robledo and Angélica Lozano. Thanks to these new provisions, today domestic workers are entitled to almost the same labour rights as all other workers, including minimum wage[47] and 13th-month payment, a compulsory contract, compulsory healthcare and social security coverage (covered entirely by the employer), family allowances and paid vacation. However, despite these notable achievements, there is still no national law specifically addressing domestic work (a basic requirement of C189), while the domestic workers' movement has denounced a lack of political commitment to implementing the Convention. In particular, the law still discriminates against live-in domestic workers, limiting the working day to ten hours (as opposed to eight hours for all other workers) and allowing for up to 30 per cent of in-kind compensation; while per-day workers still struggle to access maternity leave and sick leave.

Ecuador

Around 214,000 people were employed as domestic workers in Ecuador in 2018, representing 3 per cent of all workers and 7.3 per cent of female workers (source: National Survey on Employment, Unemployment, Subemployment, National Institute of Statistics,[48] year 2018). Overall, domestic work is a highly feminized sector, mainly employing women from lower social classes and with low education levels, often coming from the most impoverished regions of the country and whose working conditions vary greatly according to their age, ethnicity and rural or urban residence. In fact, women represent 95 per cent of domestic workers (versus 50 per cent of the workforce as a whole); 84 per cent have only pre-secondary school level education (versus 72 per cent of the total workforce).

Internal migration flows from the impoverished mountainous and coastal areas to the main cities have grown since the 1970s (Vázquez and Saltos Galarza, 2013) and mainly involve women and girls with indigenous Andean backgrounds in Quito and of Afro-Ecuadorian origin in Guayaquil. Such internal movements have long determined the current composition of this workforce. In fact, according to available census data, internal migrants represented 31 per cent of the domestic workforce in 2010. These figures peaked at 56 per cent and 44 per cent in Pichincha and Guayas, two provinces that alone host more than half (56 percent) of the domestic workers living in the country, most of them in the regions' main cities, Quito (the capital) and Guayaquil (the financial centre). International migrants from other Latin American countries are also present in the sector, notably, Peruvians, Colombian refugees and, more recently, Venezuelan refugees (source: Census, INEC, year 2010).

In terms of ethnic and racial diversity, according to the census data, in 2010 the majority of domestic workers self-identified as '*mestizas*' (69 per cent), followed by '*montubias*' (7.6 per cent), Afro-Ecuadorian (7 per cent), 'indigenous' (6 per cent) and 'white' (5 per cent).[49] Yet, significant regional differences exist, especially in relation to the presence of indigenous and Afro-Ecuadorian domestic workers. For instance, focusing on the two main cities, in Quito, 9 per cent of domestic workers self-identify as indigenous and 4.1 per cent as Black, while in Guayaquil these figures are, respectively, 1.3 per cent and 7.5 per cent (source: Census, year 2001).

As regards wages and working conditions, available data and analysis suggest that these are significantly lower than the standards set by law (Masi de Casanova et al, 2018; Masi de Casanova, 2019). For instance, in 2012 the average wage in the sector was equivalent to USD177.75 (source: National Survey on Employment, Unemployment, Subemployment, year 2012), corresponding to half the legal minimum wage for that year. According to a survey of 400 domestic workers in Guayaquil in 2014, Erin Masi de Casanova and colleagues reported that only approximately one out of three workers enjoyed some of the benefits and labour rights Ecuadorian workers are legally entitled to, such as paid holidays, after-hours payment, 13th- and 14th-month payments[50] (Masi de Casanova et al, 2018). Moreover, data by the Ecuadorian National Institute of Statistics show that the share of domestic workers affiliated to social security increased from 27 per cent in 2006 (source: Living Condition Survey) to 54.5 per cent in 2012 (source: National Survey on Employment, Unemployment, Subemployment). At the same time, these figures also show the high incidence of irregular work in the sector (almost half of all workers) and that the real situation is still far from the universal social security stipulated by law, as reflected also in qualitative accounts collected in the fieldwork.

With the new constitution in 2008, Ecuadorian domestic workers were granted the same labour rights and provisions as other workers, since it extended the right to decent work, a minimum wage and universal access to social security to all workers, and emphasized the value of reproductive labour. These constitutional norms were followed shortly after by reforms of the minimum wage and working hours in the sector, by public policies for the improvement of working conditions and access to social security, and by the ratification of C189 in December 2013. For instance, the Organic Law Defending Labour Rights (2012) equated the working times for domestic workers to those of other workers, while the government policy of salary unification extended the minimum wage provision to include domestic workers in 2010 and raised their monthly minimum wage from USD55 (established in 2005) to USD340 in 2014 (Moncayo Roldán, 2015: 111–15). Specific plans for promoting decent work in the sector were implemented by the Ministry of Labour, including measures such as capacity building and awareness raising, online and physical information points on compulsory subscription to social security and labour inspections in private households employing domestic workers (Crespo et al, 2014; Moncayo Roldán, 2015).

These achievements were the result of a recent history of state intervention and grassroots mobilization in the field. In fact, the question of domestic workers' rights entered the national public debate only in the late 2000s, as the result of two processes. On the one hand, the aforementioned legal reforms were part and parcel of the political agenda known as the 'Citizens' Revolution' promoted under the presidency of Rafael Correa (2007–17) of the leftist party Alianza País. Correa's governments promoted socioeconomic and political reforms intended to favour the working class, including people in informal and low-level jobs such as paid domestic work. His political programme was also oriented towards the expansion of social and civil rights for all citizens, but particularly for working-class women and historically excluded groups, such as the rural population, Afro-descendants and indigenous people.

Yet, the global mobilization surrounding the C189 process also had an impact on the country, fostering the politicization of the issue and the construction of a nationwide campaign for its ratification that ran from 2011 to 2013. The campaign involved international governmental and non-governmental organizations active in the fields of human rights, women's and labour rights and development (such as UN-Women, FOS-Socialist Solidarity[51] and the Latin American office of CARE International), as well as the Association of Paid Domestic Workers (ATRH).[52] The latter was created in the late 1990s in Guayaquil, but it mainly operated at the local level until this period, when it gained visibility and became active across the country.

However, the last period of the Correa administration was characterized by general discontent and division among civil society organizations as to their position with respect to the government (Profumi, 2017). In this context, in 2015–16 ATRH split into two organizations: the first kept the original name and maintained the preferential relationships established with governmental actors, while the second, the National Union of Domestic Workers and Allies (UNTHYA),[53] distanced itself from such political influence. Further, in 2016 the new incarnation of ATRH succeeded in creating the Unified Trade Union of Domestic Workers of Ecuador (SINUTRHE),[54] the first in the country formally recognized as representative of this category of workers (an institutional recognition which was not granted to UNTHYA). During those years, and up until the point of our fieldwork, the (renewed) requests by domestic workers to make formal rights a reality were not taken up by the state. Moreover, the sector still lacks a specific law on domestic workers, which is stipulated by C189.

Germany

Around 9 per cent of German households employ a domestic worker (Enste, 2017: 10). In 2016, there were nearly 347,000 regularly employed domestic workers in the country (source: Households and Family Survey, Federal Statistical Office[55]), plus an estimated 2.7 to 3 million domestic workers who work irregularly (Enste, 2017). This means that regular workers in the sector constitute 0.9 per cent of total workforce – and 1.5 per cent of the female workforce.

Regular employment in the sector is further differentiated according to the social security rules contained in each type of contract. The majority of domestic workers (around 300,000) fall under the category of so-called 'mini-jobbers'. A second group are workers regularly hired by one (or more) families, directly or via a service agency; in this case, social security contributions are shared between employers and employees. Finally there are self-employed workers for whom all social security contributions must be paid by the workers themselves.

Low wages are common in the sector, for instance, according to a recent estimate (Pusch, 2018), 42 per cent of workers do not receive the legal minimum wage. Noteworthy is the spread of mini jobs, a form of precarious labour introduced in 2003, in which workers are not allowed to work for more than 12 hours a week and have reduced social and pension benefits, while employers benefit from tax incentives (Scheiwe, 2014: 77). Mini jobs in private households require even fewer social security contributions and taxes to be paid by the employer (Minijob Zentrale, 2016: 15).

Notably, regular and irregular work is differently distributed between German and foreign citizens. The majority of regularly employed domestic workers are German citizens (72 per cent versus 27 per cent foreign citizens, in 2016) (Bundesagentur für Arbeit, 2016), as are the majority of mini-jobbers in private households (in 2016, 79 per cent versus 21 per cent foreign citizens) (Minijob Zentrale, 2016: 25), while the majority of irregular workers are estimated to be EU migrants who can live in Germany without a residence permit, as in the case of Poles, Bulgarians, Slovaks and Romanians (Lutz, 2008; Gottschall and Schwarzkopf, 2010). These trends occur in what is historically a major destination country for migrants; Germany counted 9.7 million foreigners in 2018 (around 12 per cent of the total population), of which 4.8 million were workers. There were 17.1 million German citizens of migrant descent in 2015 (around 20 per cent of the total population) (source: European Union Statistical Office, year 2015). These trends are also unsurprising for a high-income country, whose economy recovered well after the 2008 global financial crisis. In 2015, Germany ranked fourth in the Human Development Index globally. Nevertheless, inequality has been on the rise; in 2016, around every sixth person had an income of 60 per cent below average and was therefore at risk of poverty (Bundeszentrale für politische Bildung, 2016).

As for age, Germany shares similar features with the other high-income countries involved in the study, namely Italy, Spain and Taiwan. In 2018, indeed, Germany's old-age dependency ratio and the proportion of people aged 65+ in the total population stood at 32.8 per cent and 21.4 per cent, respectively (source: European Union Statistical Office, year 2018). However, the country's welfare and care model substantially differs from those of Italy, Spain and Taiwan. Germany's case constitutes what Esping-Andersen (1990) called a 'conservative-corporatist' welfare system, and what Francesca

Bettio and Janneke Plantenga (2004) referred to as a 'publicly supported private care' regime. In this setting, people in need of domestic help or care assistance receive reimbursements or monetary transfers via public-private insurance systems, either health or care insurance, with which they can pay family members (mostly women) or employ someone via intermediaries.

Yet, existing research, including the results of our fieldwork, suggests that such a system fails to cover the care needs of dependent elderly people and their families, due to the high cost of services, the low number of public benefits and the scarcity of care facilities. As a result, the care system depends heavily but tacitly on migrant care workers, many of them irregular (Lutz, 2011; Theobald, 2017). In fact, in the last few decades demographic changes and EU expansion have resulted in an increase in the circular migration of Eastern European live-in workers caring for the elderly. The working conditions of this predominantly female workforce are often precarious and far below those of other workers in Germany (Emunds and Schacher, 2012; Benazha and Lutz, 2019). The high prevalence of 'posted workers',[56] who are allowed to work for a family in Germany via contracts set out by agencies in their home countries (as employees or self-employed workers), further contributes to the lowering of wages and working conditions. In fact, even though EU legislation in principle gives these 'posted workers' the same rights as workers in the country of destination, in practice their working conditions are those of serious exploitation (Emunds and Schacher, 2012).

In Germany, a legislative framework has been in place for the sector since the 1950s. The first regulation of working hours and introduction of a rest period for those employed in private households was adopted in 1952, while the first collective agreement for the sector was approved in 1955, with the establishment of an eight-hour work day and one day off per week. The agreement was negotiated between the Union of Food Processing and Catering Workers[57] and the German Housewives Association.[58] In that decade, these two organizations began to act as, respectively, domestic workers' and employers' representatives, and they continue to fulfil this function today. Finally, in 1993 domestic work was included in general labour laws and workplace protections. Since then, most labour laws have applied to domestic workers on an equal footing with other workers, although exceptions still exist, for example the exclusion from the labour health and safety law[59] and the exclusion of live-in care workers from the general laws on working hours[60] (Trebilcock, 2018).

However, it is important to note that today this legislation applies to only a minority of people employed in the sector. In fact, legislation has not been amended in response to the fragmentation of labour status (regularly employed, self-employed and mini-jobbers) or to the migrant background of people employed in the sector, including both undocumented and temporary migrant workers. Moreover, as the numbers of foreign workers increased, so did the impact of immigration policies on the sector. Responding to this situation, the grassroots migrant domestic workers' group RESPECT Berlin became very active at the end of the 1990s and throughout the 2000s, promoting the rights of this category as part of the Europe-wide RESPECT network (Rights Equality Solidarity Power Europe Cooperation Today) (Schwenken, 2003).

Germany ratified C189 in 2013, following a quick procedure and with the unanimous support of all political parties. On the basis of a shared agreement that the existing legislation already met the C189 requirements, the government and Parliament did not foresee the need for any legal amendment, nor the development of a specific policy. This was despite the fact that a legal assessment commissioned by the Trade Union Confederation (DGB)[61] to examine the ratification recommended several improvements in working hours, wages and law enforcement (Trebilcock, 2018: 152–3).

Beside the organizations mentioned so far, other key actors in the field are church-based organizations (such as the Catholic organization Caritas, and the Protestant equivalent, Diakonie) and human rights, anti-trafficking, and migrants' rights NGOs. These organizations are mostly engaged in advice, advocacy and awareness-raising activities for domestic workers, especially migrants, and do not take part in policy negotiations for labour rights. Also of note are two remarkable feminist-inspired initiatives, the Care Manifesto, which was initiated in 2014, and the Equal Care Day initiative, launched in 2016, both calling for a global politics of care justice and equal distribution of care commitments between men and women.

Italy

Italy is another country with large numbers of households employing a domestic worker or caregiver, with latest figures indicating that 2.6 million households, or 10 per cent of Italian families, employ a domestic worker (ISMU and Fondazione Censis, 2013). This is usually explained by the combination of a rapidly ageing population and 'familistic welfare', in other words, a welfare system in which the care and support for dependent people and children is arranged by the family (Da Roit, 2010; Ambrosini, 2016; Degiuli, 2016). In fact, in 2018 Italy had Europe's oldest population, whereas the old-age dependency ratio[62] and the proportion of people aged 65+ in the total population stood at 35.2 per cent and 22.6 per cent, respectively (source: EUROSTAT, year 2018). In spite of this, national expenditure for long-term care stood at only 0.9 per cent of GDP for the preceding ten years (source: OECD.stat).

Traditionally employing women from rural regions of the country, between the 1970s and 1990s the sector increasingly became a niche for foreign workers (Andall, 2000; Catanzaro and Colombo, 2009; Vianello,

2009; Marchetti, 2011; Gissi, 2018a). This transformation was linked to major changes in Italian society, such as the growth in Italian women's education and in their participation in the labour market, and the rise in the number of women among the migrant population, a population largely employed in the care sector. In fact, in the 2000s the number of foreign residents in Italy tripled, rising from 1.3 million in 2001 to 4.6 million in 2011 (source: National Institute for Statistics ISTAT).[63] In 2018, this value peaked at 5.1 million residents, of whom 52 per cent were women.

Consistent with these changes, the share of foreign workers in the sector rose from 5.6 per cent in 1972 to 71.4 per cent in 2018. The majority of these workers are from Eastern Europe (59.1 per cent), the Philippines (11.2 per cent), South America (9.5 per cent) and East Asia (7.5 per cent) (source: National Social Security Institute INPS,[64] year 2018). The care and domestic work labour market in the country is divided between foreign and Italian workers, with Italians taking up jobs as part-time and live-out housekeepers, while migrants mostly occupy live-in and full-time jobs as caregivers to the elderly (Di Bartolomeo and Marchetti, 2016).

On the whole, domestic workers are mostly women (88.4 per cent in 2018), and almost half (49.7 per cent) are aged between 45 and 59 years, although the proportion of workers aged 60+ is significant (15.9 per cent). To understand the Italian setting, the territorial distribution of workers is also relevant. The majority are employed in the northern regions, where women's employment rates are higher and where familial welfare networks are less pronounced than in the southern and central Italian regions.

With regard to working conditions, the sector is characterized by high levels of informality and legal non-compliance. Against official data placing the number of regular domestic workers at around 860,000 people in 2018 (source: INPS),[65] estimates for the year, which include irregular workers, put the figure at around two million (Osservatorio DOMINA sul lavoro domestico and Fondazione Moressa, 2019). Already in 2013, estimates including irregular workers had put the figure as high as 1.6 million (ISMU and Fondazione Censis, 2013). Moreover, according to qualitative research, regular workers are also often hired with cheaper working contracts not corresponding to their actual jobs in terms of hours, skills and responsibilities[66] (Marchetti, 2016b: 104–6, 114). Yet the share of workers subscribed to compulsory social security increased between 2007 and 2013, from 53.7 per cent to 88.4 per cent for live-in workers, and from 58.5 per cent to 85.4 per cent for live-out and per-day workers. It is also important to note significant disparities in wages and working conditions, which favour those employed in northern versus those employed in southern regions of the country (Maioni and Zucca, 2016).

The period from the 1950s to the 1970s was marked by an intense period of activity around domestic workers' rights in Italy. Protagonists were mainly

Catholic-based domestic workers' organizations such as the Christian Associations of Italian Workers – Domestic Workers (ACLI-COLF)[67] and its spin-off API-COLF.[68] Specific legislation regulating the sector was adopted in the same period. The first law on domestic labour (still in force today) dates back to 1958,[69] followed by access to health insurance in 1971, the right to collective bargaining in 1969[70] and the first collective agreement in 1974 (Sarti, 2010; Busi, 2020). Since then, domestic workers have been granted basic labour rights and protections by law, including working and rest times, paid holidays, wages and a 13th-month payment, dismissal regulation, severance pay and matrimonial leave, among other things. The sector has been periodically subject to new collective bargaining between workers' organizations, such as the service workers sections of the three national trade union federations Filcams-CGIL,[71] Fisascat-CISL[72] and Uiltucs-UIL,[73] and other, smaller domestic workers' trade unions such as FEDERCOLF;[74] and employers' organizations. The latter include the National Federation of Italian Clergy,[75] the National Association of Domestic Work Employers New Collaboration,[76] the National Union of Domestic Work Employers (Assindatcolf),[77] the National Association of Families Employing Domestic Work (Domina),[78] the Housewives Association (Federcasalinghe) and the Italian Federation of Domestic Work Employers (Fidaldo).[79] Some of these work not only at a national level, but also at a European level, through organizations such as the European Federation for Family Employment and Home Care (EFFE).

The legislative achievements of the 1950s–1970s were encouraged by post-war economic expansion and the converging support of the two main political forces of those decades, notably the Italian Communist Party and the Catholic party Democrazia Cristiana, who sought the advancement of the conditions of the working class, including women and internal migrants. Since the 1980s, however, collective mobilizing has dropped off and there were neither legal reforms nor political interventions. This is despite the transformation the sector had undergone as a result of the radical socio-demographic changes described earlier. While the sector was becoming a niche for foreign labour, new organizations advocating for migrants' rights and representing highly feminized migrant communities, such as the association of Cape Verdeans in Italy and the Filipino Women's Council (Andall, 2000; Pojmann, 2006), among others, started to voice migrant workers' specific needs. However, their exclusion from the tripartite negotiations – that is, negotiations between workers' representatives, employers' representatives and the state, resulting in collective agreement – resulted in low institutional impact in the field of labour politics.

In later decades, the sector was increasingly affected by migration policies, especially those concerning the recruitment of foreign labour. In the 1990s, an on-call contracting and planned quota system was introduced, which became the only means of legal entry for non-EU working migrants following the 2002 immigration law (known as the Bossi-Fini law). Non-EU citizens are entitled to a residence and work permit as domestic workers only if they make the (quite small) yearly quota for on-call recruitment in this sector, and on condition of being hired with a permanent contract for at least 26 hours per week. Furthermore, ten rounds of amnesty for irregular foreign residents granted between 1981 and 2009 have had a large impact on the sector. In particular, the 2002 amnesty transformed the composition of the migrant population from predominantly male and North African, to female and Eastern European, due to the large presence of migrant women as caregivers to the elderly (Marchetti et al, 2013: 22). Meanwhile, the enlargement of the EU towards the east also had an impact on the sector, fostering the regularization of already-settled migrant workers from those countries, as well as new patterns of EU east–west migration (Triandafyllidou and Marchetti, 2013).

Italy ratified C189 in 2013 in a top-down manner, and no specific legal reform nor implementation policy followed ratification. The Italian case is often held up as good practice on the international stage, since the legislation in force is perceived to be in line with C189 requirements, especially with regard to tripartite bargaining and collective agreements for the sector (Marchetti, 2016b: 103–4). Yet, despite this public assessment, most of our interviewees from domestic workers' rights organizations stressed the need to improve the current national collective agreement on domestic work in order to fully comply with C189. This would mean giving domestic workers the same rights as others, in particular in relation to maternity leave, health and social security coverage and working hours for live-in workers. However, no organizations or institutions are taking the necessary steps in this direction. In fact, the period 2008–18 was characterized by low levels of activity in the struggle for domestic workers' rights, with trade unions and domestic workers' rights organizations not playing a particularly active or visible role.

Spain

Until the 1990s, remunerated domestic work in Spain involved rural-to-urban female migrants, often employed in upper-class households and living in their employers' home (De Dios Fernández, 2018; Monteros Obelar, 2019). Since then, as in the case of Italy, there have been major changes in relation to the emerging care needs of an ageing society and the availability of a large migrant workforce in conditions of legal and socio-economic precarity (Escriva and Skinner, 2008; León, 2010; García et al, 2011; Martínez-Buján, 2011, 2014; Agrela Romero, 2012; Oso and Parella, 2012; Arango et al, 2013; Offenhenden, 2017). Indeed, on the one hand, in 2018 Spain's old-age dependency ratio and the proportion of people aged 65+ in the total population stood at 29.2 per cent and 19.2 per cent, respectively (source: EUROSTAT, year 2018). On the other hand, the number of migrants in Spain has grown exponentially, from 1.6 per cent of the total population in 1998 to 11.4 per cent in 2008. In 2018, Spain counted five million foreign nationals, 10.7 per cent of the total population, with women representing 50.5 per cent of all migrants (source: National Institute of Statistics).[80]

Against this backdrop, the number of paid domestic workers has increased greatly since the 1990s, from 381,000 in 1990 to 630,000 in 2016, as did the proportion of foreigners among them, which rose from 48.5 per cent to 67.7 per cent (source: National Institute of Statistics, years 1990 and 2016). In the same year, the nationalities most highly represented in the sector were Romanian (20.5 per cent), Bolivian (9.9 per cent), Paraguayan (9.3 per cent), Moroccan (7.3 per cent), Ukrainian (5.6 per cent) and Ecuadorian (4.1 per cent) (source: National Institute of Statistics, year 2016). However, our interviewees pointed out that these numbers may hide a significant portion of workers who have gained Spanish citizenship and are no longer counted as part of the migrant workforce. The majority of these are from Latin America, partly due to the faster naturalization process for people from former Spanish colonies.

Domestic workers represent 3.5 per cent of the total workforce and 6.8 per cent of female workers in the country. In relation to informal labour, available data indicate that 426,000 out of the 620,000 people employed in the sector had a contract and social security coverage in 2016 (sources: Economically Active Population Survey,[81] National Institute of Statistics and National Institute of Social Security[82]). However, these numbers represent an increase in the formalization of labour, firstly, due to the widespread regularization of undocumented migrants in 2005 and to the enlargement of the EU in 2007; and secondly, thanks to the new law on domestic work in 2011, which established the requirement to have a written contract and improved social security coverage (see later). For instance, between 2011 and 2012 the share of workers who were subscribed to social security rose from 42.9 to 63.7 per cent, although in this case the increase in formalization seems to have been greater for national workers than for foreign ones (Díaz Gorfinkiel and Fernández López, 2016: 31–7). In relation to wages, the average salary tends to be far below that of other sectors, namely EUR644, as compared to EUR1,066 in 2007 (source: National Immigrant Survey,[83] National Institute of Statistics, year 2007). Domestic work is included in the inter-sectorial minimum wage established by law for all employment sectors. However, this regulation is seen as ineffective in salary negotiations, since it is below the actual cost of labour set by the market (Unión General de Trabajadores, 2017).

There is a high degree of discrepancy between Spanish and foreign workers when it comes to wages and working conditions. Firstly, as in the case of Italy, Spanish workers are more likely to be employed on a part-time basis and foreign workers on a full-time basis. Secondly, Spaniards also enjoy more permanent positions, while foreigners tend to have jobs with the lowest salaries (EUR5 per hour) (source: Household Budget Survey,[84] National Institute of Statistics, year 2014). Lastly, foreign workers, especially irregular migrants, are most represented in live-in work, which is often characterized by exploitative conditions, extended working days, low wages[85] and a lack of protection (Arango et al, 2013; Gallotti and Mertens, 2013; Asociación AD Los Molinos, 2017; Unión General de Trabajadores, 2017).

Compared to the other two European countries, Spain has a younger regulatory framework, since the first law on domestic work was passed only in 1985.[86] This is due to a number of factors, particularly the violent repression of domestic workers' early attempts at collective organizing during the Spanish Civil War (1936–39) and under Francisco Franco's fascist dictatorship (1936–76), as well as the Francoist ideology, which conceived of domestic labour as women's natural duty within the family and nation and excluded domestic workers from labour rights and laws (De Dios Fernández, 2018; Monteros Obelar, 2019). In the new democratic state, the 1985 law opened (partial) access to social security for domestic workers, but still excluded them from the general labour code. This inadequate regulation was criticized by domestic workers' organizations emerging in the late 1980s–90s, such as the Granada Domestic Workers' Association ATH-Granada[87] and the Biscayan Domestic Workers' Association (ATH-ELE)[88] in Bilbao, which are still active today. Notably, in 1985, the year when the law on domestic work was approved, the first immigration law[89] marked the beginning of policies restricting non-EU migrants' entry into employment in unqualified service jobs, including care and domestic work. Yet this did not prevent irregular entry and residence, which in fact grew in later years (Cachón Rodríguez, 2009).

According to our interviewees' accounts and the analysis conducted by our country expert, in the period during which Spain was turning into a destination country for migrants, existing groups mostly responded to the situation by providing social and legal assistance to migrant workers. This can be said for both domestic workers' groups composed of national workers and the so-called 'pro-migrant' third sector, organized by secular and church-based NGOs (such as Caritas Española, the Spanish Red Cross and Red Acoge). According to our interviewees, a new wave of domestic workers' mobilizing began in the mid-2000s, which transformed this picture by specifically focusing on labour and migrants' rights together, and for the first time included migrant domestic workers, most of them of Latin American origin. In fact, the 2005 amnesty for illegal migrants was taken by a number of political actors as an opportunity for awareness raising and networking among previously unorganized migrant workers (Monteros Obelar, 2019). It is in this context that groups such as Territorio Doméstico[90] and Servicio Doméstico Activo (SEDOAC)[91] in Madrid, and the Care and Domestic Workers' Trade Union (SINDIHOGAR/SINDILLAR)[92] in Barcelona were created.

Regulations on domestic and care work were introduced by the socialist governments of José Luis Rodríguez Zapatero (2004–11). In 2006 the Personal Autonomy and Dependent Care Law[93] was passed, with the purpose of responding to the welfare needs of the ageing Spanish society by providing public support for households with dependent family members. In 2011 a new law on paid domestic work[94] finally responded to historical demands from the sector, such as full equal access to social security and a compulsory written contract. However, this law failed to put domestic workers on a fully equal footing with other workers. Moreover, the implementation of both laws was left incomplete, due to the 2008 economic crisis and the restrictive reforms in the fields of migration law, public expenditure and social security regulations[95] approved in the years that followed by the conservative government led by Mariano Rajoy (Montserrat Codorniu, 2015; Monteros Obelar, 2019).

Throughout the 2010s, the promulgation of C189, as well as the social dynamism associated with the anti-austerity and social justice movement known as 15-M, or the Indignados Movement,[96] ignited new campaigns for domestic workers' rights and for the ratification of C189. Novel domestic workers' organizations emerged, such as the Cultural Association for Care and Domestic Work, Nosotras,[97] in Granada, and Senda de Cuidados in Madrid. This decade also saw the national scaling up of the movement, as domestic workers' groups and NGOs traditionally active at a local level converged via the National Platform of Domestic Workers' Associations[98] (beginning in 2008) and the Turin Group[99] (beginning in 2011). They also all gathered for the National Congresses on care and domestic work of 2016 and 2018 (Monteros Obelar, 2019). Lastly, at both the local and national level, new political forces championed the cause, in particular, the left-wing Podemos party.[100] Yet, despite this grassroots activity, partial political support and civil society interest on the matter, the ratification of C189 and the achievement of labour equality for domestic workers remain pending issues today. As highlighted by organized domestic workers and experts in the field, major shortcomings in the current legal framework include their exclusion from unemployment allowance, labour risks and health protection, labour inspections and collective bargaining.

3

Global Rights and Local Struggles

Our nine countries illustrate how national contextual variations can result in a transformative process at the international level being adopted, negotiated, modified or strengthened at the local level – or alternatively, ignored or rejected. With this question in mind, we look at what happened in each country during this time as regards the preparation, promulgation, ratification and, where relevant, the implementation of C189, or what we have called the 'C189 process'. We are thus asking how, and under which conditions, what we identify as a global right can be adopted at the level of local struggles. We look at the actions undertaken by local actors and the 'interpretative frames' they used to provide a narrative about their conditions and possible solutions (Benford and Snow, 2000). We also look at the alliances they established, which acquire a specific meaning in relation to the political, cultural and socioeconomic context of the country in which they take place.

We begin by elaborating on the way in which the international campaign for C189 can be seen as an example of a global agenda, combining perspectives on human rights and social movements. We provide some context to the international dimension of the C189 process, looking in particular at the preparation and promulgation phase. In the second part of the chapter we offer an analysis of the dynamics created by the C189 process in each of the nine countries under study, using a strategic action field perspective. After introducing some of the elements of the theory of strategic action fields, we describe how, in each country, the main elements of the field aiming to advocate for domestic workers' rights have evolved over the period 2008–18. We also discuss which interpretative frames have animated the field in giving meaning to the issue of domestic workers' rights in each country. In this analysis we suggest that the C189 process has been what Fligstein and McAdam (2012) call an 'external shock' which has affected each country, yet prompted different socio-political dynamics.

We then carry out a comparative assessment of the nine countries in relation to the C189 process. We describe how it has changed, depending on their respective socioeconomic, cultural and political contexts. Yet we emphasize the importance of not assessing the impact of the C189 process in terms of success or failure but, rather, as tendencies or variations, which are provoked by moving the process from the global to the local level. Thus, we have clustered our nine countries along four different variations: (1) Ecuador and the Philippines, (2) Colombia and Brazil, (3) Taiwan, India and Spain and (4) Italy and Germany. When comparing these groups, we find different objectives as well as different roles for the key actors in the C189 process at local levels. A variation between these groups can also be seen in the kinds of discourse on domestic workers and the demographic composition of the workforce in each country. This chapter also opens the way to a discussion on discourses, alliances and coalitions between actors of different kinds, continued in Chapter 5.

The rights of domestic workers as a 'global' issue

The transformation of domestic workers' movements for labour rights into a global movement compels us to consider the interplay between the national and international actors that have shaped the process. However, the interests of domestic workers seldom received much attention in the past, so, when reflecting on the growing institutional concern for their situation, a question that arose repeatedly was: 'why now?' What has motivated the changing attitudes of international actors towards paid domestic work? In other words, what has made it possible for the labour rights of domestic workers to become what Clifford Bob (2011) would call a 'new right' at the global level?

We should first consider the fact that, in reality, the issue of domestic work is not new to the ILO's agenda. Already in 1948, the ILO considered a resolution demanding minimum standards for this sector (see Schwenken et al, 2011; Boris, 2019). However, the attention given to the issue of domestic workers gradually faded away. In the post-war period it was commonly believed that the modernization of domestic life, with the growth of technology and more efficient systems to organize the household, would soon make it possible to spontaneously eliminate the traditional figure of the paid domestic worker, seen as a legacy of exploitative, premodern times (see Coser, 1973). There was thought to be no need for political intervention. It was only in the mid-1990s, when the ILO started its general campaign for the promotion of 'decent work' for flexible, informal and non-standard jobs, that the issue of paid domestic work came up again.

In 1996 an important historical precondition for the later approval of C189 was the passing of ILO Convention No. 177, setting labour standards for home work (Boris, 2019). Elisabeth Prügl (1999) demonstrates how the adoption of C177 is testament to a historical change in the conception of 'work', through its expansion of the notion in order to protect the increasing numbers of flexible home workers. These are mainly women employed by factories, especially in the small manufacturing sector, who work from their homes and are paid by piecework. Both labour rights and feminist movements that had previously tried to draw attention to this category had always been confronted with a general conception of home work as feminized labour, supplementary to that of male workers in factories, and therefore 'not real work'. Women workers' struggles over this issue intensified through the 1970s and 1980s, in parallel with the intensification of industrial production in Asia, Latin America and North Africa, where home-based workers were used by multinationals as a cheap and flexible labour force in the production of textiles, food and livestock. Indeed, it was precisely from rural women's movements in countries like India, Indonesia, Thailand and the Philippines that a new impetus to advocate for home workers' rights originated. A network of local organizations and trade unions – among them, notably, the Indian women's union SEWA – fostered a new dialogue with the ILO and successfully campaigned for the approval of Convention 177.

As we already mentioned, the ILO's decision to put the question of domestic workers' rights on its agenda for possible conventions was perceived by many as a historic moment. This was especially so from the standpoint of countries where domestic work did not have any kind of recognition as proper work, or where the legal framework protecting domestic workers' salaries and conditions was only minimal. The Convention also explicitly promotes collective organizing by domestic workers, aiming for a stronger unionization of the sector. Finally, the Convention was intended to improve the social and cultural representation of domestic workers and their economic conditions, including through an increase in salaries to level up with the minimum standards found in other sectors. The C189 process therefore promised to be something which might have real legal, cultural and economic repercussions for the lives of domestic workers.

The possibility of such historic transformation has attracted the attention of many international organizations and NGOs, from UN agencies to international trade unions and EU bodies (see Chapter 1). In the eyes of these actors, the idea of a convention on domestic work effectively combined human rights, women's rights and labour rights perspectives. In our view, the process which has brought about C189 resembles what some scholars have defined as 'the making of global agendas' (Della Porta et al, 1999; Smith and Johnston, 2002; Smith, 2004). A classic example of the construction of a global agenda has been identified in the process which was activated around the formulation of the Millennium Development Goals, with national and international NGOs and institutions working simultaneously for their preparation and later committed to their realization (Fukuda-Parr, 2004; Kabeer, 2005). Yet the literature on global agendas questions the effectiveness of the various methods, from lobbying to protests or consultations, that NGOs and civil society adopt in a bid to influence international institutions. It also debates the most effective method to foster the implementation of international frameworks at local levels, a question that is highly relevant to the drafting of ILO conventions.

Similar dilemmas have been raised by Nora McKeon (2009) looking at the efficacy of the UN, by Jan Aart Scholte (2009) analysing the World Trade Organization and by Jens Steffek, Claudia Kissling and Patrizia Nanz (2008) examining the EU. This critical perspective has also been useful in assessing the impact of normative frameworks on women's rights. Indeed, after the UN Assembly in Beijing in 1995, several studies researched the discrepancies between the international and national levels when it comes to women's issues. For example, Janet Conway (2008) has investigated how local women's movements are connected globally through the initiative of the World March of Women. Meanwhile, authors such as Sylvia Walby (2002), Martha Nussbaum (2001), Neila Kabeer (2004) and Peggy Levitt and Sally Merry (2009) have established a body of scholarship that explores the limitations, difficulties and potential developments of international norms on women's rights when they are adopted at a local level.

Along this line of analysis, we explored the impact of C189 as an instrument for the governance of global rights between local and transnational levels (Boris, 2017). An emerging literature on the Convention has begun to address this issue, looking at the impact of C189 on national or regional social movements, and on the political processes related to the campaigns for its ratification and consequent implementation (Schwenken, 2013; Blofield and Jokela, 2018; Marchetti, 2018; Cherubini et al, 2020). Research has also focused on improvements in legal advancements in various countries brought about by signing the Convention into national law (Du Toit, 2011; Albin and Mantouvalou, 2012; Gallotti and Mertens, 2013; Rosewarne, 2013; Viesel, 2013). Further, some scholars have focused on the key role played by the IDWN and that of regional and national organizations in the drafting of the Convention in 2011 in Geneva (Schwenken, 2016; Fish, 2017; Acciari, 2019).

Equally important is the work that has been done on the historical roots of C189, identified in other ILO campaigns for the promotion of decent work in flexible, non-standard and low-skilled informal sectors, as well as in the multiple debates on women's work and migrants' work which have animated the ILO agenda since the 1990s (Schwenken et al, 2011; Kott and Droux, 2013; Boris and Fish, 2014; Mahon and Michel, 2017; Boris, 2019). Promoting decent work also appeals to human rights principles, as is clearly reflected in C189, whose main prescription of equal labour rights for domestic workers is accompanied by a call for recognition of their dignity as human beings (Garofalo Geymonat et al, 2017; Marchetti, 2018). It has been rightly observed that C189 is rooted in intersectional thinking, simultaneously seeking to address issues of gender, race, ethnicity, religious and class-based discrimination at work, and calling for the protection of the most vulnerable categories of domestic workers, with special reference to migrant workers (Schwenken, 2013; Fish, 2017; Blackett, 2019).

At the local level, research on domestic workers' organizing highlights the diversity of actors and objectives involved in the struggle around the C189 process. Depending on the country, the field is populated by many institutional and non-institutional actors, playing either a supporting role in the fight for domestic workers' rights or an obstructive one. Besides domestic workers' grassroots organizations and trade unions, these actors may encompass other civil society organizations, such as general trade unions and workers' organizations (Boris and Nadasen, 2008; Chun and Cranford, 2018), women's and feminist groups, anti-racist and ethnic minority associations (Bernardino-Costa, 2014) and humanitarian NGOs (Chun and Kim, 2018). Studies have also considered organizations representing employers' interests (Chien, 2018), governmental bodies, state institutions and international organizations (Blofield, 2012). The role of these actors, their position in the field and their interactions are context-specific and deserve further empirical analysis, as we aim to provide in the following pages.

Strategic fields of action around the C189 process

In their book *A Theory of Fields* (2012), sociologists Neil Fligstein and Doug McAdam propose a comprehensive interpretative system for social movements by merging several elements from previous scholarship that studied collective actors' behaviour, their reciprocal relationships and how they frame their actions, goals and results. They use the notion of strategic action fields to describe the general level of interaction between individual and collective actors who, from their different positions and, at times, differing interests, nevertheless have the same focus.

As already discussed in Chapter 1, we consider all actors involved in domestic workers' rights issues, in each of our nine countries, to belong to the same strategic field of action. In a strategic action field perspective, it is not easy to identify the exact contours of a field. Who is in, and who is out? What exactly is the focus that they supposedly share? Actors within the same field might be in opposition to one another; some (the incumbent actors) may impose their views on the others, some (the challengers) may remain marginal, sometimes voicing dissent or proposing alternative views. When drawing the contours of the field, it is also important to understand if other fields are contiguous, with overlaps in their themes, and whether some actors have migrated from one field to another.

For Fligstein and McAdam, fields alternate between moments of internal stability and moments of crisis and change. Through these different phases, the position of actors within the field may change, as may the relationship between them. Stability, however, is only apparent, since any field is actually under constant pressure, which could be contention, a threat or an opportunity. It is this pressure that ultimately keeps the actors in the field together. Fields can be animated by coercion, competition or cooperation. They can be based on hierarchy or coalition, depending on transformations in the form of power held by each actor. Particularly determinant are what they call episodes of contention, which consist of periods during which new forms of interaction between actors emerge. Conversely, when an actor shapes new modes of interaction with others, influencing their perception about a threat or opportunity, the authors talk of an 'emergent mobilisation'. This is usually provoked by an exogenous shock and can lead to the formation of a new field that occupies a previously unorganized social space. Finally, another important characteristic of strategic fields of action is that they are socially constructed. In fact, there are no objective criteria determining whether or not an actor is included in the field, as this depends on the individual 'standing' of the actor, and the issues that are subjectively at stake at each moment. In that sense, for Fligstein and McAdam, 'fields are constructed on a situational basis' (Fligstein and McAdam, 2012: 26).

What is the role of governments and other political players in this framework? For Fligstein and McAdam, such actors often facilitate the formation of a field. This can be done, for example, by actively backing up particular groups (as in sponsorship) or, more passively, by certifying the conditions of the stability brought about by non-state actors. A new law, a new judicial ruling and so on, can create an opportunity for strategic action by established or emergent collective actors. Likewise, organized groups can go to state actors and lobby for rules that promote their interests in existing or new fields. In this chapter, we apply this framework to our nine country cases and thus try to understand the functioning of the field regarding rights for domestic workers. Different actors are included or excluded from this field in each of the contexts. The attitudes of the actors also change, depending on the country. For all cases, however, we proceed from the hypothesis that C189 can be seen as an exogenous change that shook the field.

Through this lens, in the following section we present a brief comparison between the nine countries, centred on what we have identified as key elements in a strategic action field perspective. In so doing, we aim to highlight relevant continuities and discrepancies, synergies and possible tensions in each country concerning the local impact of C189 and towards the improvement of domestic workers' rights.

C189 as an external shock

In our view, in some of the countries we examined, the C189 process has been an exogenous shock which has made it possible to think about, discuss and promote the rights of domestic workers in a new manner (Fish, 2017). In March 2008 the governing body of the ILO decided to place the topic of paid domestic work on the agenda of the forthcoming ILO Conference. Domestic workers' groups reacted promptly to this decision, strongly encouraged by international trade unions and the ILO itself. Between 2008 and 2010, grassroots domestic workers' groups, trade unions and supportive NGOs provided information to ILO offices about the circumstances in their respective countries, and they lobbied governments, employers and trade unions ahead of the vote (Schwenken et al, 2011).

In 2011, the Convention on 'decent work for domestic workers' received 396 votes in favour, 16 against and 63 abstentions. Immediately after the promulgation, a worldwide ratification campaign[1] was launched (initially called '12 by 12', aiming at 12 ratifications in 12 months). At the international level, the C189 campaign was coordinated by the ITUC and IDWN, later called International Domestic Workers Federation. In fact, an unprecedented level of direct involvement of workers themselves characterized all the steps in the ILO consultations and the drafting of the Convention (Fish, 2017), and it continues today with the aim of expanding the number of countries ratifying and implementing C189. Through this process, domestic workers' organizations have indeed extended their networks and increased their visibility at the international level.

In some of the countries in our study, C189 can be seen as the exogenous shock that has fostered the formation of new organizations and the creation of an unprecedented terrain for their action. In others it has significantly transformed an already existing movement, improving its visibility and allowing more space for action. In our view, the reason for these regional differences needs to be understood by looking at each country's tradition of political and social engagement, in a contextual perspective that we will develop further in the following section.

Goals

C189 has not always been the actual goal of the mobilizations taking place in each country. In fact, when looking at the period 2008–18, the objectives which had created the convergence between actors belonging to the strategic action field of domestic workers' rights may or may not have been directly related to C189, depending on the country and on the specific case.

In India and Taiwan, for example, the movements' goal was actually a national law on domestic work. Of course we can say that the international C189 campaign has had positive effects, initiating a debate on domestic workers' rights and giving it international legitimation, but C189 was not the main focus, for different reasons that we will clarify later. In the cases of Germany, Italy and Brazil, meanwhile, the governments have ratified in quite a bureaucratic manner, without consulting domestic workers' organizations. Yet, following the ratifications, trade unions pointed to the need to improve current national legislation in order to fully satisfy C189 demands. Conversely, prior to Brazil's ratification in 2018, domestic workers' organizations had decided not to focus on the C189 process but to fight instead for national reforms, namely the constitutional change achieved with the PEC das Domésticas, as we saw in Chapter 2.

Finally, in the Philippines, Ecuador and Colombia the goals changed several times between 2008 and 2018. At first, in all three countries, the field took shape around the issue of C189 ratification, which was successfully achieved in the years 2012, 2013 and 2014. respectively. Subsequent trajectories have, however, been different. In the Philippines, the new Kasambahay Law (2013) was introduced, which, as required by C189, was an ad hoc law on domestic work. Following its introduction, the goal of the field moved to the implementation of this new legislation, aspects of which remained lacking. In Ecuador, while demands for a national law on domestic work were frustrated, domestic workers' organizations supported other labour reforms. The same happened in Colombia, where they also campaigned for related issues, such as the right to the 13th-month payment stipulated by the Ley de Prima in 2016, although a national law on domestic work remained the ideal objective for actors in the field.

Actors

Here we set out the main actors in the strategic action field of domestic workers' rights. Of course, as we shall see, actors' roles and attitudes may change over time, as do objectives and discourses. Yet it is useful to map out the various individuals and organizations that have particular influence in the field at any one time.

In all countries where the field was at one point strongly united in pursuing the ratification of C189, namely in Ecuador, Colombia and the Philippines, we see that governments and political parties played a very important role, leading the process and building consensus around the ratification as a national goal. The political actors in these countries also had strong relationships with the ILO offices. By contrast, the ratification processes in Italy and Germany were quite different, since, as mentioned, in these two countries the path towards ratification was conducted in a particularly top-down way, without inviting wider participation.

We have also observed how governments that have been supportive of ratification have not always been as committed to its subsequent implementation. In this case, leading advocates for its implementation might be either general trade unions or, in countries where they had a strong presence (see Chapter 2), domestic workers' organizations themselves. In fact, in the majority of our nine country cases domestic workers' organizations were very active in the implementation phase.

In addition to these actors, it is also important to acknowledge the determinant role of civil society in general across all the countries in our study, including local and international NGOs, as well as the key role played by international trade unions and UN agencies. The support of international trade unions, international agencies and international NGOs tends to be more significant in the Global South, in particular those that have supported the funding or development of small domestic workers' organizations. In some contexts, international NGOs appear to also have been the intermediate actors between governments, the ILO and workers themselves. In Taiwan, the Philippines and India, the media plays a significant part in drawing attention to domestic workers' exploitation and challenging local institutions to take a stand. Finally, the role of local trade unions is essential, particularly in countries like Italy, Germany and Brazil. These countries all have strong trade unions that have traditionally covered issues relating to domestic work, such as women's work, migration and welfare.

At the same time, there are also some important absences in the strategic field of action. Actors that we may assume to be engaged in domestic workers' struggles do not always participate in the field, as is the case for some feminist and women's rights groups, indigenous movements, anti-racist groups or workers' organizations from other sectors. In Chapter 5 we will explore the question of why in many contexts feminist and women's rights organizations have not clearly supported the cause of domestic workers' rights, with exceptions in India, Brazil, Taiwan and Spain. More variegated across the nine countries is the participation of other anti-discrimination groups, which in some cases are inside the field, although in a marginal position, while in other cases they are outside. It is also interesting to look at the position of employers' organizations, including associations of disabled and chronically ill care receivers. These may range from highly committed allies of domestic workers to their antagonists, depending on the context. Moreover, the C189 process may encounter opposition from state-sponsored recruitment agencies and private brokers that are profiting from the inequalities of the current system and strive to maintain the status quo.

To summarize, focusing on the difference in the roles and positions of local actors is a useful way, in our view, to understand how the global rights of domestic workers are incorporated and realized differently at a national level. This process is greatly influenced by the types of actors involved, the relationships between them and their objectives, with outcomes that will be further discussed in the rest of this chapter.

Interpretative frames

When actors mobilize, they need to make sense of their own actions and those of others. This is done through interpretative frames, that is, the narratives used to explain problems, identify possible solutions, gain consensus and motivate actors to take action with respect to given goals (Benford and Snow, 2000). These interpretative frames also contribute to shaping the boundaries of the strategic field of action, since they help to build an (albeit temporary) consensus around what is at stake and on the objectives of the field. In our approach, such frames are important elements in making the connection between the global rights for domestic workers, and the socio-cultural and political discourses present in each of the nine countries.

In fact, in our in-depth interviews with advocates of domestic workers' rights particular attention was paid to exploring how specific discursive frames were adopted when describing domestic workers' campaigns in their countries, with the aim of identifying the meaning-making activity underpinning their struggle. In Chapter 5 we will return to the issue of frames with reference to excerpts from the interviews that draw specifically on feminist frames. Let us for now, however, briefly mention the three most commonly recurring frames which we observed.

The first centres on feminist arguments on the valorization of reproductive labour and was particularly useful in countries like Ecuador, Colombia, Brazil, India and the Philippines. Here we found that the C189 process went hand in hand with a political project emphasizing the role of women in society, especially working-class and racialized women, and the raising of their social representation.

The second frame focuses more on differences between social classes, and sees the conflict between domestic workers and their employers as a struggle between interest groups with opposing economic goals. We found this frame to be common in the majority of the countries we studied – often in ways that show inextricable links to other relevant categories such as caste, race and ethnicity. Italy, Germany and Taiwan, however, were at odds with most other countries in the study. There, class conflict appeared to be largely absent from the discussion, with issues of migration taking the foreground.

Finally, another recurrent frame is the one around the transnational commodification of care. This discourse plays on the connection between migrants' exploitation in this sector and the crisis of welfare in industrialized, ageing societies. It was thus especially common among interviewees in Italy, Spain, Germany and Taiwan as destination countries for migrants in the elder care sector. In other words, this frame is a critique of the marketization of care provision and its reliance on foreign labour.

In conclusion, it is important for us to explore the way in which these frames operate in conjunction with other elements, such as existing alliances, the roles of specific actors and so on, across a range of contexts and in response to different events. In the next section we present how various elements intertwine in translating the C189 process onto movements at a national level. This is an attempt, from our side, to understand what produces national variations in a global struggle.

Four variants of the C189 process at a national level

In the previous section we saw the numerous elements that, through a strategic action field perspective, may describe the specificities of the C189 process in each country, by looking at the main actors, their goals and the frames they recurrently used. These elements help us to articulate the way in which the C189 process is reflected practically in each country's struggle. In this section we expand our investigation through a comparative analysis of each national context, exploring how what occurred inside the field has been determined by the wider socioeconomic, political and cultural terrain.

As we will see, another important reason for these differences is the way the struggle for domestic workers' rights is perceived by society at large. In fact, the C189 process seems to have been favoured in places where domestic workers' struggles are seen as emblematic of wider campaigns for social justice in the country. Conversely, we found that in countries where domestic workers were largely seen as foreign and easily 'othered', the campaign remained isolated and issue specific, and it was difficult for activists to build a large consensus beyond direct stakeholders on domestic workers' issues. In other words, it is easier to promote the global rights of domestic workers at a national level when they are seen as part of a wider political project for social justice. Conversely, in contexts where the connection with wider political struggles was weaker or absent, the question of domestic workers' rights was framed more narrowly. Thus, giving more rights to this category was not meant to challenge the structural factors shaping this sector and the exploitation therein.

In our comparative analysis we identified four main tendencies, each produced by a different configuration of factors described in the previous section.

Ecuador and Philippines

For these two countries, it is important to emphasize the strong synergy between the ILO, national governments and civil society actors, including domestic workers' groups. In both cases the state was quick to ratify C189, legislative measures were adopted on the basis of the Convention's requirements and domestic workers' organizing was promoted – an aspect that is in itself part of the C189 goals. Other civil society actors were also responsive to the ILO campaign, thereby ensuring that it had reach beyond the institutional level.

In Ecuador, the international C189 campaign found particularly fertile ground in the political landscape inaugurated by the presidency of Rafael Correa (2007–17). Capitalizing on the cultural awareness developed in the country by social movements before his election, in 2008 Correa proposed a new constitution which, among other things, particularly emphasized the value of reproductive labour together with equality of rights between all workers. This paved the way for the ratification of C189 in 2013. Moreover, as we described in Chapter 2, between 2010 and 2014 a number of labour reforms in Ecuador equated the condition of domestic workers to that of other workers, with the support of the Ministry of Labour and the Parliament. The promulgation of these new legal norms was accompanied by awareness-raising actions aiming to improve, on the one hand, the perception of the social relevance of paid domestic work, and on the other, workers' consciousness of their own rights and position in society. In so doing, the government was able to pursue the dual goal of C189 at the levels both of legal rights and of social representation.

At the same time, some existing domestic workers' organizations were supported by the government, giving them public visibility and supporting them in their establishment as trade unions, as in the case of what is today known as SINUTRHE. Pivotal in this process was the role of several international organizations and NGOs active in the country, namely, the regional office of the ILO, humanitarian organizations such as UN-Women and the Latin American office of CARE International, and finally those affiliated with European trade unions that promote labour rights in the Global South, such as the Belgian union FOS-Socialist Solidarity. For all these actors, speaking of domestic workers' rights addressed the condition of the many working-class women performing these jobs, including internal migrants from rural contexts and/or racialized Afro-Ecuadorian and indigenous women. These different forces brought domestic workers' issues to the forefront, making them emblematic of the social reform programme of the Correa administration and his ideal of a 'citizens' revolution'.

However, even in Ecuador the C189 process was not without obstacles. In fact, by the time we completed our fieldwork (March 2018) Ecuadorian domestic workers' groups had not even achieved a fundamental aspect of the C189 implementation, that is, an ad hoc national law on domestic work. Yet the energy, the actions undertaken, the actors involved and the general discourse surrounding domestic workers' rights – very much based on the same ideals promoted by C189 – are illustrative of the Convention's strong capacity to spur local dynamics.

In our view, we believe that C189 has been an exogenous shock which has prompted mobilizations when it has encountered a suitable cultural and political ground at a local level. This is particularly the case as regards the key actors that collaborated inside the field, that is, the government and other institutional actors, NGOs and domestic workers' groups that, unlike those elsewhere, embraced C189 as a goal. Crucially, the local ILO office was fully involved in the process in collaboration with the other actors. The only notable shortcoming was the absence of grassroots Ecuadorian feminist, women's rights or indigenous organizations, which appear to have remained outside this field. Although neither against nor boycotting this process, they were not particularly engaged in the C189 campaign. In Chapter 5 we will expand on this lack of alliance with feminist and women's rights organizations, yet we will also examine the convergence that took place at the level of framing.

In the Philippines we also found a suitable terrain for synergy between local processes and the international C189 campaign. This is mainly due to growing attention towards the issue of abuses of Filipino domestic workers while employed abroad. As we saw in Chapter 2, the media coverage of such cases shocked the public even in the 1990s. This general concern about violence against migrant domestic workers was echoed in two types of policy intervention. Firstly, at the level of migration policy, the Labour Department of the Filipino government initiated a series of measures, in particular by threatening to suspend the domestic worker programme for countries with reported cases of mistreatment. Secondly, at the level of human rights protection, both governmental and non-governmental organizations focused on introducing measures against human trafficking and child labour, which affected domestic work. Further, awareness of the continuity between the violence that Filipino workers suffered abroad and the inequality affecting the country began to grow. The mass emigration of

Filipino women and girls that started in the 1970s is indicative of the poverty and lack of opportunity in the country for young women, especially in rural areas and among the part of the population ethnicized as 'Inday' or 'Bisaya' (in both cases, meaning women from the Visayan region). At the cultural level, the tendency of Filipino women to seek employment in the domestic sector is also influenced by colonial legacies (Parreñas, 2008).

Against this complex background, the idea of a convention on domestic workers' rights was embraced by the Filipino government under the administration of Liberal Party president Benigno Aquino III, who was one of the early promoters of initiatives towards C189. The Philippines was the second country in the world (after Uruguay) to ratify the Convention, and it worked on the process in close relationship with the regional ILO office. Furthermore, a national task force, the TWG, was established, which in 2013 produced a new law on domestic labour, while the same year saw the emergence of a new domestic workers' organization, UNITED. In civil society, the process was supported by a variegated landscape of actors, ranging from religious organizations and humanitarian NGOs to migrants' rights organizations, workers' centres and trade unions. All these actors had connections at the international level in the fields of human and labour rights. According to our interviewees, feminist organizations were not significantly represented in the work of the TWG and in the process leading to the approval of the Kasambahay Law. However, individual feminists were part of organizations that played an important role in the field, such as in migrants' and grassroots development organizations.

As in Ecuador, in the Philippines too we found obstacles to the process; indeed, the national law on domestic work had a great number of pitfalls and very limited efficacy. The implementation of C189 proved difficult, with stakeholders concerned that it was passed for reasons of international prestige, mostly for the sake of diplomatic relations with countries that received overseas workers. Yet it must be emphasized that, as in the case of Ecuador, the C189 process triggered a series of debates, actions and interventions that show a strong positive connection between the global and the local levels. The alignment between the ILO, the Filipino government, the Department of Labour, trade unions and much of civil society suggests that the question of domestic workers' rights assumed an emblematic role in advancing the social status of Filipino workers, especially women, whether in the diaspora or in home territory.

Colombia and Brazil

In Colombia and Brazil, we found a vibrant dynamism at civil society level, combined with the involvement of the state and other institutional actors.

We see the C189 process as embedded in a wider transformation process at play involving domestic workers as one of the key target groups – although not exclusively. At the same time, demands by domestic workers' groups explicitly went beyond C189 as such, advocating for more radical changes in the conditions of domestic workers at the legislative, social and economic levels than C189 could offer. Notably, domestic workers' organizations were already a reality in these countries, alongside a long-standing tradition of workers' and women's movements. Although C189 was the exogenous change that gave a boost to the field, the legacy of past experiences is critical to understanding these contexts.

In both Colombia and Brazil the domestic work sector is highly racialized and deeply influenced by colonial legacies in the way Afro-descendants (Afro-Colombians and Afro-Brazilians, respectively) are culturally perceived and in the positions they occupy in society. The relationship between employers and domestic workers reflects the social stratification of the country, the latter being produced by the intertwining of class-based, racial, educational and gender hierarchies, and further complicated by internal migrations towards large cities. In Colombia, since 1964 the reality of Afro-Colombian domestic workers has also been affected by the civil war, which has caused internal population displacement and led to refugee women frequently ending up in domestic work.

However, both countries also share a number of important features concerning long-lasting movements for domestic workers' rights. In Brazil, the 1930s saw the birth of a movement that would grow over the following decades and lead to the creation of domestic workers' trade unions in all Brazilian states from the 1960s onwards. Brazilian domestic workers were very active again in the late 1980s, participating in the consultations towards the new constitution (1988). In Colombia, too, the first mobilizations took place in the 1930s and 1960s, with the movement resurgent again in the 1980s.

Against this background, in both countries the domestic workers' movement gained new momentum in the 2000s and the 2010s. In Brazil this was supported in particular by the pro-worker governments of Lula da Silva (2003–11) and Dilma Rousseff (2011–16). Improving domestic workers' rights was one of the symbolic goals of the new progressive Left running the country. This phase found its apex in 2013 with the constitutional reform (PEC das Domésticas), which advanced the rights of domestic workers, with broad support in the country. International NGOs, religious and grassroots organizations (from the feminist to the anti-racist) all favoured this constitutional reform. As we described in Chapter 2, the domestic workers' movement was in fact divided over the issue of C189's ratification, since some saw it as a step back relative to Brazilian law. When ratification took place in 2018 (at the very end of our fieldwork research), it came very unexpectedly and it was seen as a diplomatic move by the then-president, Michel Temer.

Colombian domestic workers took the opportunity of the C189 process to draw attention to the most profound inequalities and discrimination affecting Black, refugee and working-class women. As we will see in Chapter 5, their organizations promoted important narratives against class- and race-based inequalities, as well as against the devaluation of women's care work. Here too, these achievements were embedded in a new political phase for the country, animated by the hopes of the peace process and the new visions for a more egalitarian society which it awakened. In 2012 the C189 ratification was supported by Juan Manuel Santos' government. Further developments such as the extension of a 13th-month payment for domestic workers (Ley de Prima) were endorsed by feminist parliamentarians from the progressive Green Party, as well as a by a wide spectrum of pro-gender-equality actors from NGOs, academia, trade unions and so forth. As in Brazil, the domestic workers' movement was given great visibility as far as it could embody the cause of Afro-descendant working-class women in the fight to end centuries of discrimination.

Both countries therefore boast a rich landscape of actors engaged in various ways in the struggle for domestic workers' rights. However, it is noticeable that, in comparison with countries like Ecuador and the Philippines, in Brazil and Ecuador the experience of domestic workers as labour organizers and trade unionists dates back to the 1930s (see Chapter 2) . Their capacity to intervene in public discourse allowed connections to be made between domestic workers' issues and a wider societal change, going beyond the mere application of the C189 process as their objective.

India, Taiwan and Spain

In Taiwan, India and Spain a different pattern emerged. A vibrant period of activity among grassroots organizations, trade unions and domestic workers did not result in the ratification of C189, nor, in the case of Taiwan, in national reforms that could incorporate C189 principles. For countries in this group, the number and strength of those opposing the C189 process is noteworthy, for domestic workers' rights were opposed not only by employers' interests but also by the conservative parties controlling Parliament, as well as by brokers who acted as market intermediaries and whose private interests were favoured by the status quo.

Let us start by looking at India. Here the majority of mobilizations around domestic workers' rights were carried out by the Platform for Domestic Workers' Rights (PDWR), a very large coalition of religious organizations, trade unions, anti-discrimination groups, anti-trafficking NGOs and the many domestic workers' organizations active in the Indian federal states. Among national trade unions, SEWA, which as we mentioned had already been very active regarding ILO Convention 177 on the rights of home workers, was again engaged in addressing the conditions of women working in informal sectors. As elsewhere, Catholic organizations and missions played a crucial role in India, and often sponsored self-organized groups of domestic workers. Some of these missions also operated shelters for young Indian women from rural areas who had been trafficked into domestic work. Important feminist commentary, from scholars to trade unionists and policy makers, has emphasized the continuing devaluation of domestic work in the country as a form of patriarchal oppression specific to India, intersecting with the legacy of the caste system and the degrading ethnicization of internal migrants as 'tribal girls'.

In 2011 the PDWR was able to lobby the Indian government to vote 'yes' for C189 in Geneva. Yet, despite the continuing mobilizations and the numerous Bills proposed by the PDWR to Parliament, nothing followed. The Convention was not ratified, and there was no real programme for a national law on domestic work. It is true that an increasing number of Indian states now have regulations, but there is still no legislation at the federal level. Domestic workers were included in several other pieces of legislation that cover important parts of their job, such as laws on sexual harassment, child labour, health insurance and so forth. However, a national law on domestic work would be an important achievement, challenging the traditional Indian mindset which postulates strong social divisions between people, in accordance with their class/caste position. The inefficacy of the C189 campaign was a major cause of frustration among pro-domestic workers actors. They saw in these continuing difficulties and the never-ending wait for answers from Parliament proof of the disinterest of the political establishment in truly changing the system of internal discrimination underpinning Indian society.

In Spain and Taiwan, similar frustrations lingered not from discrimination against a minority group, but from the discrimination against foreign workers. Our interviewees indicated that Taiwanese society overwhelmingly views foreign workers as inferior. Differential treatment is legitimated by Taiwanese policies on international labour recruitment, which have been aiding the country's industrial expansion since the 1990s. Like factory workers, foreign domestic workers – home-based caregivers in particular – have their employment regulated through a system entailing very short-term residence permits and extremely limited citizenship and social security rights for workers. The administration of this system is delegated to private recruitment agencies that manage the brokering of foreign women into Taiwanese households, with minimal legal protection against the abuses they might encounter, which sometimes results in them escaping from employers' homes at the price of losing their legal status.

The limited labour and citizenship rights of these workers compound their denigrating social representation as outsiders, easily exploitable subjects and victims of physical and psychological violence. Their well-being is scarcely considered, subordinated as they are to the needs of the many families with old and dependent members, Taiwan being a particularly ageing society. Yet many groups in Taiwan are actively challenging this status quo, campaigning for the protection of migrants' human rights and against trafficking, through lobbying, protests and support projects (for example, shelters for runaway migrant workers).

Finally, the case of Spain is different yet again, though it does share some features. As in Taiwan, the sector is almost entirely occupied by migrants, who are employed to care for an ageing population with many dependent citizens. Since the 2000s, grassroots groups advocating for the rights of migrants, including domestic workers, have gained momentum. Feminist figures have also become very vocal, from activists to feminist scholars and policy makers. As we saw in Chapter 2, this dynamism was part of a politicization of society, with the promotion of progressive causes beginning with the election of the socialist president José Luis Rodríguez Zapatero. The 15-M movement and the rise of Podemos subsequently contributed to the spread of progressive attitudes towards migrants' and women's issues.

A number of leftist political figures contributed to the visibility of domestic workers' organizations, for example the Turin Group and the National Platform of Domestic Workers' Associations. At the local level, we can find several examples of domestic workers' organizations that are visible and well regarded. Among other actors, such as academics, trade unions and NGOs, we also find a high degree of interest in domestic workers' issues, which was amplified by the international C189 campaign and related actions. However, the ratification of C189 has not yet been achieved. In fact, the domestic workers' law promulgated by Zapatero in 2011 did not fulfil the requirements on equality with other sectors, which C189 necessitates. The Rajoy government (Popular Party) further limited migrants' rights and mobility, which predictably had adverse repercussions on domestic workers. In summary, the case of Spain is frustrating, since this vibrant and vocal movement, encompassing heterogeneous and influential actors, was not able to bring about ratification. Some promises were made by the prime minister, Pedro Sanchez (Spanish Socialist Party), in office since 2018, but no actual action has been undertaken.

Thus, the cases of Taiwan, India and Spain reveal a strong level of involvement from civil society, domestic workers' groups and the ILO. However, this cannot compensate for the lack of support from the government. Moreover, in our view, another important element concerns the social perception of domestic workers' issues by society in general, in India, as lower-caste or 'tribal' people, and in Taiwan and Spain, as migrants and undocumented people; domestic workers are perceived in these countries as minority subjects whose interests are not beneficial to society as a whole and may actually conflict with the interests of the majority.

Italy and Germany

Germany and Italy represent very different cases, where we can observe an impasse in the accomplishment of the C189 process and the full promotion of domestic workers' rights. These countries' governments supported the ratification, believing it to be a mere bureaucratic formality, since their national legislation was, in their view, already in line with C189 requirements. However, that impression was not accurate. The ratification of C189 ought to have been followed by corresponding policy measures for a full implementation of C189 principles. Yet, in these countries there is now an impasse, which is at least partly due to a contradiction between the state's formal adherence to C189 and the lack of a real implementation of C189 principles.

Germany and Italy share several key characteristics that help to explain this specific variation of the C189 process. Firstly, they are countries where the population of domestic workers has been largely composed of migrant women, often undocumented. As migrants with precarious status and short-term residency, with a few exceptions, they have tended not to be very active in civil society, especially in the field of labour rights. Live-in caregivers to the elderly in particular have largely been absent from the public scene. In Italy as in Germany, traditional trade unions – which in some cases have a domestic workers' division – tended to prioritize issues concerning other labour sectors. Although they saw the relevance of care, migration and welfare issues, this did not translate to mobilization around these themes. Therefore, the question of domestic workers' rights has tended to be seen as a problem concerning foreign workers as 'others' coming to work from outside. This issue is the object of study of many scholars, especially in Italy, mostly in the field of gender and migration studies. In both countries, the case of domestic workers has been included in policy discussions concerning foreign recruitment channels through migrant quotas. Yet, such interest at the academic and policy levels was apparently insufficient to put the matter on the agenda of political parties and trade unions.

Importantly, in both countries, issues concerning domestic work and home-based care are addressed by associations of employers and care receivers (especially for disabled and long-term care patients), which favour improving the conditions of workers insofar as this can be beneficial to the employment relationship as a whole. Religious organizations protecting working women and migrants can also be found at the forefront of the movement, as in the case of the Italian ACLI-COLF, or Diakonie and Caritas in Germany. They offer information, support and even leadership training to migrant women working in these sectors, but, like activists campaigning for migrants' rights, have little leverage when it comes to labour issues as such. Feminist groups have been noticeably absent from the picture, with a few exceptions guided by abstract ideals of women's solidarity, but with little connection with migrant domestic workers in practice, as we will discuss further in Chapter 5.

In conclusion, the improvement of migrant domestic workers' rights in these countries has not generally been seen as beneficial to society as a whole. Rather, it has been deemed as something beneficial to a specific group of subjects seen as outsiders. Paradoxically, domestic workers have alternatively been perceived as already benefiting from high levels of legal protection. This is partially true, since in both countries there are national laws on domestic work dating back to the 1950s (see Chapter 2) and domestic workers have the right to contracts and other legal entitlements. However, the actual configuration of the care market in both settings has been based on large numbers of undocumented or temporary migrants and irregular workers, as well as mini-jobbers (in Germany) to whom such legal entitlements do not apply.

It is against this backdrop that the decision of the Italian and German governments to ratify C189 so soon after its promulgation was received by stakeholders as a top-down and largely bureaucratic decision. To this end, the close relationship between the two governments and ILO representatives was undoubtedly important. In the case of Italy, the ratification took place via the Italian delegation office in Geneva, thereby bypassing parliamentary discussion in Rome.

However, our activist interviewees in both Italy and Germany stressed the fact that the advancement of domestic workers' rights would, as elsewhere, need a campaign with a legal – but also a political and cultural – dimension. As stressed in Chapter 2, domestic workers are not treated as other workers in either country, albeit for different reasons. Moreover, there are few workers' organizations active in these countries; this is especially true for the migrants among them who experience a high degree of social stigma, compounded by demeaning gendered and racial stereotypes.

4

Domestic Workers
Making Intersectionality

Self-organized groups of domestic workers, that is, trade unions, associations and networks composed and led by women employed in this sector, were key actors in many of the countries included in our study. They have played a critical role in the politicization of domestic work and in the struggle for domestic workers' rights in recent decades, in particular between 2008 and 2018. They work towards enhancing the rights and the social and working conditions in the sector, through everyday actions and political interventions and by interacting with other actors in the field that either support or oppose their cause. In this chapter we focus on the domestic workers' groups that were active during the years of our study, which we encountered during our fieldwork.[1]

Domestic workers' organizing can be seen as an example of a movement putting 'intersectionality into action'. By this we mean, first of all, that this movement addresses and seeks to transform the interlocking systems of inequality that determine domestic workers' subordinated position in society. Second, we mean that in order to bring about such a transformation it deploys a series of strategies that can be defined as intersectional politics. In so doing, this movement exercises its political agency according to a complex understanding of power relations based on the interplay of social categories such as gender, class, race and so on, according to each national context. This results in a new collective identity, which is based on – and highlights – the experience of multiple forms of marginalization experienced by domestic workers. It is on this basis that we present an analysis of domestic workers' organizing through an intersectional lens and explore how different domestic workers' organizations engage with intersectionality to shape their identities and political strategies.

We will demonstrate how the various manifestations of intersectionality that emerge in domestic workers' organizing do so according to the specific characteristics of each national setting, as described in Chapter 2. These factors include the composition and regulation of the sector, and the local socioeconomic, cultural and political context. Through their efforts to politicize domestic work, organize other workers (most of them, women) and force distinct political actors and society at large to acknowledge the demands of domestic workers, the activists in these movements selectively emphasize the determinants of their social condition. That is, they attribute different meaning and political weight to gender, class, race and other factors. Through distinct elements of their activity, these movements address some forms of inequality and some intersections between social categories and social groups, while silencing or failing to address others. As a result, the meaning and political salience given to gender, race, class and other social categories varies not only across national contexts and in different domestic workers' organizations but also within the same organization in relation to various aspects of its activity, and over time. This, in our view, speaks to the situated character of the categories around which social inequalities, as well as social struggles, are articulated in each context and case (Anthias, 2012; Yuval-Davis, 2015).

In order to engage with these issues, we divide the analysis that follows into two parts. In the first, we explore the construction of a collective identity within domestic workers' organizations. We look at the discourse produced by these groups and the way their members present themselves and their organizations, drawing primarily on a narrative analysis of interviews conducted with domestic worker activists. Where relevant, this analysis is complemented by ethnographic observations collected during local workshops and other events, and by documentary analysis (see Chapter 1). For the sake of space, in the first part of the chapter we provide examples from just three of the nine countries involved in our project: Brazil, Colombia and Ecuador. A comparison of narratives from each of these countries will demonstrate how diversity in each setting has had an impact on domestic workers' processes of identity construction. While these three countries were similar in regard to the composition of and political tendencies within this sector (see Chapter 2), they nevertheless reveal important differences when it comes to distinct power relations rooted in colonial legacies, migratory phenomena, rural–urban relations, racism and other processes of social stratification that affect discrimination against domestic workers. In the second part of the chapter we explore the activities and demands elaborated by different groups, drawing primarily on a thematic analysis of interviews with every key category of interviewee, including but not limited to domestic workers' rights activists. In this section we also extend the analysis to include examples from other countries.

A new collective identity

When domestic workers organize themselves and create associations and trade unions on their own, they do so in response to the lack of rights and social recognition they experience in the labour market and in society at large. They thereby oppose the political marginalization they experience in institutional politics, civil society and single-axis social movements, which prioritize a single form of inequality (such as gender, class or racial inequality) as the primary focus of political action. This means that, at the point of reacting to this marginalization, domestic workers activate processes of political subjectification that generate a multiple-axis collective identity, being a form of political identity that integrates more than one category of difference.

In analysing these processes, we see domestic workers' organizations as examples of self-organization by social groups located at the 'neglected points of intersection between multiple structures of oppression' (McCall, 2005: 1774). It is necessary for these groups to create a new collective identity in order to find their own voice, pursue their own interests and escape social and political invisibility. In doing so, domestic workers seem to be pursuing what Éléonore Lépinard (2014: 10) calls 'intersectional recognition', which is often sought by multiply marginalized subjects who start to organize around identities that they otherwise perceive as unrepresented in mainstream organizations. In other terms, to describe the process of identity formation that Black and Chicana feminist collectives underwent during the 1960s and 1970s in the US, Benita Roth (2004) speaks of an 'organizing on one's own' ethos. According to Roth, this ethos is crucial to the founding of new organizations by subjects who identify with more than one social group, and for that reason cannot be included in a vast single-axis movement.

In a similar vein, the need for organizing on one's own was a recurrent topic in our interviews with domestic worker organizers. Speaking of their relationships with feminist, workers' or other organized groups, they pointed to a 'secondary marginalisation' (Cole, 2008: 446) in their experience in the political arena. This means they often denounce the invisibility of domestic workers' needs in political projects that promise to support them as the target group of feminist initiatives, as discriminated workers and generally as vulnerable subjects in need of others' help. Their situation resembles the case of women of colour in feminist and anti-racist movements in the US in the early 1990s, as examined by Kimberlee Crenshaw (1991). She showed the ways in which women of colour were caught between two separate movements that purported to support them either as women or as people of colour, but which in fact obscured the specific forms of violence and intersectional oppression which they experienced as a result of belonging to both groups simultaneously. The result was a gap in representation in the political sphere that reflected and reinforced the marginalization they lived in the social sphere (Crenshaw, 1991: 1245).

Returning to our study, in Chapter 5 we will see that domestic worker activists often speak of their discomfort with feminist and women's rights groups that advocate for supposedly universal principles of women's emancipation, but which in practice are biased towards the interests of economically and racially privileged women. In fact, in the eyes of domestic workers, feminist recipes for women's liberation often rest on the availability of cheap and exploited labour provided by female workers with a lower social status. A similar argument can be made to explain the scepticism of domestic workers vis-à-vis workers' movements or anti-racist movements that concentrate solely on class or race issues, leaving domestic workers' intersectional identities inadequately accounted for. In the view of many domestic workers, their struggles for equal labour rights cannot be subsumed under the 'universal' interests of the working class or migrants and racialized people. Likewise, they perceive that the interplay between gender and class works differently for them than for other workers (and women more generally), which often leads to diverging interests.

For all these reasons, we can see that in many cases these activists have set up autonomous organizations with their own identity – distinct from those of trade unions, anti-racist or feminist and women's rights groups – with the specific purpose of addressing their own problems. Such an affirmation of autonomous political agency reminds us of analogous processes undergone by other multiply marginalized subjects who were behind a new wave of activism in the early days of intersectional analysis (Anzaldúa and Moraga, 1981; Combahee River Collective, 1982; Hancock, 2016; Collins and Bilge, 2020).

The process of self-organizing around new intersectional identities that has been described so far seems to be a common element across the domestic workers' groups that we met in each of the nine countries in our study. However, our comparative analysis also reveals important differences between countries, especially in relation to the kinds of inequalities that become emphasized in the building of new collective identities as 'organized domestic workers'. Different organizations may attribute distinct political salience to the social categories shaping domestic workers' subordinated positions (such as race, gender, class or nationality). Importantly, they may also understand the relations between these categories either as separate elements that impact on domestic workers or as mutually constructed forms of discrimination that intersect and reciprocally modify one another. In other words, when comparing domestic workers' organizations, we may find distinct examples of the difference between what Ange-Marie Hancock (2007) calls 'multiple' and 'intersectional' approaches being illustrated 'in action'. In the multiple view, the effects of social categories are cumulative but remain separate from one another, while from an intersectional perspective they merge with and modify each other. This distinction guides our understanding of the way in which social movements conceive the relationship between the categories which are most relevant in shaping their own political identity. With this perspective in mind, in the following pages we explore what happened in the context of our three Latin American cases.

The legacy of slavery

In Brazil we find an outstanding example of the construction of collective identity based on the intersectional articulation of gender, race and class. As mentioned in Chapter 2, Brazil has a strong and well-structured trade union movement of paid domestic workers which is highly articulated at both the local and the national levels. All the accounts collected in our fieldwork coincide in pointing out that the struggle for rights and a better livelihood, developed by domestic workers since the 1930s, has created a new political actor that has been described in previous research as a 'black working-class women's movement' (Bernardino-Costa, 2014: 79). In fact, most of the leaders of this movement that we met during our fieldwork identified as Black women and they maintained relationships with Black feminism, as well as with the Black liberation and labour movements.

Over the decades, this movement has promoted more widespread awareness of the intersectional discrimination affecting paid domestic workers and, in particular, Black domestic workers. Unionized domestic workers have drawn attention to the interplay between racism, classism and sexism and highlighted the specific forms of oppression experienced by Black domestic workers. They point out not only that these women constitute a great proportion of employees in the sector (see Chapter 2), but that they are also subject to specific forms of exploitation, violence and misrepresentation. For instance, Creuza Maria de Oliveira, a prominent figure of the movement and secretary general of FENATRAD, describes domestic workers as follows:

> We domestic workers, we are a category made up of women, black women. [We are] women who support society and contribute to the economy although our work is not recognized – neither

as paid activity nor as unpaid domestic work at home ... Even today we suffer from domestic violence, being assaulted by the employers. In this power relationship, it is the worker who follows orders, who is under the domain of the housekeeper. She still suffers sexual violence, moral harassment, the violence of not having her rights respected. (De Oliveira, 2017a)

In this interview, De Oliveira points out the hierarchical relationship with the (male and female) employers and the widespread experience of violence lived by domestic workers. She implicitly emphasizes the importance of distinguishing between domestic workers and women in general, as the lack of recognition given to both paid and unpaid domestic work is a particular burden for racialized and low-class women. As a seasoned activist, she explains in the same interview the difficult process of unionizing people in this labour category, a task made harder by the stratified composition of the sector in terms of gender, race and education level. Moreover, this process requires undertaking the difficult task of overcoming internalized prejudices against women's participation in politics. She goes on to say:

Organising domestic workers is very difficult because we are mostly black women with low education ... We [organisers] have been struggling to get close to these workers, who were taught that women do not do politics. That unionism is something for men, not for women. (De Oliveira, 2017b)

In the case of Brazil, it is worth mentioning that domestic worker activists often elaborated on the legacy of colonial slavery to define the specific forms of intersectional discrimination and racism experienced by Black domestic workers. In doing so, they provide us with a deeper understanding of the meaning of 'race' in the construction of their identity.

Lúcia Maria Xavier, president of the Black feminist non-profit organization Criola, an ally of domestic workers' unions, explains:

'Women employed in domestic service, Black domestic workers, are the counterpoint to everything that exists in society. When you look at these women, you have a clear sense of what racial inequality means. So when someone says that there is no racism [in Brazil], it is because they are not looking at domestic workers ... Above all, this kind of work is done as it was done at the time of slavery: they look after the families, they take care of the families ... That's why it's weird to me when someone says "I didn't see racism there".' (Lúcia Xavier, Criola, Brazil)

The continuity between the figures of the Afro-descendant slave and the contemporary domestic worker is a recurrent topic in Brazilian public discourse on domestic work (Kofes, 2001; Ribeiro Corossacz, 2015: 117). The same parallels recur in the narratives we collected from domestic worker activists in their discourses around identity formation. Indeed, building on Xavier's quote, the Brazilian activists can be said to have employed two kinds of rhetorical device. Firstly, they made an analogy between the exploitative working conditions and racism endemic to contemporary domestic service and those that existed under slavery (the idea that the work is carried out "as it was done at the time of slavery") to emphasize the challenge involved in campaigning for labour rights. Secondly, they established a connection between their activity and the history of the anti-racist movement in their country. By inheriting this legacy, domestic workers' organizations achieved a unique political role insofar as they were defending the rights of those who were "the counterpoint to everything that exists in society". In other words, they successfully managed the thorny enterprise of inaugurating an original identity as an organization, while simultaneously invoking the historical genealogy of movements struggling against the oppression of women and Black people in Brazil.

Afro-descendant women in post-war society

In Colombia we found a distinctive intersectional articulation of race, gender and class in the ad hoc identity being built by UTRASD, the most visible domestic workers' organization in the country at the time of our fieldwork, with around 200 members. The Colombian domestic workers' movement is racially mixed, with organizations led and composed by both Black and mestiza workers. In this context, UTRASD represents an interesting case of an intersectional identity, which should not, however, be taken as representative of a broader national tendency. The organization was founded in Medellín in 2013 by a group of Afro-Colombian domestic workers, mainly internally displaced people who had been involved in an activist-research project on Afro-Colombian women's conditions.[2] The project gradually made them aware of their specific experiences of violence and discrimination inside and outside the workplace. This gave rise to a collective process of politicization, seeking a form of representation tailored to their specific experience as 'black Colombian domestic workers'. These events are described by María Roa Borja, UTRASD president at the time of our fieldwork, in an interview held at the organization's office:

'This process brought positive results for us as domestic workers and, in particular, for Black women: women victims of armed conflict, displaced women, female heads of households, abused women, raped women, women discriminated against. [All] women who, as domestic workers, have gone through all kind of things that this country cannot even imagine. And why are we in domestic work? We were not asked "what do you know? What is your [work] experience?" But colour, race, this marks me in a way that I have to be a domestic worker.' (María Roa Borja, UTRASD, Colombia)

In María Roa Borja's words, we hear how the identity of organized Colombian domestic workers stems from the acknowledgement of the fact that domestic workers live at the intersection of several social categories, simultaneously marked by gender, race, class, family status and regional origin. They are also especially vulnerable to violence, which was exercised against Black and rural women in particular in the context of the armed conflict that has torn the country apart since 1964. Indeed, the civil war has most negatively affected women from regions with predominantly Afro-Colombian populations. They form a large proportion of those who have been internally displaced and who have thus entered domestic work in order to make a living in cities such as Bogotá and Medellín (see Chapter 2). At the same time, her words relate to the criticism made by UTRASD of pervasive racist and sexist representations of Black women. She elaborates on how stereotypes of Black women determine their limited job opportunities and segregate Afro-Colombian women within the domestic work sector, limiting their possibility of social and labour mobility and overlooking individual characteristics and experiences.

Moreover, based on our reading of the grey literature on the union's activity and in-depth interviews with its members, we believe that UTRASD promoted an intersectional discursive repertoire in which domestic work was addressed as a simultaneously gendered, class-based and racialized activity. The specific experiences of gendered racism and racialized economic exploitation among Afro-Colombian women employed as domestic workers is at the centre of UTRASD's identity – a fact which explains the recurrent description of UTRASD as 'the first ethnically based domestic workers' union in the country'.[3]

A particular role was assigned to Afro-Colombian women internally displaced by the conflict, while indigenous, mestiza, or migrant women domestic workers seemed to be left out of UTRASD's main identity discourse. Yet UTRASD presented itself as being open to all domestic workers, walking a tightrope between a concern on the one hand with Afro-Colombian identity, and on the other with the general interests of domestic workers:

'UTRASD is an inclusive, not exclusionary, union. Even if its name says "Afro women", there are also mestizo and indigenous women in the union. We defined ourselves as Black women and so we began. When this union started, we were 28 Black women. That's the reason for its name … [But] the advocacy is not only for Afro women, women from Antioquia or Chocó[4] … We do this for the benefit of all women nationwide.' (María Boa Roja, UTRASD, Colombia)

The UTRASD leaders' discourse is based on inclusivity and the aspiration to be able to advocate for domestic workers' plurality of interests. Their capacity to fight for the advancement of this entire social category because of racial differences, rather than in spite of them, is based on the assumption that Afro-Colombians' perspectives can embrace those of all other vulnerable groups, since they are 'the ones who suffer the most'. This is how one of the activists of UTRASD explains the idea, drawing on her direct experience:

'Since I was a minor, I started to do domestic work. My first experience was before the age of 15 and I was subjected to abuse. This experience marked me … It gave me the strength to defend domestic work, because I have suffered so much … It doesn't mean that in every job I was mistreated or exploited … but I had very tough experiences which marked me as a woman and as a domestic worker.' (Anonymous interviewee, UTRASD, Colombia)

The identity formation promoted by UTRASD and primarily centred on Afro-descendant women needs to be understood within a wider political context in which the social integration of historically marginalized communities (especially Afro-Colombians) is supported on the basis of the 1991 Constitution. This includes advancing compensation policies for displaced people, mostly from Black minority communities, which have been implemented by the state since 2012 within the framework of the peace process. This process of identity formation thus pays special attention to the gendered impact of the war, both in terms of its negative effects on women as victims of violence and in terms of their potential role as peace builders in a post-conflict society.

Putting race aside

A comparative look at Ecuador reveals yet another configuration of the collective identity being elaborated by organized domestic workers. Here we see that the intersectional dimension involves only the categories of gender and class, race entering the picture as a secondary issue, which corresponds to the multiple approach described by Hancock (2007). This means that race-based discrimination is recognized as an additional burden on domestic workers (especially for indigenous and Afro-descendant communities), but not as an intrinsic feature of the social organization of domestic work or of the collective identity being promoted by the movement. This interpretation applies in particular to ATRH, the most visible and longest-running domestic workers' organization in the country, founded in 1998 in Guayaquil (Moya, 2015; Masi de Casanova, 2019) and counting around 250 members at the time of our fieldwork.

In the interviews and at the events we attended during our fieldwork, we noticed that ATRH leaders did not define themselves in racial terms. In their view, the category of the 'Ecuadorian organized domestic worker' is shaped by the interplay between two main axes of inequality: gender and class. Neither race nor other categories of difference, such as age or migration status, despite occasional inclusion in some statements, were consistently referred to as factors in their subjugation or made into central features of group identity. For instance, Lourdes Albán, an active participant of ATRH, describes the composition of the association and, more broadly, the condition of domestic workers as follows:

> 'We are from low social classes, whether Black, White, indigenous, mestiza or whatever ... We are people who decided to work in a household out of different circumstances, some of us did not have any other opportunity ... It is a hard job, it is not recognized, rights are always violated. Here we can see the patriarchal system ... just because you are a woman, you must be related to reproduction ... I would say that it is largely a job performed by low-class women.' (Lourdes Albán, ATRH, Ecuador)

For Lourdes Albán, as for other ATRH leaders, domestic workers experience a specific form of oppression rooted in the gendered construction of both paid and unpaid domestic work, as well as in the gendered and classist construction of paid domestic work as a job for women from lower social classes. A racialized component ("whether Black, White, indigenous, mestiza or whatever") is present, but underplayed. Later on in the same interview, Albán is asked to elaborate on how racist discrimination intersects with other forms of oppression in the lives of domestic workers. She says:

> 'For example, mestiza women are less mistreated, it has been seen, they have fewer problems than Black and indigenous women – far fewer ... Our comrades told us of their experiences, from which we know ... that "for being indigenous, we are called dirty

longas"[5] and that Blacks are called "dirty Blacks, thieving Blacks".[6]
I do not mean that mestiza women aren't discriminated against,
but discrimination is stronger against these other comrades.'
(Lourdes Albán, ATRH, Ecuador)

On the same topic, the president of ATRH, Maximina Salazar Peñafiel, says:

'On the issue of racism, those who suffer most from discrimination
in paid domestic work are the comrades of Esmeralda,[7] the Afros
... And the comrades who are indigenous, too ... Somehow it
affects us, because you should put yourself in the other's shoes.'
(Maximina Salazar Peñafiel, ATRH, Ecuador)

In these excerpts, both Salazar Peñafiel and Albán recognize the relative
privilege they enjoy as mestizas, in comparison to domestic workers from
Black and indigenous groups. They also acknowledge the higher risk of
exploitation and abusive behaviour to which racialized workers are exposed.
However, they seem to think that the interests and needs of these specific
groups of domestic workers can be incorporated into the general struggle
for the advancement of domestic workers' rights. In fact, ATRH claims to
represent the interests of all organized domestic workers, no matter which
sector of society they belong to. Thus, in comparison to the Colombian
and Brazilian organizations analysed here, ATRH arguably promotes a new,
inclusive collective identity by not emphasizing historical legacies (as in
Brazil), or the epistemic privilege of Black perspectives (as in Colombia).
Instead, they promote the intertwining of class and gender over and above
other social differences, to address and mobilize all domestic workers.

Overall, the analysis presented so far demonstrates the fact that, rather
than being a well-defined social identity that exists prior to mobilization,
the category of domestic worker emerges as an outcome of the organizing
processes under consideration in these pages. Indeed, although to some extent
related to the demographic composition of the sector according to each local
and national context, the collective identity being promoted by domestic
workers' groups does not automatically reflect this. Rather, it takes shape
through a creative process of politicization, in which the intersecting systems
of oppression affecting domestic workers in each local context are identified
and named in distinctive ways by activists implicated in these struggles.

Activities and political demands

In this section we explore some of the activities and political demands
put forward by the domestic workers' groups that we encountered in our

fieldwork. We show how these groups formulate demands and propose actions that simultaneously address distinct systems of power relations, thus reflecting their intersectional approach to collective identity, as explained in the previous section. Their activities and demands involve multiple domains of intervention (legal, cultural, social and political) and engage domestic workers from different backgrounds. This is accomplished not by flattening differences among them but, rather, by emphasizing wider and more inclusive claims or actions that can easily be embedded into each particular reality.

In order to show how this takes place, we focus on three types of activity: (1) sensitization or awareness raising in society in general; (2) interventions at the level of language and the cultural representation of domestic work; and (3) empowerment and training among members. As we will illustrate, such activities are based on the concept of 'domestic work as work' and range from the fields of labour law and institutional politics to the media, public discourse and the spheres of everyday life. In fact, domestic workers' groups have taken steps beyond the struggles for labour, economic and social rights and good working conditions normally promoted by organized workers and trade unions, and have tried to get to the root of their situation by pursuing equality, empowerment and recognition beyond rights.

Domestic workers' struggles draw together what Nancy Fraser (2005) calls demands for 'recognition', 'redistribution' and 'participation'. By a 'politics of recognition', Fraser means demands for acknowledgement as equal, legitimate and valued members of society. By a 'politics of redistribution', she means demands for equal access to economic and material resources allocated to different members of society. Finally, by demands for 'participation', she refers to the vindication of equal access to a political voice and the capacity to influence public decisions that affect people's lives. As Patricia Hill Collins and Sirma Bilge (2020) point out, it is difficult to separate these different aspects of struggles for social justice in political projects led by multiply marginalized groups:

> There is a vast literature documenting how disenfranchised groups tackle the issue of social justice on both fronts and view cultural empowerment (race, gender, sexuality) and economic redistribution (class) as inseparable. Out of necessity, women of colour integrated their claims for equality, recognition, and redistribution. Separating them was practically or analytically impossible when racism and sexism always structured the specific form of class exploitation that they face. (Collins and Bilge, 2020: 128)

Nira Yuval-Davis further emphasizes the specificity of demands made by multiply marginalized groups when arguing that 'the politics of intersectionality can encompass and transcend' both the 'politics of recognition' and the 'politics of redistribution' (Yuval-Davis, 2011: 155–6). Along the same lines, in this section we suggest that domestic workers' groups are able to pursue a specific kind of intersectional politics capable of transcending the dichotomy between recognition and redistribution. This may be done by addressing the combination of legal and institutional, as well as socioeconomic and cultural, fields simultaneously.

Equality beyond rights

The demand that domestic labour be recognized as a decent form of work, deserving equal labour rights, was central to all the domestic workers' movements that we met during our fieldwork. It has also been extensively described in the literature, in relation to several movements active within their countries and at the international level. For instance, Bridget Anderson (2010) describes the importance of this demand in relation to the migrant domestic workers' organization Waling Waling in the UK:

> A key feature of organizing and campaigning was Waling Waling's demand to be recognized as workers. This assertion, that they were workers, worked on several levels. First, it asserted the dignity and value of their work, for themselves, employers and the wider public. They were not 'helping' but contributing socially and economically to households and wider society; they were not 'girls' but women (and men) who were often sustaining extended families back home. It also asserted their legitimacy as public actors, their right to be heard and to be treated with respect, and it was accompanied by the demand that this labour be recognized as a route to formalized citizenship. (Anderson, 2010: 64–5)

As we saw in Chapter 3, such a demand is also central to the kind of activity and language developed by international organizations involved in the global governance of domestic work, above all the ILO. As such, it lies at the core of C189 as well as of mobilizations that took place in each of these nine countries in relation to C189's ratification, and to other legal reforms over the last decade.

Nevertheless, the focus on campaigning for legal reforms should not obscure other forms of action, in particular the concurrent engagement in cultural battles to improve the social status of domestic workers in society. Indeed, while organized domestic workers were fighting their battles in the legal field, they were also putting forward awareness-raising campaigns and engaging in outreach work.

For example, ATRH representatives in Ecuador designed an awareness-raising campaign related to domestic work in collaboration with the Ministry of Labour. They also gained public visibility following meetings with Rafael Correa in the presidential palace in 2015[8] and they were able to take advantage of such visibility to spread their message.

In Taiwan, one of the first initiatives in which the National Home-Based Workers' Union was involved was a mock 'migrants' referendum' launched in 15 locations across the country during the last two months of 2017. This was the first organization of migrant caregivers in the country, founded in 2016–17. The migrants' referendum initiative was organized by TIWA, an organization promoting the rights of all migrants in the country and which had been increasingly vocal on issues of care. The 'referendum' included three questions: whether migrant caregivers should be protected under the Labor Standards Act, whether foreign workers should be able to freely change employers and whether the government should abolish the private employment brokerage system and replace it with a nation-to-nation mechanism. This initiative enjoyed wide resonance and attracted a lot of media attention by using an alternative, tongue-in-cheek method to open space in the public debate for the serious issue of the denial of labour and political rights for migrants.

Another example comes from Spain, where the topic of domestic workers' rights was brought to wider public attention in a 2016 speech given at a TEDx event by Rafaela Pimentel Lara, of the domestic workers' grassroots collective Territorio Doméstico.[9] This group was created in 2006 and is composed of around 30 to 50 domestic workers, most of them of Latin American origin, whose repertoire of action includes public performances and the use of irony, art and theatre. In her interview, Rafaela Pimentel Lara elaborated on how forms of communication like this may help to reach people and sensitize public opinion on a 'tough' topic:

> 'So we said, this must be made visible, turning it around, making it entertaining, and that we also may have fun, since it is already tough enough. Thus in Territorio Doméstico we started to bring it up, with theatre sketches, with our "catwalks" [*pasarelas*], our radio programmes ... and the songs,[10] to change the lyrics of traditional songs and say what we were living, not having papers, the domestic work, the care work, all that was happening to us as women, for being Black, migrant women, poor women ... This was around 2008, 2010, our first public performance. We always opted for performances because everyone takes part and is visible, it makes things lighter, and we do it in a very powerful way, people are impressed ... We did cabarets, world dances,

performance, songs, reggaeton ... using the arts is powerful.'
(Rafaela Pimentel Lara, Territorio Doméstico, Spain)

Lastly, in Colombia, UTRASD was involved in the social communication activities promoted by Andrea Londoño, from the non-profit organization Bien Humano Foundation (one of the union's main allies), within the framework of an awareness-raising campaign related to domestic workers' labour and broader human rights.[11] Activists from UTRASD took part in short videos posted on their specially dedicated websites and social media platforms, illustrating domestic workers' daily lives and working conditions.[12] The core message behind these interventions, aimed at improving domestic workers' representation, is described here by Claribed Palacios García, one of the leaders of the group:

> 'God, we have to raise the alarm to the government, to the state! [We have to say] that we are here − domestic workers! − that we also exist and that we are also Colombians ... Our message? [Domestic] workers, give value to your work and do not wait for others to do so. We do it right, but we do it at the right price too. The point is: I do my job well and I demand decent treatment. Because domestic work is not a favour: domestic work − as Convention 189 states − is work.' (Claribed Palacios García, UTRASD, Colombia)

Palacio García's words evidence the way in which demands for social inclusion are being conveyed through the imperative to recognize 'domestic work as work', having the same value as any other job and, therefore, deserving of the same rights. Such a quest for equality is thus to be understood here not only in legal terms, but also at the level of social, economic and cultural life.

From the point of view of organized domestic workers, the idea that 'domestic work is work' guides their desired social transformation, casting off a rhetoric of obedience and dependency in which the best that workers can hope for is to receive favours as a reward for being at the service of a benevolent wealthy household (Marchetti, 2016a). This resonates with the spirit of C189, which Palacios García invokes to reinforce her views. From the point of view of organized domestic workers, the ideal of 'decent work' promoted by the ILO naturally means labour rights, but also human dignity, social recognition and the possibility of enjoying fair living conditions. For this reason, while the focus on labour rights may rightly be seen as a cornerstone of domestic workers' movements, it does not fully represent their struggle. Rather, domestic workers seem to define their struggle as something that goes beyond legal rights, as Rafaela Pimentel Lara explained in her interview:

> 'We make claims in which we also connect migrations, feminism, not just domestic work. On the issue of rights, we demand them, but we are not focusing just on the issue of rights, otherwise we do not dig into the history of the problem. We believe that this is not just a matter of rights; here you have to dismantle a lot of stories, a lot of stuff, you have to go in depth into the matter and this cannot be achieved with rights only ... So my struggle is not just about rights, I go beyond the right of the domestic worker because I want to go to the root of this situation.' (Rafaela Pimentel Lara, Territorio Doméstico, Spain)

In conclusion, domestic workers' organizations that promote the motto 'domestic work is work' are demanding significant transformations to the national legal framework, changes to labour laws in particular, but also radical socioeconomic changes capable of improving the conditions of domestic workers more generally. This would mean breaking away from the tendency to think of domestic work as an activity to be undertaken by people at the lowest strata of society, that is, those deemed inferior due to their intersecting gender, race and class positions and who lack access to material resources and social respectability. Finally, the demand for domestic work as decent work also singles out the reassessment of domestic work as a legitimate object of public intervention, thus pushing for its increased visibility in public policy and within the political agenda.

Naming domestic work

The cultural politics carried out by these groups also takes shape through interventions in public discourse at the level of language use. Indeed, most activists and organizations engage in debates over the choice of name when addressing domestic workers (and their employers). The leaders of ATRH in Ecuador, for instance, seem to be particularly keen on language issues. They often express their preference for the term *trabajadora remunerada del hogar* (paid household worker), instead of other common local expressions such as *doméstica* or *empleada doméstica* (literally, 'female domestic' or domestic employee) that they perceive as derogatory. This preference guided the organization's choice of its own name, as well as specific proposals made during the discussion on the reform of the labour code in 2015–16. As their president explains:

'The idea to build the Asociación de Trabajadoras Remuneradas del Hogar was with the aim of defending the labour rights of the so-called *empleadas domésticas*. I mean, this term is quite discriminatory: since then, we demand that the rights of the *trabajadoras del hogar* be respected ... For instance, in the creation of the new Labour Code, we already have a proposal ... The current code speaks of "domestic service" ... We believe that if the term is written like that, "domestic service", we are the object of discrimination, like servants, like servitude ... And all these kinds of names or nicknames that we were given at some point ... Well, thinking back a little, we do not feel at ease with this term, *empleadas domésticas* ... For this reason, we are *trabajadoras remuneradas del hogar*.' (Maximina Salazar Peñafiel, ATRH and SINUTRHE, Ecuador)

Such a militant, critical process of choosing the right name for this new identity reflects a collective effort to resignify domestic work. As such, the name has broad cultural implications, related to the reframing of domestic work as work, and far-reaching consequences for the relationships between employers and workers, as well as for the latter's sense of self.

Language disputes are important in Brazil and Colombia, too, where we often observed a critical rejection of the terms *patrão/patroa* and *patrón/patrona*, respectively, to identify employers, due to the sense of authority and consequent subordination they convey. At the same time, the activists in these contexts mostly made use of the terms *trabalhadoras domésticas* and *trabajadoras domésticas* in their accounts. These are preferred to other common terms such as *empregada doméstica* (domestic employee) in Brazil, and *muchacha* (girl), *empleada de servicio* (servant employee) or even *mi empleada* (literally, 'my employee') in Colombia.

In Spain, organized domestic workers agree on refusing colloquial phrases referring to helpers, such as *la chica que me ayuda en casa* (meaning 'the girl who helps at home'), and terms perceived as derogatory such as *chacha* (an abbreviation of *muchacha*, 'girl'). Moreover, most organizations prefer the terms *trabajadoras de hogar* or *empleadas de hogar* and reject the adjective *doméstico/a*, as in terms such as *empleada doméstica*, *servicio doméstico* and the like. The aforementioned group Territorio Doméstico is a partial exception, since it chose to use the term 'domestic' in order to invert its meaning and turn it into a source of pride and terrain of resistance.

In the Philippines, the question of language has also been of central importance for domestic workers' organizations, but dealing with this issue has led to different results. Organized domestic workers oppose the many traditional terms used there to describe this social category, loaded as they are with derogatory, infantilizing, colonial and essentializing ethnic stereotypes. In fact, some of these terms refer to women from the Visayan region, such as *Inday* ('woman' in Visayan dialect) and *Bisaya* (woman from the Visayan region). Others use the language of former colonizers, such as *muchacha*, while others refer to somebody who helps out, such as *katulong* (helper). To emphasize their distance from these terms, organized domestic workers coined the word *kasambahay*, meaning 'companion of the house' in English. Interestingly, the term was introduced in the early 2000s by the domestic workers' organization most active at that time, SUMAPI, supported by the anti-trafficking NGO Visayan Forum. They preferred to introduce a new word rather than adopt the English phrase 'domestic worker' or similar terms. The idea was to avoid emphasizing the conflict with employers, while nevertheless insisting on employers' responsibility and a sense that change can be achieved only with their cooperation. Notably, *kasambahay* indicates a close relationship to the family, while implicitly clarifying that it signifies something other than being part of a family. The choice of this word has been debated and has been a cause of contention among domestic workers' organizations and their allies. Indeed, some of our participants were ambivalent about this choice, because while most people do not mind the fact that it implies the idea that the domestic worker is considered close to the family – this is seen as a good thing – they regret that it does not connote a relationship of employment. For instance, Ellene Sana, from the Center for Migrant Advocacy, reflects on this in the following extract:

> 'In fact, in the Philippine context ... most of the domestic workers, particularly those under the age of 15 to 17, are usually the relatives of their employers. So sometimes the employers would think that they are actually doing these people a favour. "I allow them to work or help out with house chores but in return I send them to school, etc." This has become the culture here, for example the word coined for domestic workers is "kasambahay", meaning you are somebody who is a *kasama* (somebody who is considered part of the family) in the house; *kasama* doesn't connote work and it doesn't connote a relationship, like the employee–employer relationship. Maybe some would assert that in Filipino culture, that's the way we treat them – they are not others, we treated them like relatives. So during mealtimes everybody expects to sit around the table. But this is not the case. We expect them, the domestic worker, to do the housework first, then later on to find time to have their meals. Or like

when the family is going on vacation, they [the workers] are
not automatically included. This is where the risk is – when you
treat somebody working for you as a non-worker.' (Ellene Sana,
Center for Migrant Advocacy, Philippines)

The linguistic innovation promoted by the Filipino activists is reminiscent
of a similar process that took place in Italy in the 1960s, with the invention
of the term *collaboratrice familiare*, abbreviated *colf*, which translates as 'family
collaborator' (originally only in the feminine), or else 'woman (or man) who
collaborates with the family'. The term was introduced in 1961 by domestic
worker activists coming from a Catholic tradition of organizing (ACLI), who
needed a new term to substitute the words most clearly linked to a tradition
of servile relationships, such as *la donna* (the woman), *la domestica* (literally,
'female domestic') or *la serva* (the female servant), then in common use. To
do so they did not draw on the concept of employment or the identity of
the worker, but instead chose a term that puts the family at the centre. At
the same time, the term also describes a specific role vis-à-vis the family and
marks a distance from it. As someone who works together with the family,
the *colf* is not exactly part of the family. In this form, the term entered into
daily and institutional language.

We argue that what is at stake in these language disputes is something
more than the visibility and recognition of a new category of workers.
Although this is a first and very important step, the work around the issue of
language entails a radical challenge to the entire socio-cultural construction of
domestic work. It also confronts the system of intersecting power relations in
which it is immersed, and which it contributes to reproducing. Vindicating
the use of dignified language while refusing the demeaning vernacular terms
used to name domestic workers is a way of seeking legitimacy for the new
identity being created by the movement both within society at large and
in the eyes of domestic workers themselves. Through the use of innovative
words, these movements question the internalized representations of domestic
workers as performing 'dirty' work, often associated with social stigma and
shame. These internalized ideas tends to constitute an additional barrier to
domestic workers' organizing, as Geeta Menon from the Domestic Workers
Rights Union observed in the case of India:

One of the major hindrances to organising was that many women
had not told their families that they were working as domestic
workers. There is a shame, a stigma in working as domestic
workers. This stigma comes from their caste locations as well as
the notion that they go to houses where there are 'other' men. It
also comes from a societal notion of housework, which is largely

devalued, gendered, and called women's work. This further affects
perceptions of domestic workers. (Menon, 2017: 115)

From this viewpoint, the affirmations that 'we are domestic workers' and
'I am a domestic worker' advocated by these activists (under different
guises in local languages) appear in a new light. Firstly, by embracing these
statements, participants in domestic workers' groups reject the subordinate
social position they hold in societies in which home-based care and domestic
work is considered a demeaning activity, performed by low-status people.
Secondly, by affirming these statements they may also be seen to be opting
out of the ambivalent positions of identity that they occupy within their
employer families, that is, those of intimate, yet subordinate, subjects. As has
been extensively described in the literature, domestic workers usually hold
this ambivalent position in the relational and physical space of employers'
households. This is not only because they are expected to serve the family's
needs (like other members of the family, due to their gender and age) but
also due to class and racial hierarchies, and the differential immigration
status that often defines their relationship with their employers (Parreñas,
2001; Gutiérrez-Rodríguez, 2010; Brites, 2014; Marchetti, 2014). Their
work and their relationships within these households are portrayed as a sort
of extension of ascribed roles and obligations related to social reproduction
(caring, cooking, feeding, cleaning, serving and so on) that are especially
attributed to gendered, minoritized, racialized subjects. At the same time,
the deployment of what is perceived (often on both sides) as care and love
may foster the creation of intimacy with employers and care receivers.
Nevertheless, such intimate bonds often do not erase but, rather, reaffirm
the hierarchies between employers and employees, leading to what Valeria
Ribeiro Corossazc (2015: 107, 119) has called 'inequality within intimacy'.
Through their collective claims over language, organized domestic workers
refuse these ascribed attributions of social roles and to some extent dissociate
themselves from the idea that they are part of their employers' families,
something they often formerly identified with prior to the process of
subjectification we have described. On these novel grounds, they seek more
egalitarian relationships with their employers.

As we have seen in the examples in this section, this may be done in
different ways. In some of the countries in our study the focus was on
women's identity as workers: not simply helpers, nor part of the employers'
family. By claiming to be 'domestic workers', local activists wanted to
replace these representations with a new image, one of workers performing a
valuable job and, therefore, as bearers of rights. In other contexts, the idea of
being 'part of the family' was not entirely discarded, while other traditional
representations, such as that of a 'helper' deserving some 'favours' in return

for their efforts, were refused. Indeed, in the cases of the Philippines and Italy, through the terms *kasambahay* and *colf*, domestic workers' groups have tried to renegotiate their relationships with the families who employ them under new terms, implicitly recognizing the special character of such an employment relationship (that is, based on care, mutual trust and so on). While they refuse to be seen as inferior members of society and ask to be respected, they nevertheless focus on the ties that bind employers and *kasambahays* or *colf*, viewing them as a potentially convenient framework. This approach permits both individual and collective bargaining and the shared assumption of responsibility on the part of employers in what is thereby reframed as a collective struggle for the improvement of the domestic sector.

Empowering domestic workers

Finally, domestic workers' organizations conduct a number of activities aimed at supporting their members – and other domestic workers – in managing their labour relations as well as their daily lives more broadly. While limited by the financial and material resources they are able to draw upon at different times, to some extent all of these organizations provide legal support and advice for contracts, wages, contributions and access to the social security system, and other related paperwork. These groups often also function as help centres, promoting the establishment of solidarity, friendship and relations of mutual support among their members and their social networks.

Examples from our fieldwork demonstrate the resourcefulness of domestic workers' groups in carrying out these activities. Of interest in this regard was the launch of the mobile application Laudelina by the Brazilian feminist organization Themis, in collaboration with the domestic workers' national federation in 2018.[13] This app helps domestic workers to calculate salaries and severance pay, to get in contact with other workers, unions and agencies and to become more informed about their labour rights. Significantly, it takes its name from Laudelina de Campos Melo (1904–91), the Afro-Brazilian activist widely considered the first domestic worker unionist in the country (Pinto, 2015). In Spain, several domestic workers' associations were offering support services to people employed in the sector at the time of our fieldwork, while others had done so in the past. Among them, two examples include the advisory service run by ATH-ELE in Bilbao and the 24-hour helpline offering legal aid run by SEDOAC in Madrid. As we mentioned in Chapter 2, the former is one of the longest-running associations of domestic workers in the country, founded at the end of the 1980s in the Basque Country, while the latter was founded in the 2010s and attracts considerable numbers of workers of migrant origin.

The improvement of the economic conditions of people working in the sector is another significant terrain of intervention. In the Philippines, the domestic workers' organization UNITED created savings cooperatives to prevent indebtedness and foster mutual aid and solidarity among domestic workers. UNITED is an organization created in 2012 with the support of labour organizations Sentro and LEARN, which in 2017 counted approximately two thousand members and 22 chapters across the country. Notably, such a focus on economic empowerment emerged from an activist study carried out by UNITED and LEARN, involving domestic workers from lower sectors of society. This is how the president of UNITED, Himaya Montenegro, and Verna Dinah Viajar from LEARN explained the process:

> A few domestic worker organizers, including Himaya [Montenegro], went to gated neighbourhoods, urban poor areas, and schools (where domestic workers often wait for their young charges) with LEARN researchers to conduct one-on-one interviews with domestic workers. These interviews helped domestic workers network and had a snowball effect, with domestic workers referring their friends and acquaintances to each other and to LEARN. We then did house-to-house visits to create personal relationships with and among domestic workers. After these conversations and discussions with domestic workers, we decided that addressing the economic concerns of domestic workers – primarily due to low wages – was a priority, so we formed a community savings cooperative for domestic workers. The purpose was to help domestic workers avoid debt bondage and to provide them with a mutual aid programme for solidarity and support. Besides this mutual-help initiative, we also offered regular discussions and short seminars on domestic workers' rights and social protection. (Montenegro and Viajar, 2017: 122–3)

Another example of how self-organizing may facilitate empowerment is provided by the creation of workers' cooperatives. In Spain, for instance, the domestic and care workers' cooperative Senda De Cuidados was founded in 2015 in Madrid, thanks to the joint efforts of the members of Territorio Doméstico and the social work cooperative Abierto Hasta el Amanecer. The latter provides professional and capacity-building training aimed at improving both workers' skills in care work, entrepreneurship and management, and their knowledge of broader topics such as the social economy, feminist approaches to the care economy and women's labour, self-esteem and gender stereotypes. Workers' cooperatives are seen in this context as a way to improve control over working conditions through a collective learning process and a sharing of good practices. As such, they appear to be an effective way to counter both the diffuse nature of this workforce, fragmented as it is due to individual employment relationships within private households, and new forms of exploitation emerging in the market (that is, agencies, including online platforms and the sharing economy).

These examples also demonstrate that many organizations invest a great deal of effort in training activities of various kinds. Some organizations provide professional training, schooling and literacy programmes. Many of them also provide education on well-being and health, gender-based violence, reproductive rights, family care, women's rights and migrants' rights. Domestic workers themselves describe the importance of this aspect of their organizations' activities. In the words of Claribed Palacio García from Colombia:

> 'Among our internal activities, we provide gender-equality training. We also provide training in labour rights, the rights of ethnic minorities ... We also have sexual and reproductive education workshops, which are very important because, as women, all these things are going to help us. Because we cannot go on with this mindset that Black women are just there to give birth and to work in a house ... So all those programmes are designed with the real needs of our members in mind.' (Claribed Palacio García, UTRASD, Colombia)

Palacio's words align with those of other interviewees and with our fieldwork observations. She suggests how all these internal activities draw on an intersectional reading of domestic workers' realities, and recommends pathways towards their empowerment, partly in the sphere of labour relations but also at the personal, socioeconomic and political levels.

Further, many organizations also provide political and leadership training designed to bolster knowledge and strengthen abilities that are keys to active participation in the public and political sphere. These include sharing information about the way unions function, and training in public speaking. In Brazil, FENATRAD was one of the partners in the national policy initiative Trabalho Doméstico Cidadão (TDC), carried out under the Lula government (2003–11). The TDC plan was promoted by the Ministry of Labour, in partnership with the Secretariat for Policies for the Promotion of Racial Equality, the Secretariat for Policies for Women, domestic workers' organizations and other institutions.[14] It was aimed at improving domestic workers' social and professional qualifications and their awareness of their labour rights, as well as strengthening their political participation and their access to citizenship rights. In Ecuador, one of the requests advanced by

ATRH in the 2010s concerned the implementation of training programmes by public institutions after a period in which the Ministry of Labour and the Social Security Institute had provided capacity-building initiatives for domestic workers. These training and empowerment opportunities were either self-organized or created in partnership with non-profit allies (such as international and local NGOs or trade unions).

Learning processes within these organizations are also nourished by the relationships with other unionized domestic workers, and the sharing of practices that characterize their activism. An interesting narrative in this regard comes from Maria Noeli Dos Santos, a veteran Brazilian activist, leader of the Rio de Janeiro domestic workers' trade union and current secretary of the national federation FENATRAD. Remembering her first experiences in the union, after she moved to the city from the southern state of Rio Grande do Sul in the early 1980s to find work, she recounts the learning trajectory that led her to become aware of her condition of exploitation. Her view then widened to encompass the conditions of other domestic workers all over the country: "When I got to the trade union ... They started to teach me, you understand? ... They always sat and talked to me ... They took me everywhere with them, to teach me, make me see the reality. The reality of each place, each state" (Maria Noeli Dos Santos, SINDOMESTICA Rio de Janeiro and FENATRAD, Brazil).

Rafaela Pimentel Lara, from Spain, further expresses the resulting feelings of collective belonging. She provides examples of how mutual aid practices and reciprocal care define relationships among the members of many of these groups:

> 'We incorporate care among us, this is very important to us, from how we prepare the meetings ... how we welcome a comrade, the hugs, to the fact of taking care if a comrade is sick ... It is important, we call this care, taking care, we share that cake that someone brought, those candies from one's country ... We see this collective as a space for us, a space that we share, a backpack loaded with all the situations that we the women live ... Territorio Doméstico actively works in the daily life of each of us, when a woman gets sick, and she cannot work, she has no family to help, we as a collective are there ... We put a group of women in charge of going along with those who are going through sickness, heavy situations, this unites us as a group.' (Rafaela Pimentel Lara, Territorio Doméstico, Spain)

The analyses of these examples are in line with other recent comparative analyses of collective action by domestic workers and informal, unprotected and precarious workers (Agarwala and Chun, 2019b; Pratt and Migrante BC, 2019; Tilly et al, 2019). Namely, the activities of the domestic workers' groups that we studied confirm the ways in which we are confronted by special forms of labour and related forms of women's organizing, where mobilizing for labour rights and putting political pressure on institutional actors go hand in hand with cultural politics and self-help efforts focused on self-representation, self-esteem and identity. Through this process, these groups touch upon issues that transcend the field of labour and intersect with topics related to women's experience, migration, access to education, health, sexuality and participation in the public sphere.

Feminism and Domestic Workers: Different Positionalities, Discursive Convergences

The gap between feminist and domestic workers' mobilizations still remains wide. Even the most recent wave of global feminism, which has shown a distinct capacity to involve actors that are not traditionally part of the feminist movement, such as *Ni Una Menos* or #MeToo,[1] has seldom involved domestic workers and their cause. This chapter addresses the complicated relationship between the domestic workers' and the feminist and women's rights movements. As we have seen, this relationship remains troubled, not only as a theme of reflection for us as feminist researchers, but also for activists in the various countries in our study. Indeed, as we will show in the first part of this chapter, this relationship has received some attention within the emerging literature on domestic workers' organizing, which suggests that it might be ambivalent and even conflictual, rather than supportive (Boris and Nadasen, 2008; Blofield, 2012; Bernardino-Costa, 2014; Boris and Fish, 2015; Federici, 2016; Fish, 2017; Marchetti and Cherubini, 2019; Busi, 2020).

Building upon this scholarship, in the second part of the chapter we try to make sense of the different positions that feminist and women's rights organizations took in the strategic field of action of domestic workers' rights across our nine countries in the years 2008–18. Feminist and women's rights organizations have often remained marginal in this field; domestic worker activists have generally perceived them as distant, although not in opposition to their cause. In our research we came across a few cases of feminist and women's rights' organizations that have contributed in crucial ways to domestic workers' rights campaigns, such as SEWA in India, Criola, Themis and SOS Corpo in Brazil, and the Awakening Foundation in Taiwan.

In rare cases, new organizations developed from the very convergence of feminist and women's rights issues and domestic workers' rights, such as Territorio Doméstico in Spain. Much more frequent, however, were instances of individual feminist or women's rights campaigners taking an active role in these struggles, such as lawyers, politicians and NGO activists who occupied central roles in the promotion of domestic workers' rights, as we will show in the context of Colombia, Ecuador and the Philippines. In countries of the Global South, especially the Philippines and India, we often found that an important role was played by feminist and women's rights activists promoting the protection of informal workers, often as part of global organizations connected to WIEGO, such as HomeNet and StreetNet. This approach, which has been common in many parts of the Global South since the 1990s (McLaren, 2019), has often engaged with issues of domestic workers' rights by centring their activity on the improvement of the working and living conditions of women in informal work, and their access to political agency.

However, the materials we discuss in the third part of the chapter indicate that, in many contexts, the groups who are active in the field of domestic workers' rights actually draw upon classic feminist discourses, in particular those related to reproductive labour and the commodification of care. Indeed, activists regularly speak of the rights of paid domestic workers within a broader analysis of the devaluation and unequal distribution of reproductive labour, both paid and unpaid. Further, the activists we interviewed often draw upon contemporary feminist critiques of the commodification of care, especially in countries with an ageing population. Crucially, activists in the field do so by negotiating and elaborating on such discourses, and typically complicating the gender-only analytical dimension that some feminist arguments promote. This reconfiguration of existing frames arguably has the capacity to give much-needed new life to contemporary feminisms (Federici, 2016). In particular, by extending the frame of gendered inequality in reproductive labour and by centring the experience of (poorly) paid domestic work, domestic workers' rights activists provide a broader view of the unequal distribution of domestic labour across social groups. Moreover, by extending the classic frame on the commodification of care, our interviewees developed a frame that focuses on the exploitation of migrant domestic workers by showing how these migrants pay the price for the crisis of welfare and care provision in industrialized countries.

Disconnections from feminist movements

The 2010s saw a resurgence in feminist mobilizations across the globe, with a tendency to emphasize explicit anti-capitalist analyses and demands (Basu,

2010; Fraser, 2013; Luxton, 2014; Evans, 2015; Winch et al, 2019). This movement has succeeded in actively engaging a broad array of allies in the struggle, from precarious workers' groups and anti-racism campaigners to environmental activists, united under an anti-capitalist banner.

Within this confluence of struggles, the domestic workers' movement stands out as playing a central role in highlighting the contradictions of capitalism (Barbagallo and Federici, 2012; Lim, 2016; England, 2017; Teeple Hopkins, 2017). Federici argues that, in the US context in particular, migrant domestic workers' mobilizations 'have revitalized the feminist interest in the question of domestic work' and have positively contributed to questioning 'the possibility of solidarity among women and the adequacy of the once dominant feminist strategy of "emancipation through wage labor"' (Federici, 2016: 10). Yet, as Federici and others show, with regard to the relationship between feminist and domestic workers' movements, this ideal convergence is often contradicted in practice by non-collaboration and reciprocal neglect. This is as true in a time when both movements were strong and enjoying a period of growth, such as the decade 2008–18.

The possible encounters, as well as the potential distance, between domestic workers' rights and feminist and women's rights actors have begun to be explored by scholars both at the international level and in different national contexts. Among them, Jennifer Fish's ethnography of domestic workers' global organizing identifies the creation of a 'feminist-labour-activist coalition' between the then IDWN, WIEGO and international trade unions like the IUF.[2] She sees this coalition as a key factor in the success of negotiations leading to the passing of C189 (Fish, 2017). Fish views the considerable engagement of female politicians, whom she dubbed 'femocrats', who 'used their positions to voice ideologies consistent with the IDWN platform of demands' (Fish, 2017: 214), as equally critical to its creation.

Eileen Boris and Jennifer Fish (2015) identify the first steps to include domestic work within the ILO's field of vision – albeit unsuccessfully, owing to the lack of wider civil society support – as having been taken by what they termed 'individual labour feminists' working for governments, trade unions and UN agencies (Boris and Fish, 2015: 537–40). Nevertheless, the mid-2000s were a turning point, with the growing domestic workers' movement providing the basis for the formation of a coalition with transnational feminist NGOs, governments, international trade unions and human rights NGOs. Indeed, the growth of the transnational domestic workers' movement appears to have been central to the process of connecting these various actors, doing so by becoming a federation of trade unions, associations, networks and workers' cooperatives. Although not a women-only organization, this federation explicitly stresses its women's dimension, as explained by Myrtle Witbooi, president of the IDWF and one of the founders of the South African domestic workers movement:

'We launched an International Domestic Workers Federation in 2013 because, even though we had national and international labour laws, we still needed a mechanism to ensure that the voices of workers were heard and to uplift these voices, which is a big role. And then, again, history was made. This federation was for women, and led by women ... We started out as 255,000 members and 30 organizations, and today we have over 500,000 members and 62 organizations. At the beginning everybody was watching us, saying we were women and won't be able to lead, and step by step we have proved them wrong. In five years' time, we want to reach 200,000 migrant workers and double the number of domestic workers.' (Witbooi, 2017: 83)

When Myrtle Witbooi clarifies that the IDWF is 'a federation for women and led by women', and recounts how 'everybody was watching us, saying we were women and won't be able to lead', she is making important points regarding their political project. In addition to challenging the widespread prejudice that women cannot be leaders, the awareness that 'everybody was watching us' refers to other social movements and unions. Witbooi was undoubtedly describing the movement's autonomy from men – in particular men who dominate other unions. The women she refers to, as working-class, Black, migrant or from other minorities, have traditionally been denied political agency not only by these trade unions and society in general but also within feminist and women's rights organizations.

This lack of solidarity with domestic workers' movements shown by other groups, including feminist ones, has been highlighted by comparative studies focusing on the Latin American context (Chaney and Castro Garcia, 1989; Blofield, 2012). For example, Merike Blofield (2012) explored the tensions between domestic workers and what she called 'professional and elite women', feminists included, in a comparative analysis of the Bolivian, Chilean, Costa Rican and Uruguayan contexts. She emphasized that many of these women saw their own liberation and entry into the labour market as contingent on finding a low-paid substitute to carry out their chores. According to Blofield, even if this has not meant an explicit opposition to the expansion of rights for this category of workers by feminist movements, it has nevertheless affected feminist movements' priorities and agendas. Thus, in Latin America, 'domestic workers' rights have largely remained invisible and passed below the radar of most feminist movements ... Overall, feminist organizations across the region have been slow to take up the issue, although in some countries individual feminists have adopted the cause' (Blofield, 2012: 59–60).

Meanwhile, in Brazil, the campaign for a new Brazilian constitution in the late 1980s led to strong alliances between domestic workers' trade unions and the feminist movement (Bernardino-Costa, 2014). However, a distrust remains between the two movements, which Joaze Bernardino-Costa attributes not only to the significant racial and class-based differences between domestic workers and feminists but also to the ideological differences concerning the very notion of 'women's liberation'. Indeed, while (mostly White, upper- and middle-class) feminists tend to think of women's liberation as linked to emancipation from unpaid domestic work and access to the labour market, for domestic workers' activists, access to the labour market can remain exploitative and far from liberatory, given the poor employment conditions in the sector (Bernardino-Costa, 2014: 77).

Finally, the fieldwork carried out in Italy by Beatrice Busi for the DomEQUAL project has provided insight into the lack of alliance between the large Italian women's movement of the 1960s and 1970s and the domestic workers' organizations that were campaigning for their labour rights over the same period. Her work, along with other recent analyses, has elaborated on the class-based difference between the women in the two movements and it has pointed to the limitations of the Italian feminist movement in relation to women's labour issues and migrants' rights (Busi, 2020).

In the following pages we offer a contextual exploration of the relationship between these two movements in the nine countries under analysis by exploring the positions that feminist groups and individuals have taken in the strategic fields of action of domestic workers' rights in the period 2008–18.

Different feminist positionalities

There are a number of elements that can help to explain the variety of feminist positions that emerged across the nine countries in our analysis. Feminist and women's rights movements are remarkably diverse, with different positionalities coming from institutions affiliated with the state, NGOs or grassroots groups. These differences may determine their more or less intense participation in the strategic field of action of domestic workers' rights.

Furthermore, across the different countries studied, feminist and women's rights actors can at times have opposing interests. These interests may depend on whether women's rights activists delegate care and domestic duties in their private lives, especially in contexts in which there is little public provision of care and these tasks remain mainly women's responsibility. We will now briefly explore the social and economic backgrounds of domestic workers and feminist or women's rights activists across our nine countries.

Starting in the Philippines, it is worth noting that women's rights organizations were already quite active in the protection of Filipina migrants and in opposition to child labour in the mid-1990s, the period in which domestic workers' rights rose to prominence in the country. However, according to our interviewees, feminists did not widely discuss the issue of domestic work during those years, and the main tripartite body on domestic work, the TWG (see Chapter 2), itself was not particularly gender sensitive. This is confirmed by the analysis of Mylene Hega, Veronica Alporha and Meggan Evangelista (2017). However, we can identify some of the key figures responsible for the advancement of this strategic field of action as women's rights supporters. Particularly worthy of mention are Maria Cecilia Flores-Oebanda, founder of the non-governmental organization Visayan Forum, and Rosalinda Dimapilis-Baldoz, Secretary of Labour in the years 2010–16, both of whom were domestic workers in their youth. Also notable has been the role of Ellene Sana, executive director of the NGO Centre for Migrant Advocacy since 2003. Moreover, domestic workers have been a concern for women's rights activists in the Akbayan and Gabriela party lists, in labour organizations representing domestic workers in the country (LEARN, Sentro and ALLWIES), and in the context of government bodies developing policies on informal labour, such as the Workers in the Informal Sector Council of the Anti-Poverty Commission, part of WIEGO.

Our fieldwork shows that feminist activists supporting informal workers have also played an important role for domestic workers' rights in the case of India, in particular with SEWA, which has been a central actor in the struggle for domestic workers' rights in the country and has been active within the PDWR, a platform which many actors engaged in the movement. SEWA was founded in 1972, with a clear women's rights programme and a link to the Gandhian civil rights movement, and it eventually became part of the ITUC. As we mentioned in Chapter 3, SEWA was already involved in the process of ILO C177 for home-based workers, passed in 1996. The latter is a central convention for informal women workers and is considered to have prepared the ground in some respects for C189. Moreover, our participants testified to the role played by other influential feminist and women's rights NGOs that have engaged in struggles for domestic workers' rights since the late 1990s, in particular Stree Jagruti Samiti in Bangalore and Jagori in Delhi. In the decade 2008–18 their work included providing support in setting up domestic workers' trade unions, some of which are united under the National Domestic Workers' Federation. Also important was the public advocacy of organizations fighting against human trafficking, such as Shakti Vahini.

In the case of Ecuador, Rafael Correa's government established a preferential relationship with ATRH as a domestic workers' organization representative of working-class women's interests, although it excluded other women's rights movements or civil society organizations. As our interviewees clarified, grassroots feminist organizations were mainly engaged in an oppositional dynamic vis-à-vis Correa's presidency during his second and third mandates (2009–17), particularly in response to his conservative approach to reproductive rights.[3] Thus, the prominent role of Correa's government in supporting ATRH has prevented the deeper involvement of feminist grassroots organizations in the campaign for domestic workers' rights. A similar situation continued from 2017 under the government of Lenín Moreno. Yet, during the same decade individual feminists were present and active in many of the state and non-state organizations supporting the cause of domestic workers. Among them was Gina Godoy, the feminist congresswoman from the ruling party Alianza País, who advocated for the ratification of C189 in the debates at the National Assembly during the campaign for ratification in the years 2011–13.

In the case of Brazil, the domestic workers' rights movement and the feminist and women's rights movements have developed an ongoing long-term relationship. This support was seen by our participants as deriving from the fact that feminists and domestic workers fought together in the struggle against the dictatorship in the 1980s, and for the new Brazilian constitution that was ratified in 1988. Our data also demonstrates the importance of alliances between domestic workers' organizations and the feminist and Black feminist movements during the decade under analysis. In particular, some feminist organizations, such as Criola, Themis and SOS Corpo, were present and directly engaged in the campaign for the constitutional reform that had been promoted by FENATRAD since the late 2000s (PEC das Domésticas). These are feminist organizations that have been working since the 1980s (SOS Corpo) and early 1990s (Themis and Criola) to promote women's rights and social justice and to fight against gender-based violence and discrimination. Criola specifically focuses on Black women's rights and Black feminism, while SOS Corpo and Themis focus on the intersections between sexism, racism, socioeconomic exclusion and poverty, homophobia and other forms of discrimination. Also central during this period was the involvement of Senator Benedita da Silva, Afro-Brazilian feminist organizer and politician, and former domestic worker, who was the rapporteur on the PEC reform.

In Colombia, the 2010s saw not only the resurgence of domestic workers' organizing but also a noteworthy process of convergence and coalition building between individual feminist and women's rights defenders during the Ley de Prima campaign (2013–16). Indeed, the main allies of organized domestic workers in this campaign all identified as feminists – namely the activists of the Bien Humano Foundation and ENS, such as Andrea Londoño and Sandra Muñoz, and the Green Party congresswomen, Ángela María Robledo and Angélica Lozano. Further, all of these participated in the National Committee for the Care Economy,[4] a nationwide platform composed of gender-sensitive institutional and non-institutional actors. It was created in 2010 with the aim of monitoring the implementation of the National Law on the Care Economy, approved that same year.[5] This law gave full recognition to the social and economic value of unpaid care and domestic work and laid the basis for its financial and economic measurement in official statistics as a portion of the national GDP. As we have shown in previous work (Marchetti and Cherubini, 2019; Cherubini et al, 2020), the strategy of the coalition campaigning for the Ley de Prima was to extend the debate on the care economy as understood in that context, expanding its original scope to include paid work. This was pivotal in allowing for the convergence of domestic workers and the aforementioned women's rights activists.

The relationship between feminism and domestic workers' mobilizations is particularly intertwined in the case of Spain. Here, the new wave of mobilizations for domestic workers' rights that took place in the late 2000s and 2010s found common terrain with grassroots feminist groups organizing around the issues of care and social reproduction, work and precarity and migrants' rights. Such convergence is evident in the work of the migrant domestic workers' organizations created in different parts of the country in those years, in particular Territorio Doméstico, SEDOAC, SINDIHOGAR/SINDILLAR and Nosotras, as well as in the nationwide platform for domestic workers' rights known as Turin Group (which we described in Chapter 2). As can be gleaned from the views expressed by our interviewees, feminist support for domestic workers' demands has become increasingly conspicuous in the mobilizations for the ratification of C189 that have taken place between 2011 and 2018, as well as on the occasion of the first domestic workers' national congress, organized in 2016. Notably, these years of intense organizing for domestic workers' rights also correspond to large social justice mobilizations, known collectively as the 15-M movement, and to the rise of political forces that partly institutionalized this movement, such as the Podemos party. It is no coincidence that the proposal for the first EU resolution on caregivers' rights, approved in 2016,[6] was promoted by a Podemos party member, Tania González Peñas, together with the Greek MEP Kostadinka Kuneva.

In Taiwan, our interviewees informed us that the feminist NGO Awakening Foundation visibly engaged the issue of care work needs, with particular reference to long-term care provision for the elderly, which became central to the political debate of the 2010s. Awakening Foundation had been stressing the importance of women's emancipation from the family care duties ascribed to them in Confucian culture. It also supported the proposal for the Household Service Act, first formulated in 2013 by a network of migrants' rights organizations led by TIWA, to protect both Taiwanese and migrant caregivers.

Two other countries in our study, Italy and Germany, share the characteristic of having ageing societies where households tend to meet care work needs for their elderly by privately employing migrant caregivers, as we described in Chapter 2. However, the circumstances facing domestic workers migrating to these destinations differ in significant ways from those in our other case studies. Italy in particular represents an interesting context in which the feminist movement had an immense impact on society and the improvement of women's rights during the 1960s and 1970s. The International Wages for Housework Campaign of the 1970s received popular support in both countries, with a focus on promoting the valorization of unpaid reproductive labour (Toupin, 2014; Picchio and Pincelli, 2019; Busi, 2020). The more recent *Non una di meno* movement against gender-based violence has also contributed to a resurgence of activism focused on care work and a broader public debate around women's issues. On 25 November 2017, the *Non una di meno* movement was kick-started in Italy by a large demonstration for the International Day for the Elimination of Violence against Women. The movement identified the gendered division of reproductive labour as one of the root causes of women's exploitation and social vulnerability. According to Busi (2020), this may represent a favourable framework through which to build an alliance between the movements. In Germany, two notable initiatives have been the Care Manifesto,[7] started in 2014 by a group of critical scholars, and the Equal Care Day initiative,[8] launched in 2016, both calling for a global politics of care work justice and an equal distribution of caring commitments between men and women. However, so far these initiatives have not had notable repercussions on campaigns for domestic workers' rights.

On the whole, we found a large variety of positions were taken by feminist and women's rights actors, both collective and individual, in the strategic action field of domestic workers' rights across our nine countries for the period 2008–18. In most countries we found that a crucial supporting role in the domestic workers' cause was played by individual women bringing feminist and women's rights perspectives into their political and professional careers as public officials, lawyers and NGO activists, among others. Women such as Rosalinda Dimapilis-Baldoz in the Philippines and Benedita Da Silva in Brazil are exemplary in demonstrating the crucial supporting role that can be played by policy makers in these countries. They do so by overcoming the cultural stigma traditionally attached to domestic work and choosing to speak openly about their experiences of having done this form of labour in their youth.

Meanwhile, at the collective level, as we saw in Chapter 2, countries such as Spain, India, Brazil and Taiwan have all seen large mobilizations in support of domestic workers during the decade under study, and it is only in these countries that feminist and women's rights organizations engaged with issues that specifically affect this sector of society. Brazil, Spain and India all have long histories of domestic worker organizing, dating back to the 1930s, while more recent anti-racist and migrants' rights movements (in Brazil, Spain and Taiwan), as well as informal workers' mobilizations (in India), have become important new allies in struggles for domestic workers. However, as we saw in Chapter 3, the state did not support the policy changes being demanded by domestic workers' rights activists in Taiwan, Spain or India.

The situation looks rather different in the next section, where we turn our attention to the discursive frames that are employed within the strategic field of action of domestic workers' rights. We are led to a remarkable conclusion for all the countries in our study: that some of the most recurrent discursive frames in the campaigns for domestic workers' rights are actually based on feminist arguments appropriated and modified by domestic workers and other actors.

Expanding feminist discursive frames

As an issue that encompasses several social justice concerns and that has its origin in the experiences of multiply marginalized subjects, the improvement of domestic workers' rights and conditions has been framed in different ways across time and place. At times it has been framed as a women's issue, and at other times as a labour, migrant, human rights, caste or racial issue.

Scholars in many contexts have already identified the narratives employed in the field of struggles for domestic workers' rights as an important object of analysis. Jennifer Fish identifies gender equity, human rights and economic justice as complex, yet compelling, discursive frames on which domestic workers' rights activists have centred their communication strategies to promote C189 (Fish, 2017: 163). These three frameworks evoke the language of the ILO, which since the 1990s has promoted a conception of decent work that is able to combine an emphasis on human rights with a concern for the living and working conditions of labourers, especially when addressing highly gendered and ethnicized sectors, non-standard jobs and low-skilled informal workers. Particularly important in this process has been the passing of C177 in 1996 (Boris, 2019), which was promoted by a network of political actors that remobilized after the passing of C189, such as WIEGO. The ILO has since extended its work on informal labour through Recommendation 204 'concerning the Transition from the Informal to the Formal Economy' – which explicitly includes domestic workers in its definition of the informal economy and 'calls on Member States to pay special attention to domestic workers as one group that is especially vulnerable to the most serious decent work deficits in the informal economy' (paragraph 7i). Domestic workers' organizations have called upon the political and moral responsibility advocated by the UN discourse on equality and human rights in order to promote the improvement of women's and migrants' conditions (Boris and Fish, 2014; Garofalo Geymonat and Marchetti, 2017; Marchetti, 2018). This has been seen by some as a reflection of the kind of actors involved in the coalition that has been promoting domestic workers' rights at the global level. Lorenza Fontana (2020), in discussing C189, stresses the connection between the labour/human rights framework used by the Convention and the unique coalition that was mobilized in Geneva. This brought to the negotiating table not only the traditional ILO constituencies (employers' representatives, workers' organizations and governments) but also domestic workers' rights organizations and human rights NGOs (albeit without voting rights), representing a broad coalition of labour organizations, social movements and community groups (Bonner and Spooner, 2011; Blackett, 2012; Johnstone, 2012; Boris and Fish, 2014).

Other narratives have been adopted by domestic workers' groups in particular national and regional contexts (Chaney and Castro Garcia, 1989; Agarwala and Saha, 2018; Moore, 2018). For example, Agarwala and Saha (2018) show how the domestic workers' rights movement in India tends to adopt a discourse focusing on the exploitation of time and the lack of respect for personal dignity perpetuated by employers in the household. Domestic workers' rights activists have addressed both their employers and state institutions in demands for dignity, recognition and emancipation as women and as workers, in ways that modify classic anti-capitalist arguments. This in turn resonates with the frameworks employed by movements of other informal workers with whom domestic workers have developed important links. Shereen Ally (2009) and Jennifer Fish (2014) explain how, in the midst of the South African democratic transition, expanding domestic workers' rights in the country was successfully framed as integral to the wider process of 'defining features of the new nation' after the end of apartheid (Fish, 2014: 233). By contrast, in European public debates, especially since the 2000s, Bridget Anderson (2010) and Helen Schwenken (2003) have referred to two competing ways that domestic workers' struggles have been framed – namely, in terms of trafficking and in terms of rights. In ageing countries, authors have interrogated the recurrent discourses on care needs or care deficit, which, as stressed by Anderson (2014), may result in the recruitment of foreigners and therefore come into conflict with a nationalistic discourse that pushes for restrictive migration policies (Sarti, 2007; Gutiérrez-Rodríguez, 2010; Van Hooren, 2010; Triandafyllidou, 2013; Romero, 2018).

In our research we have explored the role that discursive framing plays in the relationship between domestic workers' movements and feminist groups in a range of different countries. We found that in many of our case studies activists promoting domestic workers' rights are framing their struggles within narratives that echo some classic feminist discourses, in particular those involving anti-capitalist critiques of inequality. In so doing, they utilize and modify these discourses in order to incorporate experiences of domestic workers that these discursive frames did not originally foresee, having been primarily interested in the unfair distribution of labour between men and women. Therefore, they expand these discursive frames in what could be described as an intersectional way, enlarging their scope to include racialized, low-class, migrant and other minority groups in ways which few feminist movements have achieved. In other words, they expand the scope of each of the discursive frames they mobilize – originally tied to labour, migration, gender or caste – blurring the limits that were traditionally established among them within their own national contexts.

The valorization of reproductive labour

Analysing the discursive frames mobilized within struggles for domestic workers' rights within each of the nine countries reveals a recurrent perception of the fundamental connection between the need to improve the conditions of domestic workers, on the one hand, and the need to valorize reproductive labour more generally, on the other. The concerns voiced by workers we spoke with included the professional consequences of an unequal distribution of reproductive labour between men and women, as well as the commodification of this form of work (Folbre, 2001; Boris and Parreñas, 2010). They also affirmed the imperative that societies begin to recognize the value of work being done largely by women, particularly – but not exclusively – within the home and family. Feminists have often historically organized campaigns demanding the recognition of these activities' value, both as social goods and in terms of their economic contribution to society. By implication, they have highlighted and denounced the exploitation of this form of labour within patriarchal and capitalist societies. Tasks performed by women inside their households have been emphasized as constituting 'work', deserving the same recognition as any other form of work (Sarti et al, 2018). Whether or not they explicitly acknowledge the origin of their arguments in feminist critiques, activists for domestic workers' rights also often clearly affirm the value of unpaid forms of reproductive labour, thereby challenging the general lack of social value assigned to tasks connected to caregiving and housekeeping, while simultaneously demanding improvements in their salaries, labour protections and contract rights (Dalla Costa and James, 1975; Federici, 1975; Delphy, 1984; Pateman, 1988; Picchio, 1992).

Contemporary domestic workers' rights activists are now expanding on and modifying these classic feminist arguments in favour of acknowledging the social meaning of reproductive tasks and their contribution to the economy, to include the experiences of domestic workers. This broader framework encompasses the experiences of discrimination and exploitation faced by both paid and unpaid, formal and informal workers – as women and as members of low classes, low castes and ethnic and racial minorities.

In our study, Brazil, Ecuador, Colombia, India and the Philippines were the countries in which we found these discursive reframings of feminist arguments most clearly represented. They also happened to be the places in which employers overwhelmingly occupied markedly superior ranks within local social hierarchies, and in which the labour force was overwhelmingly made up of racialized, lower-class women working almost completely in the informal labour sector. An example of the application of these novel analyses to concrete political demands relates to the historical process of implementing C189, at which time domestic workers' organizations demanded that their labour be recognized as work 'like any other work' in terms of its labour rights, protections and social and economic value; as well as 'work like no other' in relation to its unique and essential contribution to the well-being of both individual citizens and their families, and to national economies and society as a whole (Blackett, 2019).

One of the points that many of the activists we interviewed based their analyses on resonates well with the classic argument that feminists have used in their campaigns to recognize the value of unpaid reproductive labour; that is, the differentiation between a 'favour' and 'work'. It is an argument that subtracts reproductive labour from the field of personal relationships and positions it within the realm of objective value. Claribed Palacios García, a leader in the domestic workers' organization UTRASD in Colombia, describes the importance of according domestic workers proper payment and treatment in the following words: "Since I am doing my job right, I demand to be paid and be treated with dignity. Domestic work is not a favour. Domestic work – as Convention 189 says – is work" (Claribed Palacios García, UTRASD, Colombia).

These arguments around the valorization of reproductive labour challenge implicit gender-based assumptions about the natural disposition to care attributed to women, which prevent us from seeing domestic workers as 'real workers' because their activity is considered to be an extension of family duties. These interlinked arguments are briefly but poignantly described by Tania González Peñas, supporter of domestic workers' rights in Spain and a member of the political party Podemos. González Peñas makes the connection between domestic workers' rights and a broader demand to valorize domestic and care duties:

> 'It is important to give more rights to these workers, first of all, because it is a job which is necessary and therefore ought to have more dignity. Secondly, because domestic work is part of the care activities needed to support our society ... And thirdly, it is also an economic question: to invest in the care economy can produce wealth and social benefits for everybody.' (Tania González Peñas, Podemos party, Spain)

This last macroeconomic aspect – the care economy that "can produce wealth and social benefits for everybody" – is developed by a number of the activists we interviewed. Lourdes Albán, activist and member of the Ecuadorian domestic workers' organization, ATRH, explained the success of their campaign for the ratification of C189 by expanding on feminist discourses in relation to the care economy. She depicts domestic workers as pillars of society, recognizing their vital role in ensuring the well-being of Ecuadorian families, and demands more socio-economic rights for them and their households. In her words:

> 'We made them [the politicians] see that we support the country, that we are also part of the economy of the country, part of the economy of the families of Ecuador. In the same way we want the country to help us get ahead with our families, so that we feed our families ... And that is how we achieved unanimous ratification in the National Assembly.' (Lourdes Albán, ATRH, Ecuador)

With a different nuance, Sandra Muñoz, of the non-profit organization ENS, a key supporter of domestic workers' organizing in Colombia, talks about the escalation of actions and events in support of the ratification of C189. Muñoz, who identifies as a feminist, tellingly uses the concept of 'indebtedness' in her key argument:

> 'They [domestic workers] have begun to carry out a lot of actions and complaints that put Colombia in the hurricane as a country that has a social debt with the issue of gender, with women, with domestic workers. An issue that hurts everyone: it hurts

the analysts, it hurts the congressman, the president. It hurts everyone because everybody has domestic workers.' (Sandra Muñoz, ENS, Colombia)

The language of debt is used here in order to express the need to recognize the social value of domestic and care work, both on a personal level, as a debt owed to individual domestic workers exploited by the elites, and on a national level, as a debt owed to the most historically exploited sectors of society. This use of language reflects postcolonial discourses that represent the illegitimate appropriation of land, labour and resources from one class by another as historical injustices that demand reparations. Sandra Muñoz's quote highlights some of the ways in which the discursive frame of the valorization of reproductive labour, which in its most classic feminist versions is based on gender, can be utilized for the advancement of domestic workers' rights in ways that intersect with class-based and racialized discourses. Indeed, by stressing that the debt is owed to 'some women' and not all women, Sandra Muñoz's interview resonates with intersectional feminist analyses, notably that of the racial division of reproductive labour (Nakano Glenn, 1992), which have thoroughly examined the issue of the unequal distribution of domestic work between women.

Himaya Montenegro, leader of the Filipino domestic workers' organization, UNITED, argues that the contribution that paid domestic workers make to the well-being of the middle classes should represent a source of personal pride for workers:

'It is difficult to compare [with other work sectors] because, until now, although domestic work is recognised as work, we still feel the very low regard for us paid domestic workers. What we are doing to raise our self-esteem is to tell each other to be proud of what we do, that domestic work is a dignified job. We tell other paid domestic workers to remember that we are the force behind the good income that the employers have, because without us, they will worry about who will look after their houses, their children, their properties.' (Himaya Montenegro, UNITED, Philippines)

In her discussion of the dignity of domestic work she also raises the important issue of class differences between women when she implicitly refers to the delegation of unpaid domestic work to paid domestic workers. This issue is also very common in the discourses of activists in other countries in our study where class deeply intersects with race, such as Brazil, and with caste, as in India.

Indeed, many of the arguments developed around domestic workers' rights display a tension between two objectives. The first goal is to stress the commonalities between women in their position of responsibility over the sphere of reproductive work, with the aim of inserting domestic workers' labour rights within a general demand to change the understanding of reproductive labour. The second is to simultaneously visibilize the elements of inequality and conflict between women in order to highlight the exploitation of domestic workers enacted by their (female) employers. This tension is described by Maria Betânia Ávila, founder of SOS Corpo, a Brazilian feminist organization that, as we have seen, has played a crucial role as advocate for domestic workers' rights. She says: "Domestic work is considered a woman's job, that men take advantage of but simultaneously neglect. Within the relationship of paid domestic work it is the mistresses who enact the same neglect towards other women as working subjects" (Maria Betânia Ávila, SOS Corpo, Brazil). A similar set of contractions is expressed well, in another context, by Sister Lissy Joseph, organizer of the NDWM in India, the largest platform for domestic workers' rights in the country. She emphasizes how gender and caste taken together act as principles behind the devaluation of reproductive labour:

'Mainly housewives are the employers. Their own lack of dignity is also playing on the life of other women workers. And all sorts of myths are there. [For example] that certain classes of communities are coming [to Delhi] and certain types of work, cleaning and dusting have to be done by the lower castes. You know, all this discrimination is also there. Workers not having dignity.' (Lissy Joseph, NDWM, India)

It is important to point out the form of devaluation denounced in this narrative, in which the lack of recognition afforded to women's reproductive labour results in paid domestic work, the individuals who perform it and, in fact, entire social groups being devalued and seen as undignified. The employers, as women, also suffer from this lack of recognition which, in Joseph's view, is in turn negatively reflected in the lives of their employees. She also refers to the beliefs ("myths" in her words) related to cultural prescriptions about the distribution of different cleaning tasks between distinct caste groups, as is still practised in India today. Raka Ray and Seemin Qayum (2009) explain this, speaking of a 'culture of servitude' that characterizes India, where a demeaning representation of domestic workers as 'others within', separated from the rest of society, results from their association with stigmatized bodily functions and care needs.

It is important to note how domestic workers' rights activists across a wide spectrum of contexts try to reach out to women employers on the basis of 'sisterhood'. However, employers' response to sisterhood is often limited to denouncing cases of extreme and obvious physical or sexual abuse of domestic workers, rather than embracing the struggle for domestic workers' rights. This is made clear in the words of Geeta Menon, activist from the Domestic Workers Rights Union in Bangalore, who also belongs to the feminist organization Stree Jagruti Samiti:

> 'The strategies to organise residential or live-in domestic workers have evolved by trial and error. These workers are the most difficult to organise and getting information about their numbers or contacting them is sometimes impossible ... Attempts have also been made to create a forum with employers, who have shown more concern as of late for what domestic workers suffer. The sisterhood solidarity is evident in cases of domestic violence, or when neighbours ill-treat workers. But when it comes to workplace issues like wages, leave, etc., they mostly remain silent.'
> (Menon, 2017: 114)

In spite of the limits stressed by Geeta Menon ('they mostly remain silent'), the number of actions directly aimed at encouraging individual employers to act as 'good employers' has increased in many of the countries under study during the decade in question. This is the case for two ongoing global campaigns initiated in 2015, 'My Fair Home',[9] organized by the IDWF and ILO, and 'Decent Work for Domestic Workers Rights Begin at Home'[10] organized by the ILO and its employees. While arguments that aim to create alliances with employers may sound contradictory from a labour perspective, they may be better read as attempts to engage with the complexity of the positioning of domestic workers as women, and more specifically as women who perform a particular kind of labour for their female employers – namely, domestic work. In fact, these cross-class initiatives, often relying on the voluntary participation of employers, have long been part of the history of the domestic workers' rights movement (Boris and Nadasen, 2008; Agarwala and Saha, 2018).

Taken together, all these different uses of the feminist discursive frame valorizing reproductive labour demonstrate the variety of ways in which activists recurrently speak of the rights of paid domestic workers with a broader perspective in mind, focused on the unequal distribution of reproductive labour and the lack of value afforded to it – both paid and unpaid. Importantly, activists complicate the exclusively gender-oriented analytical framework that some feminist arguments tend to reproduce.

By forcibly extending the classic framework of gendered inequality to the field of domestic work, and by putting the experience of (poorly) paid domestic work in particular at the centre of their analysis, domestic workers' rights activists provide a broader view on the unequal distribution of reproductive labour.

The transnational commodification of care

Feminist critiques of the transnational commodification of care and the exploitation of migrant domestic workers have become particularly relevant following the economic crisis of 2008 (Sarti, 2007; Boris and Parreñas, 2010; Triandafyllidou, 2013; Romero, 2018). This is partly due to their simultaneous connection to what Joan Tronto (2013) identifies as two kinds of deficit: a deficit in democracy and a deficit in care. These analyses represent another related, but distinctive, feminist framework that we saw being utilized to promote domestic workers' rights in Italy, Spain, Germany and Taiwan in particular. Our interviewees in these countries – international destinations for nannies and caregivers to the elderly – emphasized the importance of promoting domestic workers' rights in terms of the expansion of care needs, and the absence of state support for women entering the labour market. In the perception of our interviewees, the need to import foreign workers into this sector was linked to the crisis of care and the failure of welfare systems to support their ageing societies (Cangiano and Walsh, 2014; Shire, 2015; Williams, 2018). Activist discourses around domestic workers' rights were therefore determined in part by macro-level trends in global mobility and migration.

It is worth pointing out that a number of the actors who have emerged in the field of domestic workers' rights in these contexts between 2008 and 2018 represent the needs of care receivers and employers. Their discursive frames also partly tap into the arguments in favour of the commodification of care. Such is the case for the EFFE, created in 2013 and bringing together thinkers and experts from the sector, as well as some domestic workers' unions and employers' unions from various European countries. Its *Manifesto for the Recognition of Household Services, Family Employment and Home Care in Europe*, published to coincide with the 2019 European elections, declares:

> The current crisis challenges the European social and economic model at its core. The crisis highlights the silent disruptions that have occurred in Europe over the past few decades, and reveals the weaknesses in our social model. ... In the face of these challenges, ... EFFE is proposing a social innovation model for the benefit of all fellow European citizens and becoming a key political negotiator

for public authorities and European, national and local institutions. It focuses on household services, family employment and home care. At the crossroads of European economic and social issues, this economic sector represents an exceptional growth potential, as well as a key development opportunity for the economic, social and solidarity-based European society we are calling for.[11]

In its campaign, EFFE reclaims the family-based model of care as a progressive alternative designed to include migrants. Indeed, in the context of nations with ageing populations in which migrants now represent the large majority of the workforce responsible for domestic work, major trends in global mobility and migration are impacting on the way activists talk about domestic workers' rights. As they frame their struggle within larger social issues, using critical tools of feminist analysis, our interviewees show an original capacity to expand feminist critiques of the commodification of care by putting the lack of rights afforded to migrant domestic workers at their centre.

Such a critical interpretation of the commodification of care will not in itself necessarily imply a link to the recognition of migrants' rights. In fact, feminist analyses of the commodification of care, even when they include the rights of domestic workers, do not necessarily make explicit the issue of citizenship rights. This is exemplified by the case of the Peng Wa Ru Foundation in Taiwan, a women's rights organization promoting good jobs and professional opportunities for unemployed women through paid domestic work. According to some of our interviewees, the foundation, which adopted a feminist perspective on the commodification of care in trying to recuperate non-market-driven care practices, mainly addresses Taiwanese caregivers and seems to favour a national workforce over foreigners.

With this background in mind, it is revealing to reproduce here a section of the interview with Su-Xiang Chen, member of TIWA, an organization founded by labour organizers in 1999, and which was a key player in the promotion of domestic workers' and other migrants' rights in Taiwan. It is worth noting how she connects the issue of migrants' rights to that of the commodification of (long-term) care, and even goes so far as to say that this process is the main reason that the exploitation of migrant domestic workers is able to persist.

Q: Do you think the labour conditions of foreign workers will be affected by the labour conditions of local workers?

A: That may be true only for the factory workers. Not for the foreign domestic workers. The labour conditions of foreign domestic workers are not related to any other kinds of workers. But their labour conditions are related to the family structure in Taiwan. If their wages rise or they have one day a week off, the cost also rises. As I said, the families who use foreign domestic workers are not all rich families, some of them struggle to make a living.

Q: So, you think the point of their labour conditions is not the lack of labour rights?

A: No. The point is the long-term care policy.
(Su-Xiang Chen, TIWA, Taiwan)

Shifting our focus to Germany, Bianca Kühl, who identifies as a feminist, is a trade unionist at the DGB (German Trade Union Confederation), a large umbrella organization of trade unions. She shares a frequent cause of concern with us:

'Regarding the question of elder care, it's basically inhumane. Nobody can be there for somebody else 24 hours, stand-by time at night, no. It is a system which is not working. But it is so normal in Germany that granny shouldn't go to a care facility, she needs to stay at home, but we cannot handle the situation either, so we get Eastern European women who leave their families behind. This cannot be the goal.' (Bianca Kühl, DGB-Berlin, Germany)

The 'inhumane' conditions to which migrant domestic workers are exposed are seen as a part of the wider phenomenon of the exploitation of commodified care. This is now being exacerbated by the collapse of public welfare provision, a tension that is particularly acute in countries with a large ageing population, like Germany.

Luciana Mastrocola is a trade unionist at Filcams-CGIL, a section of the one of the largest national trade unions in Italy that represents workers in the service, commerce and tourism sectors. She presents another account of state institutions failing to fulfil their responsibilities to workers by leaving individual households to resolve the crisis in care work by themselves, thereby obliging them to privately employ caregivers. In her view, this does not divest the state of its responsibility to protect these migrant workers:

'Families are handling something [care for the ageing] of which the state should be in charge. The fact that this care is delegated to another person [the migrant worker] has allowed the state to avoid taking responsibility for that, to acknowledge something like "I should be the one in charge".' (Luciana Mastrocola, Filcams-CGIL, Italy)

For many interviewees in ageing societies such as Taiwan, Italy, Germany and Spain, employing a caregiver was seen as a necessity by a whole range of households, including those with lower incomes, in order to face the care work needs of their elderly and disabled members. In other words, they counterposed the possible exploitation of migrant workers lacking rights to the vulnerability of their own families and the dearth of support from the state. This was the case for an activist from a disability rights' organization in Taiwan, Yu-Ji Liu, who had also been engaging in the issue of domestic workers' rights in dialogue with TIWA. He emphasized the very high level of conflict between the families of people with disabilities and migrant domestic workers:

> 'Take my family as an example, it seems the wage of our foreign domestic worker is not so good. But it still costs us NTD20,000 a month. Raising their salary will be difficult for us, because first of all, hiring foreign domestic workers cannot get tax credits, second, there is no other subsidy from the government, only a living allowance, around NTD4,000 dollars a month. It's not enough. I think the government makes us [those with disabilities and foreign domestic workers] kill each other.' (Yu-Ji Liu, Taiwan Association for Disability Rights, Taiwan)

A similar tension is described by Ana Carolina Espinoza, herself a migrant domestic worker based in Madrid, Spain. As a representative of the domestic workers' union SEDOAC, she insists on the following in relation to migration policies:

> 'We must recognise the double standard of the economy of developed countries and of migration politics above all. Because, on the one hand, they want to put a stop [to it] so that not all migrants can enter, [so] that not all foreigners can enter, but on the other hand, they let some of them enter in order to exploit them and it takes years before giving them rights.' (Ana Carolina Elías Espinoza, SEDOAC, Spain)

Ana Carolina's words echo Bridget Anderson (2014) when saying that the contrast between a societal deficit of care and nationalist tendencies to suppress the arrival of new migrants highlights the hypocrisy of states that attempt to overcome the crisis in care work by relying on a migrant workforce that is denied its full rights. Here we see the intricate connection between discourses around migrants' rights and discourses involving the criticism of gender inequalities in the organization of care work. Novel articulations of these analyses necessitate a new awareness of care work's significance beyond merely instrumental perceptions of its value as a potential 'solution' to the crisis, calling for a more general overturning of gender- and race-based inequalities within society. In fact, it is on the terrain of struggles over migration policy that most claims for migrant domestic workers' rights are now being played out. In Italy, Germany, Spain and Taiwan in particular, domestic workers' organizations are campaigning for the liberalization of migration permits, the regularization of undocumented migrants involved in domestic work and additional rights – guaranteed independently of the will of their employers – in support of their residency status (Lutz and Palenga-Möllenbeck, 2012; Kontos, 2013; Anderson, 2015).

Here we see a new awareness of migrants' rights, as an issue of central importance to the global crisis of care work, being developed through a strategic renegotiation of feminist discursive frames. Knowledge about the experiences of migrant women being exploited in the global care market is expanded, while simultaneously recognizing limitations to classic critiques of the commodification of care. By extending pre-existing feminist arguments on this dynamic, our interviewees seem to have adopted an analytic framework that successfully focuses on the exploitation of migrant domestic workers by showing how these migrants pay the price for the devolution of welfare in the Global North, and its attendant lack of social provision for care work.

6

Conclusion: Intersectionality in Action

Domestic workers globally, and in particular in the nine countries considered in this book, still experience high levels of exploitation, discrimination and exclusion from labour rights and legal protections, as compared to other workers. They also suffer forms of social stigmatization due to widespread representations of domestic work as a demeaning and 'dirty' activity, while their work fails to be recognized as such in society at large for its association with women's allegedly naturally caring and altruistic disposition. Moreover, domestic work is largely performed by people, mostly women, who belong to the most vulnerable social groups in each context, such as internal and international migrants, ethnic-minority and racialized women and low-caste and poorly educated women.

However, domestic work has become an object of governance, conflict and negotiation involving several actors. Despite being traditionally seen as 'unorganizable', domestic workers have been increasingly engaged in collective organizing via unions and other mutual aid groups. This self-organization has succeeded in heightening their visibility and garnering the attention of NGOs and other movements. This transformation accelerated in the years 2008–18, the period corresponding to what we have called the 'C189 process'.

The struggles for domestic workers' rights during this period can be interrogated with regard to how transformations of intersectional inequalities occur in a global context. By exploring these questions the present book has identified central themes that emerge not only in relation to domestic workers but also potentially for other multiply marginalized groups worldwide.

The relationship between global rights and local struggles

The first theme considered the apparent incommensurability between what can be identified as a global right and local practices. A global right may or may not be embraced at the level of local struggles. Domestic workers' rights represent a good case in this sense, for the C189 process represents what Fligstein and McAdams (2012) call an external shock to the strategic field of action of domestic workers' rights, impacting the field at the national level in different ways depending on local contextual factors.

Rather than assessing the C189 process in terms of success or failure, we have instead explored the variations of the C189 process which national adoption gave rise to. We have therefore looked at the main actors, their goals and the interpretative frames they used. These elements supported our interpretation of the way in which the C189 process is practically reflected in each country's struggle, in relation to the wider socioeconomic, political and cultural elements of each national context. Thus, we have clustered our nine countries according to four types of impact. It is hoped that this classification may aid in understanding similar cases of the relationship between global rights and local struggles.

1. Ecuador and the Philippines showed a strong synergy between the ILO, national governments and civil society actors, including domestic workers' groups. The state was quick to ratify C189, and legislative measures were adopted on the basis of its requirements. Domestic workers' organizing was promoted. Other civil society actors were also responsive to the ILO campaign and, as a result, the campaign has exceeded institutional confines. C189 has therefore encountered a suitable cultural and political environment at the local level.
2. In Colombia and Brazil we found the combination of a vibrant dynamism at the level of civil society with the involvement of the state and other institutional actors. The C189 process was embedded in a wider process of transformation taking place within the country, involving domestic workers as one of the key target groups, although not exclusively. Demands by domestic workers' groups explicitly went beyond C189 as such, advocating for more radical changes to the conditions of domestic workers at the legislative, social and economic levels. Although C189 was the exogenous change that gave a boost to this field of struggle, an awareness of the legacy of past experiences is vital to understanding developments in these contexts, since domestic workers' organizations were already a reality in these countries, alongside a long-standing tradition of workers' struggles, Black liberation movements and women's movements.

3. In Taiwan, India and Spain there was a high degree of involvement of domestic workers' organizations, civil society groups more generally and the ILO (with the exception of Taiwan in the last case). Yet this cannot compensate for the lack of government support. Domestic workers' rights were opposed not only by employers' interests but also by the conservative parties dominating Parliament and opposing egalitarian reforms, as well as by brokers who acted as market intermediaries and whose private interests were favoured by the status quo. Indeed, domestic workers were perceived as minority subjects (lower-caste and 'tribal' people in India, and migrants and undocumented people in Taiwan and Spain) whose interests were seen as being at odds with those of society as a whole.

4. In Italy and Germany we observed an impasse in the accomplishment of the C189 process and the full promotion of domestic workers' rights, partly due to a contradiction between a formal adherence by the state to C189 and the lack of a real implementation of C189 principles. These countries did ratify C189, since they believed their national legislation to already be in line with C189 requirements. However, the ratification of C189 ought to have been followed by corresponding policy measures for a full implementation of the C189 principles, which was not the case. Moreover, social movements tend not to mobilize around the issue of domestic workers' rights in these locations, which is largely seen as a problem concerning (often undocumented) foreign workers, and therefore beyond the concern of the majority of society.

Domestic workers' rights are fought for and developed in different ways at the local level, all of which ultimately inform the C189 process. Among them, we have emphasized that the effectiveness of the C189 process seems to have been greater in countries where improving the conditions of domestic workers is seen as emblematic of social justice struggles in the country as a whole. Conversely, we found that in countries where domestic workers were easily associated with 'others' from foreign countries the campaign remained isolated and issue specific, and it was difficult for activists to build a large consensus beyond direct stakeholders on domestic workers' issues. Giving more rights to this category of workers has not been intended as a challenge to the structural inequalities in society of which the exploitation of domestic workers is part and parcel.

Making change happen from an intersectional perspective

The second theme we have explored is the way in which groups that organize based on multiply marginalized social positions may make intersectional change; or, in other words, how intersectional politics may actually be practised on the ground. In the case of domestic workers, this book has shown how, through their efforts to politicize their conditions, activists from these movements selectively attribute different political salience and meaning to gender, class, race, caste, migration status and so on. This varies not only between different national contexts or between different domestic workers' organizations, but also within the same organization in relation to distinct aspects of its activity, and over time. In particular we found that separating the different elements of groups' intersectional politics – such as the process of identity making, demands and activities – allows for a deeper exploration of intersectionality as enacted by organizations composed of multiply marginalized people. In particular, it ensures that one avoids the trap of assuming that there should be a coherence between intersectionality in terms of identity making, the formulation of demands and the ways activities are carried out.

We also discussed the general reluctance by domestic workers to engage in mobilizations that concentrate solely on issues of class, race or gender, or with approaches that tend to subsume their struggles for rights and dignity under the 'universal' interests of women, migrants, working-class or racialized people. Reacting to these marginalizing structures, activists have set up autonomous groups around the identity of 'organized domestic workers'. Notably, we have shown how this collective identity emerges as an outcome of such organizing processes, rather than being a well-defined, pre-existing identity which automatically reflected the gender, class, ethnic and racial composition of the sector. In fact, different organizations attribute distinct political salience to the social categories shaping domestic workers' subordinate positions, and may understand the relations between these categories differently. This demonstrates a creative process of politicization in which the intersecting systems of oppression affecting domestic workers in each local context are differently identified and named by the activists.

To illustrate this process, we have discussed examples from Brazil, Colombia and Ecuador. Brazilian activists – in particular from the national federation FENATRAD – mobilized two kinds of rhetorical devices: firstly, the analogy between today's racism and exploitation of Black domestic workers, and that which pervaded under slavery; secondly, they established an ideal relation with the legacy of the anti-racist movement in the country. In so doing they have been able to develop a novel identity while simultaneously mobilizing the genealogy of Brazilian movements against the oppression of women and Black people. In Colombia we found that the Afro-Colombian domestic workers' union UTRASD promoted an intersectional discursive repertoire in which domestic work is understood as at once a gendered, class-based and racialized activity. The specific experiences of Afro-Colombian women, especially internal migrants and refugees, are central to UTRASD's self-definition as 'the first ethnically-based domestic workers' union in the country'. Ecuador reveals yet another configuration, with race-based discrimination recognized as an additional burden, but not as an intrinsic feature of the social organization of domestic work and of the collective identity promoted by the movement. In particular, the activists of the domestic workers' association ATRH appear to see the category of 'organized Ecuadorian domestic workers' as shaped primarily by the interplay of gender and class inequalities.

If these can be seen as the challenges to the 'making of intersectionality' at the level of identity construction, a different scenario emerges when considering the demands and actions of these groups, which can be summarized in the following instances. Firstly, we have looked at awareness-raising activities promoting the slogan 'domestic work is work' and demanding improvements to the legal framework, in particular concerning labour laws, but also radical socioeconomic changes which may improve the conditions of domestic workers more generally. These campaigns sought recognition and equal rights for domestic workers: the same demands which are central to the discourses on 'decent' work used by the ILO and the other international organizations involved in the global governance of domestic work.

Secondly, we have highlighted key interventions concerning the use of language both in public discourse and in everyday interactions. Indeed, most of the organizations we studied have engaged in debates over adequate terminology to address domestic workers. Refusing the demeaning terms commonly used in their local languages, they have sought legitimacy for the new identity created by the movement, that is, that of workers performing a valuable job in society. This challenges the representations of domestic work as 'intimate' yet 'dirty', which are often internalized by the workers themselves. Even in the cases in which the family remains central to semantic innovations, such as in the Philippines with the term *kasambahay* (companion of the house) and in Italy with *colf* (collaborator in the family), these new terms challenge the ambivalence of their position within their employers' families.

Finally, we have looked at the capacity of domestic workers' groups to carry out empowering activities for their members and for domestic workers as a whole. We have shown how many organizations, besides providing legal support, information regarding contracts and working conditions, and access to professional training, also provide schooling and literacy programmes, education against gender-based violence and for women's health and well-being. Further, some deliver political and leadership training designed to strengthen knowledge and build capacities that are key to active participation in the public and political sphere, such as collective bargaining strategies or public speaking skills. Others aim to improve the economic conditions and bargaining power of their members by creating savings cooperatives or workers' cooperatives. Depending on the circumstances and opportunities in the field, a number of these activities and programmes were created and delivered autonomously from below, while others emerged in collaboration with allies, both non-profit organizations and public institutions. We have shown how these organizations also function as solidarity and mutual support groups that support domestic workers both in their labour relations and in other aspects of their lives.

To summarize, our research has revealed unique forms of labour and women's organizing, where the struggle for labour rights goes hand in hand with cultural politics. In other words, the function of these groups transcends a mono-dimensional struggle for labour rights and expands their focus to include broader issues related to women's experiences, self-esteem and identity, including migration, anti-racism, access to education, political participation, economic autonomy, health, sexuality and personal and family well-being.

The role of feminist and women's rights activists

The third theme we have explored is that of the role that feminist and women's rights organizations can play in the struggles for the rights of multiply marginalized women. What we found was that these organizations were generally perceived by domestic workers' activists as distant, although not in opposition to their cause. We found a few exceptions to this, among feminist organizations explicitly committed to domestic workers' rights, notably in India, Brazil, Spain and Taiwan. These differences may be explained by context-specific characteristics, especially in relation to the particular history of the feminist movement in each setting. At the same time, we found a number of feminists and women's rights activists who promoted domestic workers' issues on an individual basis, in particular as lawyers, NGO activists or politicians, and managed to play a key role in Colombia, Ecuador and the Philippines in particular.

In spite of this marginal involvement at the practical level, we discovered that, at the level of discourse, feminist argumentations are present in this field, with activists for domestic workers' rights incorporating the classic repertoire of feminist critiques into their own narratives. In particular, activists recurrently spoke of the rights of paid domestic workers within broader feminist and anti-capitalist critiques of inequality and exploitation of women's work. First, we considered the feminist notion of the valorization of reproductive labour. This was often invoked by domestic workers' rights advocates when they spoke of their desire to see their compatriots recognize the value of their work, starting with appreciating the reproductive labour done by women inside their homes and within their families. In other words, as they seek the recognition of 'domestic work as work' they not only demand the right to have contracts, better salaries and labour protection but also challenge the devaluation of tasks connected to caregiving and housekeeping more generally. However, they also modify and expand this traditional feminist argument, originally developed around unpaid labour, to include the case of paid workers and their experiences of discrimination and exploitation as women who are simultaneously lower class and from ethnic, racialized and caste minorities. This framing is predominantly used in Brazil, Ecuador, Colombia, India and the Philippines, where domestic workers are mostly citizens from disadvantaged social groups employed by privileged women.

Indeed, many of these arguments developed around domestic workers' rights show a tension between two goals. The first is the need to stress the commonalities between women in their responsibility for the sphere of reproductive work, in order to promote the issue of domestic workers' labour rights within a general demand to change the understanding of reproductive labour. The second is to simultaneously visibilize the elements of difference and conflict between women, in order to emphasize the exploitation of domestic workers by their female employers. Interestingly, domestic workers' rights activists across a large number of contexts try to reach out to women employers on the basis of 'sisterhood'. However, in response, the sisterhood is often limited to denouncing cases of overt and extreme abuse, including the sexual abuse of domestic workers, rather than embracing the struggle for domestic workers' rights.

In countries where, by contrast, the majority of domestic workers are migrant caregivers for the elderly, we have observed a more frequent use of another feminist frame relating to the commodification of care, which in turn connects to feminist critiques of welfare and the care crisis. In countries such as Italy, Spain, Germany and Taiwan, the way activists spoke about domestic workers' rights was affected by major trends in global mobility and migration. It is worth pointing out that in these contexts some of the actors that have emerged in the field of domestic workers' rights, particularly between 2008 and 2018, are those representing care receivers and employers, and their frames also at least partly tap into the argument on the commodification of care. Class differences in these contexts are indeed complicated by the fact that employers occupy a wide range of social positions. These include those with lower incomes, since hiring a home-based caregiver is often the only option, given the lack of state support for the elderly, chronically ill and disabled. In this context, domestic worker activists tend to expand feminist arguments on care and welfare issues by centring the experience of migrants and arguing that they bear the burden of the scarcity of social provision in the Global North.

It is important to highlight how, in these different applications of feminist frames, domestic worker activists transform and enrich these arguments by adding an intersectional dimension. Indeed, they enlarge the capacity of these perspectives to also include racialized, lower-class, migrant and other minority groups in ways which few feminist movements have achieved. In fact, domestic worker activists tend to expand the scope of the interpretative frames they draw upon – whether these are originally tied to labour, migration, gender or caste – and blur the limits that are traditionally established between them. We have discussed this capacity as a creative force in the domestic workers' movement which may facilitate the building of alliances with other groups for domestic workers' sake, while expanding the scope of contemporary feminisms.

Beyond domestic workers

The results of our research invite us to look beyond domestic workers' struggles and explore the implications they may have for research on other multiply marginalized groups organizing to demand more rights and recognition. In line with previous feminist scholarship on intersectionality and social movements discussed at length in this book, we have argued against the tendency to think of social struggles through a categorical perspective, namely by separating women's movements from those based on class or anti-racism. To this end, we have discussed the struggles of groups whose experiences of discrimination and paths towards recognition would be difficult to describe on the basis of any of these categories alone. In other words, as their experience of oppression is multidimensional, so too is their struggle to end it. We have also shown that there isn't a singular way to pursue this path, since the configuration of such dimensions changes from place to place and from time to time.

What are some of the broader implications of these findings for research practice in relation to other multiply marginalized groups and their struggles? Firstly, it is important to always remain open to new interpretations of the complex realities in which these groups live. This may require the development of a deeper understanding of the interconnections between categories of identity, or the identification of new categories which emerge in different situations. This may or may not parallel configurations found in other times and places.

Secondly, it means exploring the ways in which the realities of multiply marginalized groups are reflected in the organizations aiming to represent them. What is the composition of these organizations? What are their demands? What are their activities and actions? What is their agenda? In addressing these questions, it is important to ask whether some elements of complexity have been lost. One may consider their political activities – both day to day and in the long term – through intersectional lenses. Furthermore, since these organizations are internally heterogeneous, it is important to consider whether the struggle leaves some of their members behind or renders them invisible. This invisibility might be the consequence of a strategic decision to pursue a political goal, or it could be an unintended effect. Indeed, we should not make assumptions about the capacity of organizations to adequately represent the multiply marginalized identities of their members at every level of their political projects.

We also need to be aware of the difficulty these groups may have in making alliances with other kinds of organizations, including feminist, labour and anti-racist movements, all of which tend to focus on single-issue struggles. The relationships with these other organizations can be frustrating, as they may need to compromise with other organizations' tendencies towards essentialist approaches, hierarchy and simplified views on the complexity of their multiply marginalized realities. Researching organizing cultures among multiply marginalized groups can be helpful in identifying spaces for dialogue and collaboration with other single-issue organizations and in developing a better understanding of how they may work together towards a shared political view. The intersectionality of oppressions which affects the lives of multiply marginalized groups can indeed turn from being an insurmountable burden into being one of the most powerful tools they have towards liberation, both for themselves and for their allies.

Appendix: List of Interview Participants

Names and affiliations of interviewees at the time of the interview. The date of the interview is indicated in parentheses.

Brazil

Mário Avelino, Doméstica Legal (27 March 2018)

Maria Betânia Ávila, SOS Corpo Feminist Institute for Democracy (10 August 2017)

Alexandre Barbosa Fraga, Federal University of Rio de Janeiro (6 June 2017)

Jefferson Belarmino de Freitas, State University of Rio de Janeiro (8 March 2018)

Joaze Bernadino-Costa, University of Brasilia (6 July 2017)

Myllena Calasans de Matos, FENATRAD National Federation of Domestic Workers (1 August 2017)

Nair Jane de Castro Lima, Domestic Workers' Trade Union of Nova Iguaçu Rio de Janeiro (11 September 2017)

Creuza Maria de Oliveira, FENATRAD National Federation of Domestic Workers and Domestic Workers' Trade Union of Bahia (2 August 2017)

Ana Gilda dos Santos, ACIERJ Association of Elderly Caregivers of the State of Rio de Janeiro (28 August 2017)

Carli Maria dos Santos, Domestic Workers' Trade Union of Rio de Janeiro (14 September 2017)

Maria Noeli dos Santos, FENATRAD National Federation of Domestic Workers and Domestic Workers' Trade Union of Rio de Janeiro (29 June 2017)

Jurema Gorski Brites, Federal University of Santa Maria (29 June 2017)

Rachel Gouveia Passos, Federal Rural University of Rio de Janeiro (30 March 2018)

Graziela Moraes Silva, Federal University of Rio de Janeiro (19 March 2018)

Laura Murray, Coletivo Davida and Federal University of Rio de Janeiro (3 March 2018)

Hildete Pereira de Melo, Federal University of Fluminense (retired) (14 July 2017)

Felicia Picanço, Federal University of Rio de Janeiro (17 August 2017)

Valeria Ribeiro Corossacz, University of Modena and Reggio Emilia (4 September 2017)

Jana Silverman, Solidarity Center of São Paulo (12 September 2017)

Bila Sorj, Federal University of Rio de Janeiro (24 July 2017)

Antônio Teixeira, Institute of Economic and Applied Research IPEA (23 October 2017)

Roberto Véras de Oliveira, Federal University of Paraíba (10 November 2017)

Lúcia Maria Xavier, Criola (10 November 2017)

Livia Zanatta, Themis Gender, Justice and Human Rights (29 March 2018)

Colombia

Ligia Inés Alzate, CUT Colombian Workers' Central Trade Union (31 October 2017)

Luz Gabriela Arango Gaviria, National University of Colombia (14 June 2017)

Ana Isabel Arenas Saavedra, National Committee for the Care Economy (15 March 2018)

María Teresa Aristizábal, Ruta Pacífica de las Mujeres (15 March 2018)

María Aideé Cárdenas, UTRAHOGAR Domestic Workers' Trade Union of Santiago de Cali (26 April 2018)

Yenni Hurtado, SINTRASEDOM Domestic Workers' National Trade Union (11 November 2017)

Magdalena León, National University of Colombia (retired) (14 September 2017)

Andrea Londoño, Bien Humano Foundation, Hablemos de Empleadas Domèsticas and National Committee for the Care Economy (25 July 2017 and 15 March 2018)

Pascale Molinier, University of Paris XIII (30 August 2017)

Sandra Milena Muñoz, Colombian National Trade Union School ENS and CARE International (25 July 2017 and 9 March 2018)

Viviana Osorio, CARE International (15 September 2017)

Claribed Palacios García, UTRASD Afro-Colombian Domestic Workers' Trade Union (24 and 25 July 2017)

Laura Penagos, EAFIT University (16 September 2017)

Ramón Emilio Perea, Carabantú Association for Afro-Colombian Social and Cultural Development (4 August 2018)

Javier Pineda, Andes University (18 September 2017)

Jeanny Posso, University del Valle (8 August 2017)

María Roa Borja, UTRASD Afro-Colombian Domestic Workers' Trade Union (25 July 2017)

Ángela María Robledo, Green Party (23 August 2017)

Fidelia Suarez, Sindacato de Trabajadoras Sexuales de Colombia SINTRASEXCO (20 October 2018)

Ana Teresa Vélez Orrego, ENS Colombian National Trade Union School (25 July 2017)

Bertha Yolanda Villamizar Jaimes, SINTRAIMAGRA Domestic workers' Chapter of the National Union of Food Workers (19 August 2017)

Mara Viveros Vigoya, National University of Colombia (9 March 2018)

Ecuador

Lourdes Albán, ATRH Domestic Workers' Association (2 August 2017)

Ivonne Amores, Secretaría Nacional de la Gestión de la Política (31 October 2017)

Diana Barrezueta, Independent scholar (17 October 2017)

Bladimir Chicaiza, ILO International Labour Organization Peru and Ecuador (8 August 2017)

Judith Flores, Asamblea de Mujeres Populares y Diversas (27 February 2018)

Gina Godoy, Alianza País Party (18 October 2017)

Gioconda Herrera, FLACSO Ecuador (16 February 2018)

Pablo Lastra, Secretaría Nacional de la Gestión de la Política (31 October 2017)

Katy Betancourt Machoa, CONAIE Confederación de Nacionalidades Indígenas del Ecuador (25 October 2017)

Magali Marega, FOS Socialist Solidarity (8 March 2017)

Erynn Masi de Casanova, University of Cincinnati (9 June 2017)

Clara Merino, Luna Creciente (16 August 2017)

Karla Moncayo, Independent legal expert (13 October 2017)

Miriam Moya, CARE International (14 June 2017)

María Alexandra Ocles Padilla, Alianza País Party (21 February 2018)

Santiago Ortiz, FLACSO Ecuador (23 October 2017)

Lenny Quiroz, UNTHYA National Union of Domestic Workers and Allies (17 October 2017)

Franklyn Ramirez, FLACSO Ecuador (14 March 2018)

Maximina Salazar Peñafiel, ATRH Domestic Workers' Association (8 September 2017)

Cristina Vega Solís, FLACSO Ecuador (30 June 2017)

Cristina Vera, FLACSO Ecuador (8 September 2017)

Byron Vernaza, JOCI International Young Christian Workers (24 October 2017)

Jo Vervecken, FOS Socialist Solidarity (13 June 2017)

Antonio Zena, JOCI International Young Christian Workers (24 October 2017)

Germany

Sigrid Arnade, ISL Interessenvertretung Selbstbestimmt Leben in Deutschland (15 March 2017)

Isabel Arnedo, Caritas Hamburg (15 September 2017)

Marta Böning, DGB German Trade Union Confederation (10 June 2017)

Elisabeth Bothfeld, NGG Union of Food Processing and Catering Workers (retired) (23 August 2017)

Johannes Flothow, Diakonisches Werk Württemberg (14 September 2017)

Karin Gottschall, University of Bremen (28 August 2017)

Eva Kocher, European University of Viadrina (8 April 2017)

Bianca Kühl, DGB German Trade Union Confederation (11 September 2017)

Uta Meier-Gräwe, University of Gießen (21 August 2017)

Barbara Miranda Caro, Oficina Precaria Berlín (30 October 2017)

Gisela Notz, Independent scholar (1 November 2017)

Mónica Orjeda, Verikom Hamburg (15 August 2017)

Karin Pape, WIEGO Women in Informal Employment: Globalizing and Organizing, and IDWF International Domestic Workers Federation (26 September 2017)

Representative, Union of Food Processing and Catering Workers NGG (8 August 2017)

Maria S. Rerrich, University of Munich (retired) (10 November 2017)

Helen Schwenken, University of Osnabrück (16 June 2017)

Magret Steffen, Ver.di United Services Trade Union (26 June 2017)

Sylwia Timm, DGB German Trade Union Confederation (14 July 2017)

Sebastian Walter, University of Kassel (19 June 2017)

Yevgenia Wirz, Technical University Munich and University of Frankfurt (6 November 2017)

Mareike Witkowski, University of Oldenburg (23 June 2017)

India

Swapna M. Banerjee, CUNY (12 June 2019)

Mewa Bharati, Rajasthan Mahila Kamgar Union (21 August 2018)

Basu Dev Burman, Tata Institute of Social Sciences (31 July 2017)

Suneetha Eluri, ILO International Labour Organization India (31 July 2017)

Anchita Ghatak, Parichiti A Society for Empowerment of Women (13 June 2017)

Aditi Gupta, Human Rights and Law Network (4 August 2018)

Netha Hui, University of Reading (18 June 2017)

Jonita (sister), Adivasi Jivantika Sangstha (27 March 2018)

Lissy Joseph (sister), NDWM National Domestic Workers' Movement (30 April 2018)

Ramendra Kumar, Delhi Gharelu Kamgar Sangathan (8 July 2018)

Geeta Menon, Stree Jagruti Samiti and Domestic Workers Rights Union (18 July 2017)

Neetha Pillai, Centre for Women's Development Studies (4 August 2017)

Parvati Raghuram, Open University UK (31 May 2019)

Kalai Selvi (sister), NDWM National Domestic Workers' Movement (12 August 2017)

Asha Sharma, AIDWA All India Democratic Women's Association (22 August 2018)

Sonal Sharma, Johns Hopkins University (31 July 2017)

Noli Nivedita Tirkey, Tata Institute of Social Sciences (23 July 2017)

Shobha Tirki, Tata Institute of Social Sciences (28 June 2017)

Neha Wadhawan, Independent scholar (31 July 2017)

Pallavi Xalxo, Tata Institute of Social Sciences (18 July 2017)

Italy

Claudia Alemani, University of Milano-Bicocca (17 July 2017)

Anna Badino, Institute for Advanced Study of Aix-Marseille University (11 November 2017)

Pina Brustolin, ACLI-COLF Associazioni Cristiane Lavoratori Italiani-Collaboratrici Domestiche (retired) (24 October 2017)

Pia Covre, Committee for Civil Rights of Prostitutes (15 November 2017)

Alisa Del Re, University of Padua (retired) (24 August 2017)

Silvia Federici, Hofstra University (retired) (21 September 2017)

Leopoldina Fortunati, University of Udine (13 November 2017)

Anna Frisone, University of Paris I (10 November 2017)

Lorenzo Gasparrini, CAS.SA.COLF and DOMINA National Association of Domestic Workers' Employers' Families (5 April 2018)

Alessandra Gissi, University of Naples L'Orientale (6 September 2017)

Loredana Ligabue, CARER Family Caregivers Emilia-Romagna (4 September 2018)

Daniela Loi, IRS Institute for Social Research (11 April 2018)

Raffaella Maioni, ACLI-COLF Associazioni Cristiane Lavoratori Italiani-Collaboratrici Domestiche (19 June 2017)

Luciana Mastrocola, FILCAMS-CGIL Federazione Italiana dei Lavoratori del Commercio, Alberghi, Mense e Servizi-Confederazione Generale Italiana del Lavoro (6 September 2017)

Michele Peri, ASC InSieme (30 April 2018)

Alessandra Pescarolo, Istituto Regionale Programmazione Economica della Toscana (retired) (17 October 2017)

Antonella Picchio, University of Modena and Reggio-Emilia (retired) (23 March 2018)

Raffaella Sarti, University of Urbino (15 and 19 July 2017)

Olga Turrini, ISFOL Istituto per lo sviluppo della formazione professionale dei lavoratori (retired) (17 July 2017)

Gianfranco Zucca, IREF Istituto di Ricerche Educative e Formative (18 July 2017)

Philippines

Analyn Aguda Marcato, DSWD Department of Social Welfare and Development (6 October 2017)

Ronahlee Asuncion, University of the Philippines (17 August 2017)

Julius Cainglet, FFW Federation of Free Workers (12 July 2017)

Jeanne Marie Calubaquib, ALU Associated Labour Unions (12 July 2017)

Rosalinda Dimapilis-Baldoz, Department of Labor and Employment (retired) (26 October 2017)

Jurgette Honculada, PILIPINA Philippines Women's Movement PILIPINA and NCRFW National Commission on the Role of Filipino Women (retired) (1 July 2017)

Aurora Javate-de Dios, Miriam College (17 August 2017)

Ahmma Charisma Lobrin-Satumba, DOLE Department of Labor and Employment (20 July 2017)

Angelina Ludovice-Katoh, SIM-CARRD Sustainable Integrated Area Development Initiatives in Mindanao-Convergence for Asset Reform and Regional Development (12 November 2017)

Mariquit Melgar, Akbayan Citizens' Action Party (22 June 2017)

Himaya Montenegro, UNITED United Domestic Workers of the Philippines (21 June 2017)

Rene Ofreneo, University of the Philippines (retired) (14 November 2017)

Rosalinda Ofreneo, University of the Philippines (14 November 2017)

Roland Pacis, Visayan Forum Foundation (18 June 2017)

Josephine Parilla, NAPC WISC National Anti-Poverty Commission – Workers in the Informal Sector Council (11 July 2017)

Reynaldo Rasing, LEARN Labour Education and Research Network (7 July 2017)

Djohanna Delia Ravelo, QC-PESO Quezon City Public Employment Service Office (9 October 2017)
Ellene Sana, Center for Migrant Advocacy (26 July 2017)
Rex Varona, Migrant Forum Asia (6 June 2018)

Spain

Mamen Briz Hernández, Colectivo Hetaira (12 March 2018)
Esperanza Camarasa, Cooperative Abierto Hasta el Amanecer and Turin Group (17 August 2017)
Ana María Corral Juan, UGT Workers' General Trade Union (19 October 2017)
Eider de Dios Fernández, University of the Bascque Countries (19 October 2017)
Rocio de Frutos, PSOE Spanish Socialist Workers' Party (17 October 2017)
Magdalena Díaz Gorfinkiel, University Carlos III of Madrid (19 June 2017)
Ana Carolina Elías Espinoza, SEDOAC Servicio Doméstico Activo (19 June 2017)
Celia García, Nosotras Association for migrant domestic workers in Granada (9 October 2017)
Tania García Sedano, Territorio Doméstico and Comillas Pontifical University of Madrid (2 October 2017)
Tania González Peñas, Podemos Party (27 September 2017)
Alberto Guerrero, CC.OO. Workers' Commissions (retired) (8 September 2017)
Laura Guillén Ramón, National Platform of Domestic Workers Associations (30 October 2017)
Ana Haba, USO Unión Sindicalista Obrera (27 September 2017)
Raquel Martínez Buján, University of Coruña (26 July 2017)
Carlota Merchán, PSOE Spanish Socialist Workers' Party (17 October 2017)
Belén Navarro, USO Unión Sindicalista Obrera (27 September 2017)
Joaquín Nieto Sainz, ILO International Labour Organization Spain (17 October 2017)
María Offenhenden, University Rovira i Virgili (27 July 2017)
Amaia Pérez Orozco, Independent scholar and activist (18 October 2017)
Rafaela Pimentel Lara, Territorio Doméstico (26 July 2017)
Isabel (Liz) Quintana, ATH-ELE Biscayan Domestic Workers' Association (26 March 2018)
Ismael Sánchez Jiménez, IUS24 Lawyers cooperative (13 September 2017)
Begoña San José, Feminist Political Forum of Madrid (16 October 2017)
Arantxa Zaguirre Altuna, Territorio Doméstico (21 June 2017)

Taiwan

Cheng Chang, Newspaper 4-Way Voice (5 November 2017)

Chin-Fen Chang, Academia Sinica (9 August 2017)

Chiung-Chih Chen, National Chiao Tung University (4 March 2018)

Jun-Jou Chen, TIWA Taiwan International Workers' Association (20 June 2017)

Su-Xiang Chen, TIWA Taiwan International Workers' Association (19 July 2017)

Zhi-Yue Cheng, National Chengchi University (21 July 2017)

Cing-Kae Chiao, Academia Sinica (18 September 2017)

Lung-Ying Chiu, Legal Aid Foundation (20 September 2017)

Yu-Rung Chyn, Awakening Foundation (15 June 2017)

Guang-Yu Du, SPA Serve the People Association (17 July 2017)

Yi-Bee Huang, Covenants Watch (16 March 2018)

Pei-Yu Kuo, COSWAS Collective of Sex Workers and Supporters (6 April 2018)

Pei-Chia Lan, National Taiwan University (22 September 2017)

Kai-Li Lee, The Garden of Hope Foundation (8 January 2018)

Li-Fang Liang, National Yang-Ming University (14 September 2017)

Yu-Ping Lin, Peng Wan-Ru Foundation (28 June 2017)

Mei-Chun Liu, National Chengchi University (9 August 2017)

Yu-Ji Liu, Taiwan Association for Disability Rights (17 June 2017)

Joy Tajonera (father), Ugnayan Center of Tanzi Catholic Church (9 November 2017)

Chao-Ahing Wang, Peng Wan-Ru Foundation (20 June 2017)

Sherry Macmod Wang, SPA Serve the People Association (11 August 2017)

Si Wang, Taiwan Association for Human Rights (6 September 2017)

Lennon Ying-Dah Wong, SPA Serve the People Association (2 July 2017)

Yi-Ting Xiao, COSWAS Collective of Sex Workers and Supporters (6 April 2018)

Li-Qi Yu, Taiwan Access for All Association (27 February 2018)

Notes

Chapter 1

[1] The first DomEQUAL Venice Symposium 'Global View on Paid Domestic Work', was held on 17 March 2017, and the second, 'The Global Struggle for Domestic Workers' Rights', took place on 15–16 June 2017.

[2] Out of these, 23 occurred in the Global South, and 8 in the Global North (all in Europe). www.ilo.org/dyn/normlex/en/f?p=NORMLEXPUB:11300:0::NO::P113 00_INSTRUMENT_ID:2551460 (last accessed 31 January 2021).

[3] Brazil ratified C189 in 2018, after our fieldwork came to an end.

[4] We held eight local workshops as follows: in Rio de Janeiro and Quito in September 2017, in Bogotà and Hamburg in October 2018, in Rome and Madrid in December 2018 and in Taipei and Quezon City in January 2018.

[5] The documentary is available at https://www.youtube.com/watch?v=FgwSO1hwf0c (last accessed 13 July 2021).

Chapter 2

[1] This is a conservative number based on official national employment statistics, and includes domestic workers aged 15 years and older.

[2] This estimate does not include undocumented migrants. This represents 17.2 per cent of all domestic workers and 7.7 per cent of all migrant workers worldwide. About 74 per cent (or around 8.5 million) of all migrant domestic workers are women (Fudge and Hobden, 2018).

[3] Since 1999, several bills have been filed in the country for a law on informal labour or Magna Carta of Workers in the Informal Economy, which could have a major impact on domestic workers.

[4] In the Philippines, family drivers, who are mostly men, have been excluded from the definition of 'domestic workers' under the Kasambahay Law.

[5] Samahan at Ugnayan ng mga Manggagawang Pantahanan sa Pilipinas.

[6] The recruitment of foreign labourers, first introduced in the country in 1989 to import workers for construction and factories from the Philippines, Vietnam and Thailand, was extended to the private sector and families, and in 1992 care and domestic workers were included in the Employment Service Act. From 1,032 in 1992, the total number of migrant care and domestic workers working in private households reached 246,975 in 2017, representing about a third of the total 657,983 migrant workers employed in Taiwan (source: Ministry of Labour, year 2017).

[7] Caregivers and domestic workers employed by individual households, both migrants and Taiwanese, were explicitly excluded from the Labour Standard Act in 1998, after having

been included in it for some time. The care workers employed by institutions, on the other hand – both nationals and migrants – are covered by the Labour Standard Act.

[8] The TIP Report has been published annually since 2000 by the US State Department's Office to Monitor and Combat Trafficking in Persons. It ranks countries in four groups (Tier 1, Tier 2, Tier 2 Watchlist, Tier 3), starting from those perceived as fully complying to the minimum standard of the US Trafficking Victims Protection Act (2000), down to those perceived as non-compliers.

[9] Kapulungan ng Samahang Pilipino.

[10] Ikatan Pekerja Indonesia di Taiwan.

[11] The names of the migrants' rights rallies organized by TIWA and the Migrants Empowerment Network in Taiwan are quite significant: in 2003: 'Anti-slave'; in 2005: 'Valuing foreign workers' contribution'; in 2007 'I want my day off'; in 2009: 'I want may day off – still not allowed'; in 2011: 'Where is my day off?'; in 2013: 'Say NO to sweatshop long-term care, say YES to minimum wage'; in 2015: 'Where is the justice of care policies?'; in 2017: 'Recognizing Non-Citizens'.

[12] In the field of education, for instance, in 2011 scheduled caste women had a literacy rate of 41.9 per cent, and scheduled tribe women had a literacy rate of 34.8 per cent (versus 65.5 per cent of all women) (source: National Sample Survey, year 2011–12).

[13] 'Scheduled castes', 'scheduled tribes' and 'other backward classes' castes', are officially designated groups in the Indian constitution, which sets out general principles of positive discrimination towards them. The scheduled castes were formerly known as untouchables, and are also referred to as Dalit.

[14] Pesquisa Nacional por Amostra de Domicílios Contínua, Instituto Brasileiro de Geografia e Estatística. The survey also includes irregular domestic workers and distinguishes between monthly (mensalistas) and daily (diaristas) workers.

[15] The remaining part includes domestic workers who self-identified as 'indigenous' (0.35 per cent), 'yellow' (0.2 per cent) and missing values (7.4 per cent)

[16] Pesquisa de Orçamentos Familiares, IBGE.

[17] Proposta de Emenda à Constituição.

[18] Constitutional Amendment 72/2013 and Complementary Law 150/2015.

[19] Law 5859/1972.

[20] Federação Nacional de Trabalhadoras Domésticas, founded in 1997.

[21] Central Única dos Trabalhadores.

[22] On the 19th-century history of the Brazilian domestic workers' movement see, among others: Carvalho, 1999; Bernardino-Costa, 2007, 2013, 2014; Oliveira, 2008; Pinho and Silva, 2010; Fraga, 2016; Monticelli, 2017; Acciari, 2019.

[23] Domestic Workers Professional Association in Santos, Associação de Trabalhadoras Domésticas em Santos.

[24] Juventude Operária Católica.

[25] Full name Themis Gender, Justice and Human Rights, Themis Gênero, Justiça e Direitos Humanos, founded in 1993 in Porto Alegre (Rio Grande do Sul state).

[26] Full name SOS Corpo Feminist Institute for Democracy, SOS Corpo Instituto Feminista para a Democracia, created in 1981 in Recife (Pernambuco state).

[27] Created in 1992 and based in Rio de Janeiro.

[28] Partido dos Trabalhadores.

[29] Gran Encuesta Integrada de Hogares, Departamento Administrativo Nacional de Estadística.

[30] Afro-Colombian and indigenous people, respectively, comprised 10.62 per cent and 2.83 per cent of the total population in 2017 (source: National Institute of Statistics, year 2017).

[31] In Colombia, the socioeconomic position of individuals and households is classified into six *estratos* (levels) on the basis of the conditions of the family home and the surroundings. Strata 1 to 3 comprise people with a very low to medium-low level of resources, while strata 5 and 6 correspond to medium-high and high positions.

[32] Domestic Service Union (Sindicato del Servicio Doméstico) and the Obra de Nazaret, in Bogotá.

[33] Sindicato Nacional de Trabajadoras del Servicio Doméstico, founded in Bogotá in 1977 and formalized in 1985.

[34] Unión de Trabajadoras Remuneradas del Hogar, founded in 1984 in Cali.

[35] Decree 824/1988 and Law 11/1988 (the latter was derogated in 2003).

[36] The first exploratory talks with the FARC-EP were announced by the government in 2012; in November 2016 the congress approved the peace agreement between the Colombian government and the FARC. Although violence, clashes and assassinations have not ceased in the post-accord period, the peace process has continued up until today, involving several civil society and state actors.

[37] Law 1448/2011 (Ley de víctimas y restitución de tierras). The law 975/2005 (Ley de justicia y paz) was a relevant antecedent.

[38] Central Unitaria de Trabajadores de Colombia.

[39] Escuela Nacional Sindical.

[40] Fundación Bien Humano.

[41] Friedrich Ebert Stiftung.

[42] Unión de Trabajadoras Afrocolombianas del Servicio Doméstico.

[43] Sindicato Nacional de Trabajadores de la Industria de Alimentos.

[44] Law 1595/2012. The convention entered into force in 2014.

[45] Decree 2616/2013 expanding access to social security to domestic workers hired 'per day'; Decree 721 giving access to family benefits.

[46] Law 1778/2016.

[47] In 2018 the monthly minimum wage for full-time workers was COP781,242.00 (USD188.07, EUR175.20) plus a monthly transport subsidy of COP88.21. For per-day workers, it is COP26,041.40 daily and COP3,255.18 hourly (ordinary working days and hours), plus transportation assistance.

[48] Encuesta Nacional de Empleo, Desempleo y Subempleo, Instituto Nacional de Estadística y Censos.

[49] Most of the Ecuadorian population self-identify as '*mestizo/a*', meaning of mixed European and indigenous descent; the country has a large Afro-Ecuadorian and indigenous population, mostly concentrated in the coastal region (which includes the city of Guayaquil) and the Sierra area (including the city of Quito), while people identifying as '*montubios/as*' live in the rural areas on the coast. On the racial dynamics in contemporary Ecuador see, among others, De La Torre and Striffler, 2008.

[50] Of the surveyed workers, 62 per cent reported not enjoying any of these benefits; 14 per cent reported that they receive overtime payment, 28 per cent have paid holidays, 29 per cent receive a partial or full 13th- and 14th-month salary. These figures refer to people who are currently employed in the sector, while former workers show lower figures.

[51] Full name: Development Cooperation Fund – Socialist Solidarity, Fonds voor Ontwikkelingssamenwerking.

[52] Asociación de Trabajadoras Remuneradas de Hogar.

[53] Unión Nacional de Trabajadoras del Hogar y Afines.

[54] Sindicato Unitario de Trabajadoras Remuneradas del Hogar de Ecuador.

[55] Mikrozensus, Statistisches Bundesamt.

⁵⁶ The system of 'posting' migrant workers was developed during the transition period of EU enlargement (2003–11), in particular for factory work, but at the same time it was, and remains largely, used in the domestic and care sector to circumvent the limitations on new EU citizens from Eastern Europe working in Germany and other EU countries.

⁵⁷ Gewerkschaft Nahrung Genuss Gaststätten.

⁵⁸ Deutscher Hausfrauenbund, renamed Netzwerk Haushalt, Berufsverband der Haushaltsführenden in 2009.

⁵⁹ Worker Protection Act, *Arbeiterschutzgesetz*, 1996 (last amended in 2015).

⁶⁰ Act on Working Hours, *Arbeitszeitgesetz*, 1994 (last amended in 2016).

⁶¹ Deutscher Gewerkschaftsbund.

⁶² The number of people conventionally considered economically inactive (aged 65 years and over) to the number of people of working age (15–64 years).

⁶³ Istituto Nazionale di Statistica.

⁶⁴ Istituto Nazionale di Previdenza Sociale.

⁶⁵ Corresponding to 3.9 per cent of total workers and 8.1 per cent of female workers.

⁶⁶ Wages and social security quotas are regulated by the national collective agreement and are classified by eight employment levels (according to their housekeeping or care tasks and professional skills). In Italy, wages are regulated through collective agreements for each professional sector, and not through the setting of a minimum wage standard.

⁶⁷ Founded in 1946 within the Catholic workers' organization ACLI (Associazioni Cristiane Lavoratori Italiani) with the name Gruppi Acli Domestiche (GAD); renamed ACLI-COLF (Collaboratrici Familiari) in 1964.

⁶⁸ Associazione Professionale Italiana dei Collaboratori Familiari, born in 1971 after a split from the ACLI-COLF, under the influence of the Italian Episcopal Conference.

⁶⁹ Law 339/1958 Tutele del rapporto di lavoro domestico.

⁷⁰ Constitutional Court decision 68, March–April 1969.

⁷¹ Federazione Italiana dei Lavoratori del Commercio, Alberghi, Mense e Servizi, part of the Confederazione Generale Italiana del Lavoro.

⁷² Confederazione Italiana Sindacati Lavoratori.

⁷³ Unione Italiana del Lavoro.

⁷⁴ Sindacato dei Lavoratori al Servizio della Persona, founded in 1971 and connected to API-COLF.

⁷⁵ Federazione Nazionale del Clero Italiano.

⁷⁶ Associazione Nazionale Datori di Lavoro Domestico (Nuova Collaborazione).

⁷⁷ Associazione Nazionale Sindacale dei Datori di Lavoro Domestico (Assindatcolf).

⁷⁸ Associazione Nazionale Famiglie Datori di Lavoro Domestico (Domina).

⁷⁹ Federazione Italiana Datori di Lavoro Domestico.

⁸⁰ Instituto Nacional de Estadística.

⁸¹ Encuesta de Población Activa.

⁸² Instituto Nacional de la Seguridad Social.

⁸³ Encuesta Nacional de Inmigrantes.

⁸⁴ Encuesta de Presupuestos Familiares.

⁸⁵ For instance, according to the law, the hours a worker is required to be present must be agreed upon by all parties and compensated in money or time, but this often results in arbitrariness. Further, up to 30 per cent of the salary that exceeds the minimum wage can be paid in kind (comprising food and lodging). As a result, wages for live-in workers often barely meet the level of the minimum wage.

⁸⁶ Real Decreto 1424/1985.

⁸⁷ Asociación de Trabajadoras del Hogar de Granada, created in 1996.

88 Asociación de Trabajadoras de Hogar de Bizkaia / Etxeko Langileak Elkartea, founded in 1986 and formally recognized in 1991.

89 Ley Orgánica de Extranjería, 7/1985.

90 Literally, 'Domestic Territory'.

91 Literally 'Active Domestic Service', created in 2008.

92 Sindicato Autónomo de Trabajadoras de Hogar y del Cuidado / Sindicat Independent de Dones Treballadors de la Llar i les Cures, created in 2011 in Barcelona.

93 Ley 39/2006 de Promoción de la Autonomía Personal y Atención a las personas en situación de dependencia, known as the Ley de Dependencia.

94 Real Decreto 1620/2011 and Ley 27/2011.

95 Real Decreto Ley 29/2012, on social security; Real Decreto Ley 20/2012, on budget stability.

96 The name 15-M comes from the date of the first major protest in Madrid, on 15 May 15 2011.

97 Asociación Socio Cultural Nosotras (literally 'ourselves') por los Cuidados y el Empleo del Hogar, created in 2015 in Granada.

98 Plataforma Estatal de Asociaciones de Trabajadoras de Hogar.

99 Grupo Turin.

100 For instance, Tania González Peñas, a feminist politician from the left-wing Podemos party and member of the European Parliament since 2014, together with Konstadinka Kuneva, promoted the first Resolution on domestic workers and caregivers, approved in April 2016 by the European Parliament. See 'Resolution on domestic workers and carers in the EU' 2015/2094(INI). Full text: www.europarl.europa.eu/doceo/document/TA-8–2016–0203_EN.html (last accessed 13 July 2021).

Chapter 3

1 Information regarding the ratification campaign can be found on the IDWF website: https://idwfed.org/en/campaigns/ratify-c189 (last accessed 13 July 2021).

Chapter 4

1 As shown in Chapter 2, in the decade under analysis, groups led by and composed of domestic workers or former domestic workers were active in Brazil, Colombia, Ecuador, India, the Philippines and Spain, and had begun to emerge in Taiwan. On the other hand, in Italy, and to a lesser extent in Germany, they had already been present in the preceding decades.

2 The project was carried out by two national non-profit organizations: ENS, active in the field of labour rights and union empowerment, and Carabantú (Corporación Afrocolombiana de Desarrollo Social y Cultural), promoting rights and cultural recognition for Afro-Colombian minorities. Together with a third non-profit organization active in education and social communication (Fundación Bien Humano), they supported the first organizing process that led to the creation of UTRASD. See Morales Mosquera and Muñoz Cañas (2013).

3 www.trabajadorasdomesticas.org/empleadas-xm-domesticas-xm/sindicato-utrasd.html (last accessed 30 October 2018).

4 The regions with the highest percentage of Black and Afro-Colombian groups; also among the poorest in the country.

5 Longa is a racist epithet for indigenous girls and women.

[6] *Negra* in the original (feminine form). A common racial epithet for Black women, here used in a derogatory way.

[7] One of the regions with a large Afro-descendant population, from which many internal migrants who are employed as domestic workers in the big cities come.

[8] www.larepublica.ec/blog/politica/2015/04/20/correa-almuerza-sindicato-oficialista-carondelet/ (last accessed 30 November 2019).

[9] 'Sin nosotras no se mueve el mundo' (Without us the world cannot run), available from: www.youtube.com/watch?v=891gV9iENMc (last accessed 6 April 2020).

[10] She refers to performances in public space, mostly in the Lavapiés neighbourhood in Madrid, where they dramatize a situation, dress up, parade as models of domestic workers and sing protest songs.

[11] www.trabajadorasdomesticas.org/el-movimiento/quienes-somos.html (last accessed 20 October 2019).

[12] The aforementioned web page www.trabajadorasdomesticas.org; the Facebook page and YouTube channel Hablemos de Empleadas Domésticas (Let's talk about domestic workers); and the Twitter account @Empleadas_hogar (Domestic workers).

[13] The Laudelina app is one of the outcomes of the project Trabalho Doméstico: Construindo Igualdade no Brasil, carried out by Themis, ELAS Fund and UN Women in Brazil (2015–16). https://play.google.com/store/apps/details?id=br.org.laudelina&hl=pt_BR; www.facebook.com/aplicativolaudelina/ (last accessed 20 October 2019).

[14] The Ministries of Education, Cities, Social Security, the Federal Savings Bank and the General Secretariat of the Presidency of the Republic.

Chapter 5

[1] The movements against gender-based violence that arose in Argentina and the US in 2016 and 2017, respectively, and have since spread worldwide.

[2] International Union of Food, Agricultural, Hotel, Restaurant, Catering, Tobacco and Allied Workers' Associations.

[3] For instance, under the Ecuadorian penal code approved in 2014 (Código Orgánico Integral Penal, COIP) abortion is sanctioned as a crime, with only a few exceptions (such as cases of rape involving women with learning difficulties or when pregnancy may result in serious danger to the woman's health).

[4] Mesa intersectorial de economía del cuidado.

[5] Law 1413/2010.

[6] See 'Resolution on domestic workers and carers in the EU' 2015/2094(INI). Full text: www.europarl.europa.eu/doceo/document/TA-8-2016-0203_EN.html (last accessed 13 July 2021).

[7] https://care-macht-mehr.com (last accessed 13 July 2021).

[8] https://equalcareday.de (last accessed 13 July 2021).

[9] https://idwfed.org/myfairhome (last accessed 13 July 2021).

[10] www.ilo.org/global/topics/domestic-workers/events-and-training/WCMS_371983/lang--en/index.htm (last accessed 13 July 2021).

[11] www.effe-homecare.eu/wp-content/uploads/2014/10/EFFE_MANIFESTE.pdf (last accessed 13 July 2021).

References

Acciari, L. (2019) 'Decolonising Labour, Reclaiming Subaltern Epistemologies: Brazilian Domestic Workers and the International Struggle for Labour Rights', *Contexto Internacional*, 41(1): 39–64.

Agarwala, R. and Saha, S. (2018) 'The Employment Relationship and Movement Strategies among Domestic Workers in India', *Critical Sociology*, 44(7–8): 1207–23.

Agarwala, R. and Chun, J.J. (eds) (2019a) *Gendering Struggles against Informal and Precarious Work*, Bingley: Emerald Publishing Limited.

Agarwala, R. and Chun, J.J. (2019b) 'Gendering Struggles against Informal and Precarious Work', in R. Agarwala and J.J. Chun (eds) *Gendering Struggles against Informal and Precarious Work*, Bingley: Emerald Publishing Limited, pp 1–28.

Agrela Romero, B. (2012) 'Towards a Model of Externalisation and Denationalisation of Care? The Role of Female Migrant Care Workers for Dependent Older People in Spain', *European Journal of Social Work*, 15(1): 45–61.

Alberti, G., Holgate, J. and Tapia, M. (2013) 'Organising Migrants as Workers or as Migrant Workers? Intersectionality, Trade Unions and Precarious Work', *International Journal of Human Resource Management*, 24(22): 4132–48.

Albin, E. and Mantouvalou, V. (2012) 'The ILO Convention on Domestic Workers: From the Shadows to the Light', *Industrial Law Journal*, 41(1): 67–78.

Alcoff, L. (1991) 'The Problem of Speaking for Others', *Cultural Critique*, 20(winter): 5–32.

Ally, S.A. (2009) *From Servants to Workers: South African Domestic Workers and the Democratic State*, Ithaca: Cornell University Press.

Alzate Arias, L.I. (2005) *El Trabajo Doméstico*, Bogotá: Central Unitaria del Trabajo CUT.

Ambrosini, M. (2016) *Irregular Migration and Invisible Welfare*, London: Palgrave Macmillan.

Andall, J. (2000) *Gender, Migration and Domestic Service: The Politics of Black Women in Italy*, Farnham: Ashgate.

Anderson, B. (2010) 'Mobilizing Migrants, Making Citizens: Migrant Domestic Workers as Political Agents', *Ethnic and Racial Studies*, 33(1): 60–74.

Anderson, B. (2014) 'Nations, Migration and Domestic Labor: The Case of the UK', *Women's Studies International Forum*, Pergamon, 46(September–October): 5–12.

Anderson, B. (2015) 'Migrant Domestic Workers: Good Workers, Poor Slaves, New Connections', *Social Politics: International Studies in Gender, State & Society*, 22(4): 636–52.

Anthias, F. (2012) 'Hierarchies of Social Location, Class and Intersectionality: Towards a Translocational Frame', *International Sociology*, 28(1): 121–38.

Anzaldúa, G. and Moraga, C. (eds) (1981) *This Bridge Called My Back: Radical Writings of Women of Color*, Watertown: Persephone Press.

Arango, J., Díaz Gorfinkield, M. and Moualhi, D. (2013) *Promover la integración de las trabajadoras y los trabajadores domésticos migrantes en España*, Estudios sobre migraciones internacionales No. 114, ILO, Genève.

Asociación AD Los Molinos (2017) *Estudio la mujer inmigrante en el servicio doméstico. Análisis de la situación laboral e impacto de los cambios normativos*, Madrid: Taller de Impresión Mundocopia.

Barbagallo, C. and Federici, S. (2012) 'Introduction to "Care Work" and the Commons', *Commoner*, 15: 1–21.

Barbary, O. and Urrea Giraldo, F. (eds) (2004) *Gente negra en Colombia. Dinámicas sociopolíticas en Cali y el Pacífico*, Medellín: Editorial Lealon.

Barua, P., Waldrop, A. and Haukanes, H. (2017) 'From Benevolent Maternalism to the Market Logic: Exploring Discursive Boundary Making in Domestic Work Relations in India', *Critical Asian Studies*, 49(4): 481–500.

Bassel, L. and Lépinard, É. (2014) 'Introduction: The Theory and Politics of Intersectionality in Comparative Perspective', *Politics & Gender*, 10(1): 115–17.

Basu, A. (ed) (2010) *Women's Movements in the Global Era: The Power of Local Feminisms* (2nd edn), Philadelphia: Westview Press.

Benazha, A.V. and Lutz, H. (2019) 'Intersektionale Perspektiven auf die Pflege: Geschlechterverhältnisse und Migrationsprozesse', in C. Rudolph and K. Schmidt (eds) *Interessenvertretung und Care. Voraussetzungen, Akteure und Handlungsebenen*, Münster: Verlag Westfälisches Dampfboot, pp 146–60.

Benford, R.D. and Snow, D.A. (2000) 'Framing Processes and Social Movements: An Overview and Assessment', *Annual Review of Sociology*, 26(1): 611–39.

Bernardino-Costa, J. (2007) 'Sindicatos das trabalhadoras domésticas no Brasil: teorias da descolonização e saberes subalternos', PhD thesis, Departamento de Sociologia, Instituto de Ciências Sociais, Brasília.

Bernardino-Costa, J. (2013) 'Controle de vida, interseccionalidade e política de empoderamento: as organizações políticas das trabalhadoras domésticas no Brasil', *Estudos Históricos (Rio de Janeiro)*, 26(52): 471–89.

Bernardino-Costa, J. (2014) 'Intersectionality and Female Domestic Workers' Unions in Brazil', *Women's Studies International Forum*, 46(C): 72–80.

Bettio, F. and Plantenga, J. (2004) 'Comparing Care Regimes in Europe', *Feminist Economics*, 10(1): 85–113.

Blackett, A. (2012) 'The Decent Work for Domestic Workers Convention and Recommendation, 2011', *The American Journal of International Law*, 106(4): 778–94.

Blackett, A. (2019) *Everyday Transgressions. Domestic Workers Transnational Challenge to International Labor Law*, Ithaca and London: ILR Press.

Blofield, M. (2012) *Care Work and Class: Domestic Workers' Struggle for Equal Rights in Latin America*, University Park: Penn State Press.

Blofield, M. and Jokela, M. (2018) 'Paid Domestic Work and the Struggles of Care Workers in Latin America', *Current Sociology*, 66(4): 531–46.

Bob, C. (ed) (2011) *The International Struggle for New Human Rights*, Philadelphia: University of Pennsylvania Press.

Bonner, C. and Spooner, D. (2011) 'Organizing Labour in the Informal Economy', *Labour, Capital and Society*, 44(1): 127–52.

Boris, E. (2017) 'The Intimate Knows no Boundaries: Global Circuits of Domestic Worker Organizing', in S. Michel and I. Peng (eds) *Gender, Migration, and the Work of Care: A Multi-Scalar Approach to the Pacific Rim*, Cham: Palgrave Macmillan, pp 245–68.

Boris, E. (2019) *Making the Woman Worker: Precarious Labor and the Fight for Global Standards, 1919–2019*, New York: Oxford University Press.

Boris, E. and Nadasen, P. (2008) 'Domestic Workers Organize!', *Working USA: The Journal of Labor and Society*, 11(4): 413–43.

Boris, E. and Parreñas, R.S. (eds) (2010) *Intimate Labors: Cultures, Technologies, and the Politics of Care*, Redwood City: Stanford University Press.

Boris, E. and Klein, J. (2012) *Caring for America: Home Health Care Workers in the Shadow of the Welfare State*, New York: Oxford University Press.

Boris, E. and Fish, J. (2014) '"Slaves no More": Making Global Labor Standards for Domestic Workers', *Feminist Studies*, 40(2): 411–43.

Boris, E. and Fish, J. (2015) 'Decent Work for Domestics: Feminist Organizing, Worker Empowerment, and the ILO', in D. Hoerder, E. van Nederveen Meerkerk and S. Neunsinger (eds) *Towards a Global History of Domestic and Caregiving Workers*, Leiden: Brill, pp 530–52.

Brites, J. (2014) 'Domestic Service, Affection and Inequality: Elements of Subalternity', *Women's Studies International Forum*, 46: 63–71.

Bundesagentur für Arbeit (2016) *Zeitreihe Beschäftigte nach der WZ 2008 (Monatszahlen), Klassifikation T-97 (Private Haushalte mit Hauspersonal)*, Bundesagentur für Arbeit, Germany, Available from: https://statistik. arbeitsagentur.de/ (last accessed 13 July 2021).

Bundeszentrale für politische Bildung (2016) *Ausgewählte Armutsgefährdungsquoten (Selected at-risk-of-poverty rates)*, Bundeszentrale für politische Bildung, Bonn, Available from: www.bpb.de/nachschlagen/zahlen-und-fakten/ soziale-situation-in-deutschland/61785/armutsgefaehrdung (last accessed 13 July 2021).

Busi, B. (ed) (2020) *Separate in casa. Lavoratrici domestiche, femministe e sindacaliste: una mancata alleanza*, Rome: Ediesse.

Cachón Rodríguez, L. (2009) *La "España inmigrante": Marco discriminatorio, mercado de trabajo y políticas de integración*, Barcelona: Anthropos Editorial.

Cangiano, A. and Walsh, K. (2014) 'Recruitment Processes and Immigration Regulations: The Disjointed Pathways to Employing Migrant Carers in Ageing Societies', *Work, Employment and Society*, 28(3): 372–89.

Carastathis, A. (2013) 'Identity Categories as Potential Coalitions', *Signs: Journal of Women in Culture and Society*, 38(4): 941–65.

Carvalho, L. (1999) *A luta que me fez crescer*, Recife: Deutscher Entwicklungsdienst.

Castro, M.G. (1993) 'The Alchemy between Social Categories in the Production of Political Subjects: Class, Gender, Race and Generation in the Case of Domestic Workers Union Leaders in Salvador-Bahia, Brazil', *The European Journal of Development Research*, 5(2): 1–22.

Catanzaro, R. and Colombo, A. (eds) (2009) *Badanti & Co: Il lavoro domestico straniero in Italia*, Bologna: Il Mulino.

Chaney, E. and Castro Garcia, M. (eds) (1989) *Muchachas no more. Household workers in Latin America and the Caribbean*, Philadelphia: Temple University Press.

Chavez, J. and Piper, N. (2015) 'The Reluctant Leader: The Philippine Journey from Labor Export to Championing a Rights-Based Approach to Overseas Employment', in E. Berman and M.S. Haque (eds) *Asian Leadership in Policy and Governance*, Bingley: Emerald Publishing Limited, pp 305–44.

Chen, C.-F. (2016) *General Assembly Report of the Taiwan Association of Family Caregivers*, Taipei: Taiwanese Association of Family Caregivers Publishing.

Chen, Y.-J. (2019) 'Isolated but Not Oblivious: Taiwan's Acceptance of the Two Major Human Rights Covenants', in J.A. Cohen, W.P. Alford and C. Lo (eds) *Taiwan and International Human Rights. Economics, Law, and Institutions in Asia Pacific*, Singapore: Springer, pp 207–25.

Cheng, I. and Momesso, L. (2017) 'Look, the World is Watching How We Treat Migrants! The Making of the Anti-Trafficking Legislation during the Ma Administration', *Journal of Current Chinese Affairs*, 46(1): 61–99.

Cherubini, D. (2018) *Nuove cittadine, nuove cittadinanze? Donne migranti e pratiche di partecipazione*, Rome: Meltemi.

Cherubini, D. and Tudela-Vázquez, M.P. (2016) 'Beyond Victims and Cultural Mediators: An Intersectional Analysis of Migrant Women's Citizenship Practices in Spain and the United States', *Rassegna Italiana di Sociologia*, 57(3): 461–80.

Cherubini, D., Garofalo Geymonat, G. and Marchetti, S. (2020) 'Intersectional Politics on Domestic Workers' Rights: The Cases of Ecuador and Colombia', in E. Evans and É. Lépinard (eds) *Intersectionality in Feminist and Queer Movements: Confronting Privileges*, Abingdon: Routledge, pp 236–54.

Chesters, G. (2012) 'Social Movements and the Ethics of Knowledge Production', *Social Movement Studies*, 11(2): 145–60.

Chien, Y.C. (2018) 'The Struggle for Recognition: The Politics of Migrant Care Worker Policies in Taiwan', *Critical Sociology*, 44(7–8): 1147–61.

Cho, S., Crenshaw, K.W. and McCall, L. (2013) 'Toward a Field of Intersectionality Studies: Theory, Applications, and Praxis', *Signs: Journal of Women in Culture and Society*, 38(4): 785–810.

Chun, J.J. and Cranford, C. (2018) 'Becoming Homecare Workers: Chinese Immigrant Women and the Changing Worlds of Work, Care and Unionism', *Critical Sociology*, 44(7–8): 1013–27.

Chun, J.J. and Kim, Y.-S. (2018) 'Feminist Entanglements with the Neoliberal Welfare State: NGOs and Domestic Worker Organizing in South Korea', in R. Agarwala, and J.J. Chun (eds) *Gendering Struggles against Informal and Precarious Work*, Bingley: Emerald Publishing Limited, pp 147–68.

Chun, J.J., Lipsitz, G. and Shin, Y. (2013) 'Intersectionality as a Social Movement Strategy: Asian Immigrant Women Advocates', *Signs: Journal of Women in Culture and Society*, 38(4): 917–40.

Cobble, D.S. (2005) *The Other Women's Movement: Workplace Justice and Social Rights in Modern America*, Princeton: Princeton University Press.

Cole, E.R. (2008) 'Coalitions as a Model for Intersectionality: From Practice to Theory', *Sex Roles*, 59(5–6): 443–53.

Coll, K.M. (2010) *Remaking Citizenship: Latina Immigrants and New American Politics*, Redwood City: Stanford University Press.

Collins, P.H. (2015) 'Intersectionality's Definitional Dilemmas', *Annual Review of Sociology*, 41(1): 1–20.

Collins, P.H. and Bilge, S. (2020) *Intersectionality* (2nd edn), Cambridge: Polity Press.

Combahee River Collective (1982) 'A Black Feminist Statement', in G. Hull, P. Bell and B. Smith (eds) *All the Women Are White, All the Blacks Are Men, but Some of Us Are Brave*, Old Westbury: Feminist Press.

Conway, J. (2008) 'Geographies of Transnational Feminisms: The Politics of Place and Scale in the World March of Women', *Social Politics*, 15(2): 207–31.

Coser, L.A. (1973) 'Servants: The Obsolescence of an Occupational Role', *Social Forces*, 52(1): 31–40.

Costa, J.S., Barbosa, A.L.N. de H. and Hirata, G.I. (2016) *Effects of Domestic Worker Legislation Reform in Brazil*, Working Paper No. 149, International Policy Centre for Inclusive Growth (IPC-IG), United Nations Development Programme, Brasília, Available from: www.econstor.eu/bitstream/10419/173803/1/869879804.pdf.

Crenshaw, K.W. (1991) 'Mapping the Margins: Intersectionality, Identity Politics, and Violence against Women of Color', *Stanford Law Review*, 43(6): 1241–99.

Crespo, P.U., Peredo Beltrán, P., Flores Chamba, J. and Guillén, R. (2014) *Situación organizativa de las trabajadoras remuneradas del hogar en la región andina y procesos de incidencia política para la ratificación del Convenio 189*, Quito: CARE América Latina.

Cruells López, M. and Ruiz García, S. (2014) 'Political Intersectionality within the Spanish Indignados Social Movement', in L.M. Woehrle (ed) *Intersectionality and Social Change*, Bradford: Emerald Publishing Limited, pp 3–25.

Da Roit, B. (2010) *Strategies of Care: Changing Elderly Care in Italy and the Netherlands*, Amsterdam: University Press.

Dalla Costa, G.F. (2008) *The Work of Love. Unpaid Housework, Poverty and Sexual Violence at the Dawn of the 21st Century*, Williamsburg: Autonomedia.

Dalla Costa, M. and James, S. (1975) *The Power of Women and the Subversion of the Community*, Bristol: Falling Wall Press.

Daway, P.R.P.S. (2014) *Primer on Kasambahay rights and Obligations under the Batas Kasambahay*, Diliman, Quezon City: University of the Philippines Law Complex.

De Dios Fernández, E. (2018) *Sirvienta, empleada, trabajadora de hogar. Género, clase e identidad en el franquismo y la transición a través del servicio doméstico (1939–1995)*, Malaga: Universidad de Malaga.

Degiuli, F. (2016) *Caring for a Living: Migrant Women, Aging Citizens, and Italian Families*, Oxford: Oxford University Press.

De la Torre, C. and Striffler, S. (eds) (2008) *The Ecuador Reader: History, Culture, Politics*, Durham: Duke University Press.

Della Porta, D., Ruch, D. and Kriesi, H. (eds) (1999) *Social Movements in a Globalizing World*, London: Macmillan.

Delphy, C. (1984) *Close to Home: A Materialist Analysis of Women's Oppression*, Amherst: University of Massachusetts Press.

De Oliveira, C.M. (2017a) 'A luta foi para equiparar nossos direitos aos dos trabalhadores, mas seguem as desigualdades, afirma Creuza Oliveira sobre a PEC das Domésticas', published on 4 May 2017 in 'Trabalhadoras Domésticas: Direitos e Desafios – Uma Conversa com Creuza Oliveira', ELAS – Fundo de Investimento Social website, Available from: www.fundosocialelas.org/noticias-conteudo.asp?cod=374 (last accessed 13 July 2021).

De Oliveira, C.M. (2017b) 'Temos feito malabarismo para conseguir chegar perto dessas trabalhadoras, que foram ensinadas que a mulher não faz política', published on 12 May 2017 in 'Trabalhadoras Domésticas: Direitos e Desafios – Uma Conversa com Creuza Oliveira', ELAS – Fundo de Investimento Social website, Available from: http://www.fundosocialelas.org/noticias-conteudo.asp?cod=376 (last accessed 13 July 2021).

Díaz Gorfinkiel, M. and Fernández López, C. (2016) *Impacto de las reformas legislativas en el sector del empleo del hogar en España*, Conditions of work and employment series No. 82, ILO, Genève, Available from: www.ilo.org/wcmsp5/groups/public/---ed_protect/---protrav/---travail/documents/publication/wcms_519719.pdf (last accessed 13 July 2021).

Di Bartolomeo, A. and Marchetti, S. (2016) 'Migrant Women's Employment in Paid Reproductive Work through the Crisis: The Case of Italy (2007–2012)', *Investigaciones Feministas*, 7(1): 57–74.

DIEESE (2013) *O Emprego Doméstico no Brasil*, Estudos e Pesquisas No. 68, Departamento Intersindical de Estatística e Estudos Socioeconômicos, São Paulo, Available from: www.dieese.org.br/estudosetorial/2013/estPesq68empregoDomestico.pdf (last accessed 13 July 2021).

Donaldson, J.K. (1992) 'Finding Common Ground: Redefining Women's Work in Colombia', *Grassroots Development*, 16(1): 2–11.

D'Souza, A. (2010) *Moving towards Decent Work for Domestic Workers – an Overview of the ILO's Work*, Working paper No. 2, ILO Bureau for Gender Equality, Genève.

Du Toit, D. (2011) 'Domestic Workers' Convention: A Breakthrough in Human Rights', *Law, Democracy and Development*, 15(1): 4–7.

Emunds, B. and Schacher, U. (2012) *Ausländische Pflegekräfte in Privathaushalten*, Frankfurter Arbeitshefte zur gesellschafts ethischen und sozialwissenschaftlichen No. 61, Oswald von Nell-Breuning-Institut für Wirtschafts- und Gesellschaftsethik der Philosophisch-Theologischen Hochschule Sankt Georgen, Frankfurt am Main, Available from: https://nbi.sankt-georgen.de/assets/typo3/redakteure/Dokumente/FAgsFs/Pflege_HBS_Endfassung.pdf (last accessed 13 July 2021).

England, K. (2017) 'Home, Domestic Work and the State: The Spatial Politics of Domestic Workers' Activism', *Critical Social Policy*, 37(3): 367–85.

Enste, D.H. (2017) *Schwarzarbeit und Schattenwirtschaft – Argumente und Fakten zur nicht angemeldeten Erwerbstätigkeit in Deutschland und Europa*, IW Report No. 9, Institute of German economy, Köln, Available from: www.iwkoeln. de/studien/iw-reports/beitrag/dominik-h-enste-schwarzarbeit-und-scha ttenwirtschaft-324737 (last accessed 13 July 2021).

Escriva, A. and Skinner, E. (2008) 'Domestic Work and Transnational Care Chains in Spain', in H. Lutz (ed) *Migration and Domestic Work. A European Perspective on a Global Theme*, London: Routledge, pp 113–26.

Esping-Andersen, G. (1990) *The Three Worlds of Welfare Capitalism*, Cambridge: Polity Press.

Evans, E. (2015) *The Politics of Third Wave Feminisms. Neoliberalism, Intersectionality and the State in Britain and the US*, London: Palgrave Macmillan.

Evans, E. (2016) 'Diversity Matters: Intersectionality and Women's Representation in the USA and UK', *Parliamentary Affairs*, 69(3): 569–85.

Evans, E. and Lépinard, É. (eds) (2020a) *Intersectionality in Feminist and Queer Movements Confronting Privileges*, London: Routledge.

Evans, E. and Lépinard, É. (2020b) 'Confronting Privileges in Feminist and Queer Movements', in E. Evans and É. Lépinard (eds) *Intersectionality in Feminist and Queer Movements: Confronting Privileges*, London: Routledge, pp 1–26.

Federici, S. (1975) *Wages Against Housework*, Bristol: Falling Wall.

Federici, S. (2009) 'Education and the Enclosure of Knowledge in the Global University', *ACME: An International E-Journal for Critical Geographies*, 8(3): 454–61.

Federici, S. (2016) '"We Have Seen Other Countries and Have Another Culture." Migrant Domestic Workers and the International Production and Circulation of Feminist Knowledge and Organization', *WorkingUSA*, 19(1): 9–23.

Ferree, M.M. and Roth, S. (1998) 'Gender, Class and the Interaction between Social Movements', *Gender & Society*, 12(6): 626–48.

Fish, J.N. (2014) 'Organizing through State Transitions and Global Institutions: Crafting Domestic Labour Policy in South Africa', in M. Romero, V. Preston and W. Giles (eds) *When Care Work Goes Global. Locating the Social Relations of Domestic Work*, Farnham: Ashgate, pp 233–56.

Fish, J.N. (2017) *Domestic Workers of the World Unite! A Global Movement for Dignity and Human Rights*, New York: New York University Press.

Fligstein, N. (2008) 'Theory and Methods for the Study of Strategic Action Fields', paper presented at the Institutional Development and Change Conference, Max Planck Institute and Northwestern University, 16–19 July, Chicago, USA.

Fligstein, N. and McAdam, D. (2012) *A Theory of Fields*, Oxford: Oxford University Press.

Folbre, N. (2001) *The Invisible Heart. Economics and Family Values*, New York: The New Press.

Fontana, L. (2020) 'The Contentious Politics of Labour Rights as Human Rights: Lessons from the Implementation of Domestic Workers Rights in the Philippines', *Human Rights Quarterly*, 42(4): 859–77.

Fraga, A.B. (2016) 'O Serviço Doméstico Sob os Holofotes Públicos: Alterações e Articulações entre Trabalho Produtivo e Reprodutivo no Brasil (Estado, Mercado e Família)', PhD thesis, Instituto de Filosofia e Ciências Sociais, Universidade Federal do Rio de Janeiro, Brazil, Available from: www.escavador.com/sobre/6936501/alexandre-barbosa-fraga.

Fraser, N. (2005) 'Reframing Justice in a Globalizing World', *New Left Review*, 36(Nov/Dec): 69–88.

Fraser, N. (2013) *Fortunes of feminism. From State-managed Capitalism to Neoliberal Crisis*, London: Verso.

Fudge, J. and Hobden, C. (2018) *Conceptualizing the Role of Intermediaries in Formalizing Domestic Work*, Conditions of Work and Employment Series No. 95, ILO, Genève, Available from: www.ilo.org/wcmsp5/groups/public/---ed_protect/---protrav/---travail/documents/publication/wcms_631587.pdf (last accessed 13 July 2021).

Fukuda-Parr, S. (2004) 'Millennium Development Goals: Why They Matter', *Global Governance*, 10(4): 395–402.

Fundación José Antonio Galán (2013) *Trabajadoras del hogar en Colombia – Bucaramanga, Bogotá y Cartagena – Contextualización y mapeo de organizaciones (Informe Regional)*, ENS and CARABANTÚ, Bucaramanga, Available from: http://sintraimagra.org/visor_archivos2.php?cat=5&arch2=Files/inf_trab_rem_hog.pdf&arch1=../Files/inf_trab_rem_hog.pdf (last accessed 13 July 2021).

Gallo, E. and Scrinzi, F. (2016) 'Outsourcing Elderly Care to Migrant Workers: The Impact of Gender and Class on the Experience of Male Employers', *Sociology*, 50(2): 366–82.

Gallotti, M. and Mertens, J. (2013) *Promoting Integration for Migrant Domestic Workers in Europe: A Synthesis of Belgium, France, Italy and Spain*, International Migration Papers No. 118, ILO, Genève, Available from: https://digitalcommons.ilr.cornell.edu/intl/291 (last accessed 13 July 2021).

García Sáinz, C., Santos Pérez, M.L. and Valencia Olivero, N.Y. (eds) (2011) *Inmigrantes en el servicio doméstico. Determinantes sociales, jurídicos e institucionales en la reorganización del servicio doméstico*, Madrid: Talasa.

Garofalo Geymonat, G. and Marchetti, S. (2017) 'A global landscape of voices for labour rights and social recognition', in G. Garofalo Geymonat, S. Marchetti and P. Kyritsis (eds) *Domestic Workers Speak: A Global Fight for Rights and Recognition*, OpenDemocracy, pp 12–17, Available from: https://drive.google.com/file/d/0B2lN4rGTopsaZ0VLdmZuYnBuc0U/view (last accessed 13 July 2021).

Garofalo Geymonat, G., Marchetti, S. and Kyritsis, P. (eds) (2017) *Domestic Workers Speak: A Global Fight for Rights and Recognition*, OpenDemocracy, Available from: www.opendemocracy.net/en/beyond-trafficking-and-slavery/global-landscape-of-voices-for-labour-right/ (last accessed 13 July 2021).

Geertz, C. (1973) *The Interpretation of Culture: Selected Essays*, New York: Basic Books.

Gissi, A. (2018a) ' "Le estere". Immigrazione femminile e lavoro domestico in Italia (1960–80)', *Meridiana*, 91: 37–56.

Gissi, A. (2018b) 'The Home as a Factory: Rethinking the Debate on Housewives' Wages in Italy, 1929–1980', in R. Sarti, A. Bellavitis and M. Martini (eds) *What Is Work? Gender at the Crossroads of Home, Family, and Business from the Early Modern Era to the Present*, New York: Berghahn Books, pp 152–77.

Gottschall, K. and Schwarzkopf, M. (2010) *Irreguläre Arbeit in Privathaushalten – Rechtliche und institutionelle Anreize zu irregulärer Arbeit in Privathaushalten in Deutschland. Bestandsaufnahme und Lösungsansätze*, Arbeitspapier No. 217, Hans Böckler Stiftung, Düsseldorf, Available from: www.econstor.eu/handle/10419/116677 (last accessed 13 July 2021).

Gutiérrez-Rodríguez, E. (2010) *Migration, Domestic Work and Affect: A Decolonial Approach on Value and the Feminization of Labor*, New York: Routledge.

Hancock, A.-M. (2007) 'When Multiplication Doesn't Equal Quick Addition: Examining Intersectionality as a Research Paradigm', *Perspectives on Politics*, 5(1): 63–79.

Hancock, A.-M. (2011) *Solidarity Politics for Millennials: A Guide to Ending the Oppression Olympics*, New York: Palgrave Macmillan.

Hancock, A.-M. (2016) *Intersectionality. An Intellectual History*, New York: Oxford University Press.

Haraway, D. (1988) 'Situated Knowledges: The Science Question in Feminism and the Privilege of Partial Perspective', *Feminist Studies*, 14(3): 575–99.

Haskins, V. (2001) 'On the Doorstep: Aboriginal Domestic Service as a "Contact Zone"', *Australian Feminist Studies*, 16(34): 13–25.

Hega, M.D., Alporha, V.C. and Evangelista, M.S. (2017) *Feminism and the Women's Movement in the Philippines: Struggles, Advances, and Challenges*, Pasig City: Friedrich-Ebert-Stiftung.

Hochschild, A.R. (2002) 'Love and Gold', in B. Ehrenreich and A.R. Hochschild (eds) *Global Woman: Nannies, Maids, and Sex Workers in the New Economy*, New York: Holt, pp 15–30.

Huyette, P. (1994) 'L'emploi domestique dans la Colombie des années 80', in B. Lautier (ed) *La mise en forme de la mobilité par l'emploi: les travailleurs du bâtiment et les employées domestiques en Amérique Latine (Brésil, Colombie, Chili)*, Paris: Rapport de recherche remis au ministère de l'Enseignement et de la recherche par le GREITD/CREPPRA/ARTE, pp 269–348.

ILO (2009) *Narrative report on the Philippine Campaign on Decent Work for Domestic Workers*, ILO, Genève, Available from: www.ilo.org/asia/publications/WCMS_120013/lang--en/index.htm (last accessed 13 July 2021).

ILO (2011) *Domestic Workers in the Philippines: Profile and Working Conditions*, ILO, Genève, Available from: www.ilo.org/wcmsp5/groups/public/---ed_protect/---protrav/---travail/documents/publication/wcms_167021.pdf (last accessed 13 July 2021).

ILO (2013) *Domestic Workers across the World. Global and Regional Statistic and the Extent of Legal Protection*, ILO, Genève, Available from: www.ilo.org/travail/Whatsnew/WCMS_173363/lang--en/index.htm (last accessed 13 July 2021).

ILO (2015) *Global Estimates of Migrant Workers and Migrant Domestic Workers: Results and Methodology*, ILO, Genève, Available from: https://www.ilo.org/wcmsp5/groups/public/---dgreports/---dcomm/documents/publication/wcms_436343.pdf (last accessed 13 July 2021).

ILO (2017a) *Decent Work Country Diagnostics: Philippines 2017*, International Labour Organization Country Office for the Philippines, Genève, Available from: www.ilo.org/manila/publications/WCMS_588875/lang--en/index.htm (last accessed 13 July 2021).

ILO (2017b) *Practical Guide to Ending Child Labour and Protecting Young Workers in Domestic Work*, ILO, Genève.

IPEA (2013) *Duas décadas de desigualdade e pobreza no Brasil medidas pela Pnad/IBGE*, Comunicados do IPEA No. 159, Instituto de Pesquisa Econômica Aplicada, Brasília, Available from: www.ipea.gov.br/portal/images/stories/PDFs/comunicado/131001_comunicadoipea159.pdf.

Irvine, J.A., Lang, S. and Montoya, C. (2019) *Gendered Mobilizations and Intersectional Challenges: Contemporary Social Movements in Europe and North America*, London: Rowman & Littlefield.

ISMU and Fondazione Censis (2013) *Elaborazione di un modello previsionale del fabbisogno di servizi assistenziali alla persona nel mercato del lavoro italiano con particolare riferimento al contributo della popolazione straniera*, Ministero del Lavoro e delle Politiche Sociali, Rome, Available from: www.agenziaiura.it/fonti/documenti/168/ (last accessed 13 July 2021).

Johnston, H. and Noakes, J.A. (2005) *Frames of Protest: Social Movements and the Framing Perspective*, Lanham: Rowman & Littlefield Publishers.

Johnstone, L. (2012) 'Organising Domestic Workers: For Decent Work and the ILO Convention No. 189', MA thesis in International Social Welfare and Health Policy, Faculty of Social Sciences, Oslo and Akershus University College of Applied Sciences, Norway.

Kabeer, N. (2004) 'Globalization, Labor Standards, and Women's Rights: Dilemmas of Collective (in)Action in an Interdependent World', *Feminist Economics*, 10(1): 3–35.

Kabeer, N. (2005) 'Is Microfinance a "Magic Bullet" for Women's Empowerment? Analysis of Findings from South Asia', *Economic and Political Weekly*, 40(44/45): 4709–18.

King-Dejardin, A. (2018) *The Philippines: Contribution of Social Dialogue to the Formalisation of Domestic work and Agenda 2030*, ILO, Genève, Available from: www.ituc-csi.org/IMG/pdf/sd_philippines_en.pdf. (last accessed 13 July 2021)

Kofes, S. (2001) *Mulher, mulheres: identidade, diferença e desigualdade na relação entre patroas e empregadas domésticas*, Campinas: Editora da Unicamp.

Kofman, E. and Raghuram, P. (2015) *Gendered Migrations and Global Social Reproduction*, London: Palgrave Macmillan.

Kontos, M. (2013) 'Negotiating the Social Citizenship Rights of Migrant Domestic Workers: The Right to Family Reunification and a Family Life in Policies and Debates', *Journal of Ethnic and Migration Studies*, 39(3): 409–24.

Kott, S. and Droux, J. (eds) (2013) *Globalizing Social Rights. The International Labour Organization and Beyond*, Houndmills: Palgrave Macmillan.

Lan, P.-C. (2006) *Global Cinderellas: Migrant Domestics and Newly Rich Employers in Taiwan*, Durham, NC and London: Duke University Press.

Larguía, I. and Dumoulin, J. (1976) *Hacia una ciencia de la liberación de la Mujer*, Barcelona: Anagrama.

Lasalle, A. (2020) 'Bringing Epistemology into Intersectional Methodology', *European Journal of Politics and Gender*, 3(3): 409–26.

León, M. (2010) 'Migration and Care Work in Spain: The Domestic Sector Revisited', *Social Policy & Society*, 9(3): 409–18.

León, M. (2013) 'Proyecto de Investigación-acción: trabajo doméstico y servicio doméstico en Colombia', *Revista de Estudios Sociales*, 45: 198–211.

Lépinard, É. (2014) 'Doing Intersectionality: Repertoires of Feminist Practices in France and Canada', *Gender and Society*, 28(6): 877–903.

Levitt, P. and Merry, S. (2009) 'Vernacularization on the Ground: Local Uses of Global Women's Rights in Peru, China, India and the United States', *Global Networks*, 9(4): 441–61.

Lim, A. (2016) 'Transnational Organising and Feminist Politics of Difference and Solidarity: The Mobilisation of Domestic Workers in Hong Kong', *Asian Studies Review*, 40(1): 70–88.

Lutz, H. (2008) *Vom Weltmarkt in den Privathaushalt. Die neuen Dienstmädchen im Zeitalter der Globalisierung* (2nd edn), Opladen: Verlag Barbara Budrich.

Lutz, H. (2011) *The New Maids: Transnational Women and the Care Economy*, London: Zed Books.

Lutz, H. and Palenga-Möllenbeck, E. (2012) 'Care Workers, Care Drain, and Care Chains: Reflections on Care, Migration, and Citizenship', *Social Politics: International Studies in Gender, State & Society*, 19(1): 15–37.

Luxton, M. (2014) 'Marxist Feminism and Anticapitalism: Reclaiming Our History, Reanimating Our Politics', *Studies in Political Economy*, 94(1): 137–60.

Mahon, R. and Robinson F. (2011) *Feminist Ethics and Social Policy: Towards a New Global Political Economy of Care*, Berkeley: University of British Columbia Press.

Mahon, R. and Michel, S. (2017) 'Out of Focus: Migrant Women Caregivers as Seen by the ILO and the OECD', in S. Michel and I. Peng (eds) *Gender, Migration, and the Work of Care: A Multi-Scalar Approach to the Pacific Rim*, Cham: Palgrave Macmillan, pp 269–91.

Maioni, R. and Zucca, G. (eds) (2016) *Viaggio nel lavoro di cura. Chi sono, cosa fanno e come vivono le badanti che lavorano nelle famiglie italiane*, Rome: Ediesse.

Marchetti, M. (2013) 'Intersezionalità', in C. Botti (ed) *Le etiche della diversitàculturale*, Firenze: Le Lettere, pp 133–48.

Marchetti, S. (2011) *Le ragazze di Asmara. Lavoro domestico e migrazione postcoloniale*, Rome: Ediesse.

Marchetti, S. (2014) *Black Girls: Migrant Domestic Workers and Colonial Legacies*, Leiden-Boston: Brill.

Marchetti, S. (2016a) 'Citizenship and Maternalism in Migrant Domestic Labour: Filipina Workers and Their Employers in Amsterdam and Rome', in B. Gullikstad, G.K. Kristensen and P. Ringrose (eds) *Paid Migrant Domestic Labour in a Changing Europe*, London: Palgrave Macmillan, pp 147–68.

Marchetti, S. (2016b) 'Domestic work is work? Condizioni lavorative delle assistenti familiari in Italia, tra finzioni e realtà', in R. Maioni and G. Zucca (eds) *Viaggio nel lavoro di cura. Chi sono, cosa fanno e come vivono le badanti che lavorano nelle famiglie italiane*, Rome: Ediesse, pp 101–23.

Marchetti, S. (2018) 'The Global Governance of Paid Domestic Work: Comparing the Impact of ILO Convention No. 189 in Ecuador and India', *Critical Sociology*, 44(7–8): 1191–205.

Marchetti, S. and Cherubini, D. (2019) '"Domestic Work Is Work": But for Whom? Tensions around Labour Rights and the Valorisation of Care in Ecuador and Colombia', *Rassegna Italiana di Sociologia*, 60(4): 721–47.

Marchetti, S., Piazzalunga, D. and Venturini, A. (2013) *Costs and Benefits of Labour Mobility between the EU and the Eastern Partnership Countries Country Study: Italy*, IZA Discussion Paper No. 7635, IZA, Bonn, Available from: www.iza.org/publications/dp/7635/costs-and-benefit s-of-labour-mobility-between-the-eu-and-the-eastern-partnership -countries-country-study-italy (last accessed 13 July 2021).

Martínez Buján, R. (2011) 'La reorganización de los cuidados familiares en un contexto de migración internacional', *Cuadernos de Relaciones Laborales*, 29(1): 93–123.

Martínez Buján, R. (2014) '¡El trabajo doméstico cuenta! Características y transformaciones del servicio doméstico en España', *Migraciones. Publicación Del Instituto Universitario De Estudios Sobre Migraciones*, 36: 275–305.

Masi de Casanova, E. (2019) *Dust and Dignity: Domestic Employment in Contemporary Ecuador*, Ithaca: Cornell University Press.

Masi de Casanova, E., Rodriguez, L. and Roldán, R.B. (2018) 'Informed but Insecure: Employment Conditions and Social Protection among Paid Domestic Workers in Guayaquil', *Latin American Perspectives*, 45(1): 163–74.

May, V. (2011) *Unprotected Labor. Household Workers, Politics, and Middle-Class Reform in New York, 1870–1940*, Chapel Hill: University of North Carolina Press.

McCall, L. (2005) 'The Complexity of Intersectionality', *Signs: Journal of Women in Culture and Society*, 30(3): 1771–800.

McKeon, N. (2009) *The United Nations and Civil Society: Legitimating Global Governance – Whose Voice?*, London: Zed Books.

McLaren, M.A. (2019) *Women's Activism, Feminism, and Social Justice*, Oxford: Oxford University Press.

Meertens, D., Viveros, M. and Arango, L.G. (2008) 'Discriminación étnico-racial, desplazamiento y género en los procesos identitarios de la población negra en sectores populares de Bogotá', in M. del C. Zabala Argüelles (ed) *Pobreza, exclusión social y discriminación étnico-racial en América Latina y el Caribe*, Bogotá: Siglo del Hombre Editores y Clacso, pp 181–214.

Mehrotra, S.T. (2010) *A Report on Domestic Workers: Conditions, Rights and Responsibilities*, New Delhi: Jagori.

Menon, G. (2017) 'Dignity and Visibility for Domestic Workers: No Longer Workers in the Shadow!', in G. Garofalo Geymonat, S. Marchetti and P. Kyritsis (eds) *Domestic Workers Speak: A Global Fight for Rights and Recognition*, OpenDemocracy, pp 112–19, Available from: https://drive.google.com/file/d/0B2lN4rGTopsaZ0VLdmZuYnBuc0U/view. (last accessed 13 July 2021)

Michel, S. and Peng, I. (2012) 'All in the Family? Migrants, Nationhood, and Care Regimes in Asia and North America', *Journal of European Social Policy*, 22(4): 406–18.

Michel, S. and Peng, I. (2017) *Gender, Migration, and the Work of Care: A Multi-Scalar Approach to the Pacific Rim*, Cham: Palgrave Macmillan.

Minijob Zentrale (2016) *Aktuelle Entwicklungen im Bereich der geringfügigen Beschäftigung, IV. Quartal 2016*, Minijob Zentrale/Deutsche Rentenversicherung Knappschaft-Bahn-See, Essen, Available from: www.minijob-zentrale.de/DE/02_fuer_journalisten/02_berichte_trendreporte/quartalsberichte_archiv/2016/4_2016.pdf?__blob=publicationFile&v=1 (last accessed 13 July 2021).

Molyneux, M. (2001) *Women's Movements in International Perspective: Latin America and Beyond*, Basingstoke: Palgrave Macmillan.

Momsen, J.H. (1999) *Gender, Migration and Domestic Service*, London: Routledge.

Moncayo Roldán, K.E. (2015) *Análisis histórico jurídico de la condiciones laborales del trabajador doméstico ecuatoriano*, MA thesis, Facultad de Jurisprudencia, Pontificia Universidad Católica del Ecuador, Quito, Ecuador.

Montenegro, H. and Viajar, V.D.Q. (2017) 'The Filipino Kasambahay's Long Struggle against Invisibility', in G. Garofalo Geymonat, S. Marchetti and P. Kyritsis (eds) *Domestic Workers Speak. A Global Fight for Rights and Recognition*, OpenDemocracy, pp 120–5, Available from: www.opendemocracy.net/en/beyond-trafficking-and-slavery/global-landscape-of-voices-for-labour-right/. (last accessed 13 July 2021)

Monteros Obelar, S. (2019) 'El empleo de hogar como campo de batalla: breve historia de los movimientos de las luchas en España', *AFIN*, 111: 1–11.

Monticelli, T.A. (2017) *'Eu não trato empregada como empregada': empregadoras e o desafio do trabalho doméstico remunerado*, PhD thesis in Sociology, Setor de Ciências Humanas, Universidade Federal do Paraná, Curitiba, Brazil.

Monticelli, T.A. and Seyffarth, M. (2017) *Paid Domestic Workers in Brazil – an Analysis of the Political and Cultural Conjunctures of Labor Rights*, paper presented at the XIII Global Labour University Conference: The Future of Work: Democracy, Development and the Role of Labour, 7–9 August, São Paulo, Brazil.

Montserrat Codorniu, J. (2015) 'Impactos de las medidas de estabilidad presupuestaria en el Sistema de Autonomía y Atención a la Dependencia: retos del futuro', *Revista de servicios sociales*, 60: 9–30.

Moore, L. (2018) 'Transformative Labor Organizing in Precarious Times', *Critical Sociology*, 44(7–8): 1225–34.

Morales Mosquera, M.E. and Muñoz Cañas, S.M. (2013) *Barriendo la Invisibilidad de las Trabajadoras Domésticas Afrocolombianas en Medellín*, ENS and CARABANTÚ, Bucaramanga, Available from: www.ens.org.co/wp-content/uploads/2017/04/Barriendo-invisibilidades.pdf (last accessed 13 July 2021).

Mosquera, C. (2015) 'La progresiva emergencia de las víctimas como agentes políticos en Colombia', in A. Vargas (ed) *Transición, democracia y paz*, Bogotá: Universidad Nacional de Colombia, pp 203–28.

Moya, M. (2015) 'Situación de las trabajadoras remuneradas del hogar y su organización', *Ecuador Debate*, 94: 81–97.

Nakano Glenn, E. (1992) 'From Servitude to Service Work: Historical Continuities in the Racial Division of Paid Reproductive Labor', *Signs: Journal of Women in Culture and Society*, 18(1): 1–43.

Naples, N.A. (2003) *Feminism and Method: Ethnography, Discourse Analysis, and Activist Research*, New York: Routledge.

National Commission for Enterprises in the Unorganized Sector (2007) *Report on the Conditions of Work and Promotion of Livelihoods in the Unorganized Sector*, National Commission for Enterprises in the Unorganised Sector, New Delhi, Available from: https://dcmsme.gov.in/Condition_of_workers_sep_2007.pdf (last accessed 13 July 2021).

NDWTU (2015) *A Handbook on Unionizing Domestic Workers*, Mumbai: NDWTU, Available from: https://idwfed.org/en/resourc es/a-handbook-on-unionizing-domestic-workers/@@display-file/ attachment_1.

Nussbaum, M.C. (2001) *Women and Human Development: The Capabilities Approach*, Cambridge: Cambridge University Press.

Oelz, M. and Rani, U. (2015) *Domestic Work, Wages, and Gender Equality: Lessons from Developing Countries*, Working paper No. 5, ILO, Genève, Available from: www.ilo.org/global/publications/working-papers/ WCMS_430902/lang--en/index.htm (last accessed 13 July 2021).

Offenhenden, M. (2017) ' "Si hay que romperse una, se rompe" El trabajo del hogar y la reproducción social estratificada', PhD thesis, Departament d'Antropologia, Filosofia i Treball Social, Universitat Rovira i Virgili, Tarragona, Spain.

Ogaya, C. (2020) 'The Rights Movement for Domestic Workers in the Philippines. Its Local and Transnational Path to Decent Work', *Revue internationale des études du développement*, 242(2): 169–89.

Okechukwu, A. (2014) 'Shadows of Solidarity: Identity, Intersectionality, and Frame Resonance', in L.M. Woehrle (ed) *Intersectionality and Social Change*, Bradford: Emerald Publishing Limited, pp 153–80.

Oliveira, C.M. (2008) 'A Organização Política das Trabalhadoras Domésticas no Brasil', in M.B. Ferreira, M. Ávila, T. Prado, V. Souza and V. Soares (eds) *Reflexões Feministas Sobre Informalidade e Trabalho Doméstico*, Recife: SOS Corpo, pp 109–15.

Oso, L. and Parella, S. (2012) 'Inmigración, género y Mercado de trabajo: una panorámica de la investigación sobre la inserción Laboral de las mujeres inmigrantes en España', *Cuadernos de Relaciones Laborales*, 30(1): 11–44.

Osservatorio DOMINA sul lavoro domestico and Fondazione Leone Moressa (2019) *Primo rapporto annuale sul lavoro domestico*, DOMINA, Rome, Available from: www.osservatoriolavorodomestico.it/documenti/Rapporto-annuale-DOMINA-lavoro-domestico-2019.pdf (last accessed 13 July 2021).

Paarlberg-Kvam, K. (2019) 'What's to Come Is More Complicated: Feminist Visions of Peace in Colombia', *International Feminist Journal of Politics*, 21(2): 194–223.

Paes de Barros, R., Foguel, M.N. and Ulyssea, G. (eds) (2006) *Desigualdade de renda no Brasil: Uma análise da queda recente*, Brasília: IPEA.

Palmer, P. (1989) *Domesticity and Dirt: Housewives and Domestic Servants in the United States, 1920–1945*, Philadelphia: Temple University Press.

Palriwala, R. and Neetha, N. (2010) 'Care Arrangements and Bargains: Anganwadi and Paid Domestic Workers in India', *International Labour Review*, 149(4): 511–27.

Pardo Rojas, M., Mosquera, C. and Ramírez, M.C. (eds) (2004) *Panorámica afrocolombiana. Estudios sociales en el Pacífico*, Bogotá: Instituto Colombiano de Antropología e Historia, Universidad Nacional de Colombia.

Parreñas, R.S. (2001) *Servants of Globalization: Women, Migration and Domestic Work*, Stanford: Stanford University Press.

Parreñas, R.S. (2008) *The Force of Domesticity: Filipina Migrants and Globalization*, New York: New York University Press.

Pateman, C. (1988) *The Sexual Contract*, Stanford: Stanford University Press.

Peng, I. and Wong, J. (2010) 'East Asia', in F.G. Castles, S. Leibfried, J. Lewis, H. Obinger and C. Pierson (eds) *The Oxford Handbook of the Welfare State*, Oxford: Oxford University Press, pp 656–70.

Picchio, A. (1992) *Social Reproduction. The Political Economy of the Labour Market*, Cambridge: Cambridge University Press.

Picchio, A. and Pincelli, G. (eds) (2019) *Una lotta femminista globale. L'esperienza dei gruppi per il Salario al Lavoro Domestico di Ferrara e Modena*, Milano: Franco Angeli.

Pinho, P. de S. and Silva, E.B. (2010) 'Domestic Relations in Brazil: Legacies and Horizons', *Latin American Research Review*, 45(2): 90–113.

Pinto, E.A. (2015) *Etnicidade, gênero, e educação: trajetória de vida de Laudelina de Campos Mello*, São Paulo: Anita Garibaldi.

Pitch, T. (2004) 'Tess e io. Differenze e disuguaglianze nella differenza', *Ragion Pratica*, 23: 339–62.

Plata Quezada, W.E. (2013) 'El Sindicato del Servicio Doméstico y la Obra de Nazareth: entre asistencialismo, paternalismo y conflictos de interés, Bogotá, 1938–1960', *Revista de Estudios Sociales*, 45: 29–41.

Pojmann, W.A. (2006) *Immigrant Women and Feminism in Italy*, Aldershot: Ashgate.

Posso, J. (2008) 'Mecanismos de discriminación étnico-racial, clase social y género: la inserción laboral de mujeres negras en el servicio doméstico de Cali', in M.C. Zabala Argüelles (ed) *Pobreza, exclusión social y discriminación étnico-racial en América Latina y el Caribe*, Bogotá: Siglo del Hombre Editores y Clacso, pp 215–40.

Pratt, G. and Migrante BC (2019) 'Organizing Filipina Domestic Workers in Vancouver, Canada: Gendered Geographies and Community Mobilization', in R. Agarwala and J.J. Chun (eds) *Gendering Struggles against Informal and Precarious Work*, Bingley: Emerald Publishing Limited, pp 101–20.

Pratt, L. (2012) *Families Apart: Migrant Mothers and the Conflicts of Labor and Love*, Minneapolis: University of Minnesota Press.

Predelli, L.N., Halsaa, B., Sandu, A., Thun, C. and Nyhagen, L. (2012) *Majority–Minority Relations in contemporary Women's Movements: Strategic Sisterhood*, London: Palgrave Macmillan.

Profumi, E. (2017) 'La Revolución tradita di Rafael Correa', *Left*, 18 February: 46–8.

Prügl, E. (1999) 'What Is a Worker? Gender, Global Restructuring, and the ILO Convention on Homework', in M.K. Meyer and E. Prügl (eds) *Gender Politics in Global Governance*, Lanham: Rowman & Littlefield, pp 197–209.

Pusch, T. (2018) *Bilanz des Mindestlohns: Deutliche Lohnerhöhungen, verringerte Armut, aber auch viele Umgehungen*, Policy Brief WSI No. 19, Wirtschafts- und Sozialwissenschaftliches Institut, Düsseldorf, Available from: www. boeckler.de/pdf/p_wsi_pb_19_2018.pdf (last accessed 13 July 2021).

Rao, N. (2011) 'Respect, Status and Domestic Work: Female Migrants at Home and Work', *European Journal of Development Research*, 23(5): 758–73.

Ray, R. and Qayum, S. (2009) *Cultures of Servitude. Modernity, Domesticity, and Class in India*, Stanford: Stanford University Press.

Rettberg, A. (2015a) 'Ley de víctimas en Colombia: un balance', *Revista de Estudios Sociales*, 54: 185–8.

Rettberg, A. (2015b) 'Victims of the Colombian Armed Conflict: The Birth of a Political Actor', in B.M. Bagley and J.D. Rosen (eds) *Colombia's Political Economy at the Outset of the 21st Century: From Uribe to Santos and Beyond*, New York: Lexington Books, pp 111–39.

Ribeiro Corossacz, V. (2018) *White Middle-class Men in Rio de Janeiro. The Making of a Dominant Subject*, Lanham: Lexington Books.

Roberts, D.E. (1997) 'Spiritual and Menial Housework', *Yale Journal of Law and Feminism*, 9(1): 51–80.

Romero, M. (2017) *Introducing Intersectionality*, New York: John Wiley & Sons.

Romero, M. (2018) 'Reflections on Globalized Care Chains and Migrant Women Workers', *Critical Sociology*, 44(7–8): 1179–89.

Rosewarne, S.C. (2013) 'The ILO's Domestic Worker Convention (C189): Challenging the Gendered Disadvantage of Asia's Foreign Domestic Workers?', *Global Labour Journal*, 4(1): 1–25.

Roth, B. (2004) *Separate Roads to Feminism: Black, Chicana, and White Feminist Movements in America's Second Wave*, Cambridge: Cambridge University Press.

Sarti, R. (2007) 'The Globalisation of Domestic Service in a Historical Perspective', in H. Lutz (ed) *Migration and domestic work: a European perspective on a global theme*, Aldershot: Ashgate, pp 77–98.

Sarti, R. (ed) (2010) *Lavoro domestico e di cura: quali diritti?*, Rome: Ediesse.

Sarti, R., Bellavitis, A. and Martini, M. (eds) (2018) *What is Work? Gender at the Crossroads of Home, Family, and Business from the Early Modern Era to the Present*, New York: Berghahn.

Scheiwe, K. (2014) 'Arbeitszeitregulierung für Beschäftigte in Privathaushalten – entgrenzte Arbeit, ungenügendes Recht?', in K. Scheiwe and J. Krawietz (eds) *(K)Eine Arbeit wie jede andere? Die Regulierung von Arbeit im Privathaushalt*, Berlin: De Gruyter, pp 60–84.

Scholte, J.A. (2009) *IMF Interactions with Member Countries: The Civil Society Dimension*, IEO Background Paper, BP/09/08, IEO, Washington.

Schwenken, H. (2003) 'RESPECT for All: The Political Self-organization of Female Migrant Domestic Workers in the European Union', *Refuge: Canada's Journal on Refugees*, 21(3): 45–52.

Schwenken, H. (2013) *Speedy Latin America, Slow Europe? Regional Implementation Processes of the ILO Convention of Decent Work for Domestic Workers*, United Nations Research Institute for Social Development, Genève, Available from: www.unrisd.org/80256B3C005BCCF9/search/9 7AA08A7519A3BA9C1257D39005B8205?OpenDocument (last accessed 13 July 2021).

Schwenken, H. (2016) 'The Emergence of an Impossible Movement. Domestic Workers Organize Globally', in D. Gosewinkel and D. Rucht (eds) *Transnational Struggles for Recognition: New Perspectives on Civil Society since the 20th Century*, New York: Berghahn, pp 205–28.

Schwenken, H., Prügl, E., Pabon, R., Hobden, C. and Shireen, A. (2011) 'An ILO Convention for Domestic Workers', *International Feminist Journal of Politics*, 13(3): 437–61.

SEWA (2014) *Domestic Workers' Laws and Legal Issues in India*, WIEGO Law and Informality Resources, Cambridge: WIEGO.

Sharma, S. (2014) *Pollution, Household-space and Stigma from the Perspective of Women Domestic Workers*, Paper presented at X International Conference on Labour History, 22–24 March, V.V. Giri National Labour Institute, Noida/New Delhi.

Sharma, S. and Kunduri, E. (2015) 'Of Law, Language and Labour: Situating the Need for Legislation in Domestic Work', *Economic and Political Weekly*, 50(28): online, Available from: www.epw.in/journal/2015/28/web-exclusives/law-language-and-labour.html (last accessed 13 July 2021).

Shire, K. (2015) 'Family Supports and Insecure Work: The Politics of Household Service Employment in Conservative Welfare Regimes', *Social Politics*, 22(2): 193–219.

Smith, J. (2004) 'Transnational Processes and Movements', in D.A. Snow, S.A. Soule and H. Kriesi (eds) *The Blackwell Companion to Social Movements*, Hoboken: Wiley-Blackwell, pp 331–35.

Smith, J. and Johnston, H. (2002) *Globalization and Resistance: Transnational Dimensions of Social Movements*, Lanham: Rowman & Littlefield.

Soares Leivas, P.H. and Moreira Aristides dos Santos, A. (2018) 'Horizontal Inequality and Ethnic Diversity in Brazil: Patterns, Trends, and Their Impacts on Institutions', *Oxford Development Studies*, 46(3): 348–62.

Steffek, J., Kissling, C. and Nanz, P. (eds) (2008) *Civil Society Participation in European and Global Governance. A Cure for the Democratic Deficit?*, London: Palgrave Macmillan.

Strolovitch, D.Z. (2007) *Affirmative Advocacy: Race, Class, and Gender in Interest Group Politics*, Chicago: University of Chicago Press.

Teeple Hopkins, C. (2017) 'Mosty Work, Little Play: Social Reproduction, Migration, and Paid Domestic Work in Montreal', in T. Bhattacharya (ed) *Social Reproduction Theory. Remapping Class, Recentering Oppression*, London: Pluto Press, pp 131–47.

Theobald, H. (2017) 'Care Workers with Migration Backgrounds in Formal Care Services in Germany: a Multi-level Intersectional Analysis', *International Journal of Care and Caring*, 1(2): 209–26.

Tilly, C., Rojas-García, G. and Theodore, N. (2019) 'Intersectional Histories, Overdetermined Fortunes: Understanding Mexican and US Domestic Worker Movements', in R. Agarwala and J.J. Chun (eds) *Gendering Struggles against Informal and Precarious Work*, Bingley: Emerald Publishing Limited, pp 121–45.

Toupin, L. (2014) *Le Salaire au Travail Menager: Chronique d'une lutte féministe internationale (1972–1977)*, Montréal: les éditions du remue-ménage.

Townsend-Bell, E. (2011) 'What Is Relevance? Defining Intersectional Praxis in Uruguay', *Political Research Quarterly*, 64(1): 187–99.

Trebilcock, A. (2018) 'Challenges in Germany's Implementation of the ILO Decent Work for Domestic Workers Convention', *International Journal of Comparative Labour Law and Industrial Relations*, 34(2): 149–76.

Triandafyllidou, A. (2013) *Irregular Migrant Domestic Workers in Europe: Who Cares?*, Abingdon: Routledge.

Triandafyllidou, A. and Marchetti, S. (2013) 'Migrant Domestic and Care Workers in Europe. New Patterns of Circulation?', *Journal of Immigration and Refugee Studies*, 11(4): 339–46.

Tronto, J. (2002) 'The "Nanny" Question in Feminism', *Hypatia*, 17(2): 34–51.

Tronto, J. (2013) *Caring Democracy. Markets, Equality, and Justice*, New York: New York University Press.

Tudela-Vázquez, M.P. (2016) *'La organización de nosotras'. Procesos de ciudadanía a partir de experiencias de 'Ilegalidad' en Estados Unidos. Aprendizajes con Mujeres Unidas y Activas*, PhD thesis, Department of Anthropology, University of Granada, Granada, Spain.

Unión General de Trabajadores (2017) *Radiografía del empleo de las Trabajadoras del Hogar. Desafíos y medidas para avanzar en la equiparación de derechos*, Pamplona: Unión General de Trabajadores de Navarra.

Urrea Giraldo, F., Viafara, C. and Viveros Vigoya, M. (2015) 'From Whitened Miscegenation to Triethnic Multiculturalism: Race and Ethnicity in Colombia', in E. Telles (ed) *Pigmentocracies. Ethnicity, Race and Color in Latin America*, Chapel Hill: University of Carolina Press, pp 81–126.

Valenzuela, M.E. and Sjoberg, C. (2012) 'Situación del trabajo doméstico remunerado en América Latina', in *Panorama Laboral 2012. América Latina y El Caribe*, Lima: OIT, pp 59–67.

Van Hooren, F. (2010) 'When Families Need Immigrants: The Exceptional Position of Migrant Domestic Workers and Care Assistants in Italian Immigration Policy', *Bulletin of Italian Politics*, 2(2): 21–38.

Vásquez, L.S. and Saltos Galarza, N. (2013) *Ecuador: Su Realidad*, Quito: Fundación José Peralta.

Verloo, M. (2013) 'Intersectional and Cross-Movement Politics and Policies: Reflections on Current Practices and Debates', *Signs: Journal of Women in Culture and Society*, 38(4): 893–915.

Vianello, F. (2009) *Migrando sole: legami transnazionali tra Ucraina e Italia*, Milano: Franco Angeli.

Viesel, S. (2013) 'Who Cares? The ILO Convention "Decent Work for Domestic Workers"', *Transnational Social Review*, 3(2): 229–43.

Wade, P. (1993) *Blackness and Race Mixture: The Dynamics of Racial Identity in Colombia*, Baltimore: Johns Hopkins University Press.

Walby, S. (2002) 'Feminism in a Global Era', *Economy and Society*, 31(4): 533–57.

Walby, S. (2007) 'Complexity Theory, Systems Theory, and Multiple Intersecting Social Inequalities', *Philosophy of the Social Sciences*, 37(4): 449–70.

Williams, F. (2011) 'Towards a Transnational Analysis of the Political Economy of Care', in R. Mahon and F. Robinson (eds) *Feminist Ethics and Social Policy: Towards a New Global Political Economy of Care*, Vancouver: University of British Columbia Press, pp 21–38.

Williams, F. (2018) 'Care: Intersections of Scales, Inequalities and Crises', *Current Sociology*, 66(4): 547–61.

Winch, A., Forkert, K. and Davison, S. (2019) 'Editorial: Neoliberalism, Feminism and Transnationalism', *Soundings: A Journal of Politics and Culture*, 71: 4–10.

Woehrle, L.M. (ed) (2014) *Intersectionality and Social Change*, Bradford: Emerald Publishing Limited.

Yeates, N. (2004) 'Global Care Chains', *International Feminist Journal of Politics*, 6(3): 369–91.

Yeoh, B. and Huang, S. (1999) 'Negotiating Public Space: Strategies and Styles of Migrant Female Domestic Workers in Singapore', *Urban Studies*, 35(3): 583–602.

Yuval-Davis, N. (2011) 'Beyond the Recognition and Re-distribution Dichotomy: Intersectionality and Stratification', in H. Lutz, M.T.H. Vivar and L. Supik (eds) *Framing Intersectionality: Debates on a Multi-faceted Concept in Gender Studies*, London: Ashgate, pp 155–69.

Yuval-Davis, N. (2015) 'Situated Intersectionality and Social Inequality', *Raisons politiques*, 2(58): 91–100.

Zelizer, V. (2009) *The Purchase of Intimacy*, Princeton: Princeton University Press.

Index

References to endnotes show both the page number and the note number (139n96).